World Bank Group interactions with environmentalists

MANCHESTER
1824
Manchester University Press

Issues in Environmental Politics

series editors Mikael Skou Andersen and Duncan Liefferink

At the start of the twenty-first century, the environment has come to stay as a central concern of global politics. This series takes key problems for environmental policy and examines the politics behind their cause and possible resolution. Accessible and eloquent, the books make available for a non-specialist readership some of the best research and most provocative thinking on humanity's relationship with the planet.

already published in the series

Science and politics in international environmental regimes *Steinar Andresen, Tora Skodvin, Arild Underdal and Jørgen Wettestad*

Animals, politics and morality (2nd edn) *Robert Garner*

Implementing international environmental agreements in Russia *Geir Hønneland and Anne-Kristin Jørgensen*

Implementing EU environmental policy *Christoph Knill and Andrea Lenschow (eds)*

Environmental politics in the European Union: policy-making, implementation and patterns of multi-level governance *Christoph Knill and Duncan Liefferink*

Sweden and ecological governance: straddling the fence *Lennart J. Lundqvist*

Bounded rationality in decision-making: how cognitive shortcuts and professional values may interfere with market-based regulation *Helle Nielsen*

Global warming policy in Japan and Britain: interactions between institutions and issue characteristics *Shizuka Oshitani*

North Sea cooperation: linking international and domestic pollution control *Jon Birger Skjærseth*

Climate change and the oil industry: common problem, varying strategies *Jon Birger Skjærseth and Tora Skodvin*

Environmental policy-making in Britain, Germany and the European Union *Rüdiger K. W. Wurzel*

World Bank Group interactions with environmentalists

Changing international organisation identities

Susan Park

Manchester University Press

Published by Manchester University Press
Altrincham Street, Manchester M1 7JA, UK
www.manchesteruniversitypress.co.uk

British Library Cataloguing-in-Publication Data is available

ISBN 978 0 7190 7947 4 hardback

First published by Manchester University Press 2010

Typeset by Action Publishing Technology Ltd, Gloucester

For Matt

Contents

List of figures and boxes

Figures

Boxes

Preface

I became interested in the World Bank during the height of the second generation of reforms within the organisation – the shift from the mass protest campaigns of the 1980s to ongoing campaigns for policy, information disclosure and accountability reforms in the 1990s. I was roused by the early ferocity of anti-Bank campaigners and the widespread challenge to the orthodoxy of the institution whose mandate of reconstruction and development was surely positive. It became clear throughout my research into the World Bank Group that there is much more than a simple pro- or anti- position on the role of international financial institutions in developing countries. That the Bank has wrought damage on the natural environment and facilitated the forcible movement of peoples is clear. That it has since improved its policies, procedures, environmental funding and oversight mechanisms is also evident. That it can do more is not in doubt. Organisational change, as scholars of bureaucracies know only too well, is neither fast nor necessarily linear.

Yet change is possible. Whether financial instruments can be wielded for positive environmental outcomes remains open for serious investigation. At this stage, mitigating environmental damage is central to viewing the importance of interactions between environmentalists, the organisations of the World Bank Group, and the member states that direct them. Some of the history of the environmental campaigns against the World Bank may be familiar to you. These are discussed in chapter 3, which provides a comprehensive account of the project, policies and institutional changes within the organisation from the 1970s to the present. This recounting is important because the activities of environmentalists that shaped the World Bank are now used by environmentalists to challenge other components of the World Bank Group, bilateral export credit agencies and private banks.

The rapid opening up of developing countries to direct foreign investment and trade demonstrates the importance of examining how private sector operations in developing countries have been facilitated by institutions such as the International Finance Corporation (IFC) and the Multilateral Investment Guarantee Agency (MIGA). That these institutions have also come under the scrutiny of environmentalists demonstrates not only an expansion of development investment and underwriting, but the possibility of 'greening' these industries.

Chapters 4 on IFC and 5 on MIGA unpack the layers of these institutions again through their project, policy and institutional changes. Their stories, like the World Bank's, are very much bound by how those operating them view the world through the prism of the organisation's identity. Environmental ideas, first derided and rejected, then engaged with and adopted, can be seen as a positive sign for those wishing to influence the future of project investment lending and underwriting. The shift in the project investment industry through the Equator Principles is a positive step, spearheaded by IFC's engagement with environmentalists. MIGA's belated and top down response is rooted in the belief that the natural environment is not part of what political risk insurers do, although change is coming. Environmentalists' engagement with these organisations is based on shaping these institutions to influence broader industry practice. Both the Bank and IFC demonstrate that this can happen; whether MIGA chooses to take on this mantle remains to be seen.

Perhaps more important however, is how environmental ideas are understood within international political economy. Industrialised states developed first and then began to address environmental problems. Official development assistance may aid sustainable development but it will not instigate ecological innovation. Developing countries continue to face significant development obstacles while beginning to grapple, to varying degrees, with environmental problems. Yet lending institutions like the World Bank Group are still dominated by industrialised states and are seen to be the owners of some environmental ideas, including environmental and social safeguard policies. The history of the World Bank in developing countries and the North–South political divide both indicate that spreading environmental norms through these organisations, in spite of, or even because of, their expertise is not enough to make development ecologically sustainable. The proliferation of financing mechanisms in the international development market further indicates that borrowers, either through the World Bank Group or through other financing instruments, increasingly have the power to fundamentally reconstitute sustainable development. This is the challenge for the twenty-first century.

Acknowledgements

Books are never the work of just the author. Thank you to everyone who helped this project through its various stages, particularly Jason Sharman and Peter Dauvergne for shepherding me through the process from its initial conception to completion and for giving support and intellectual stimulation. I owe a great debt to staff at the World Bank, IFC and MIGA, as well as the many activists that have given me their time. I have tried to capture your observations to the best of my abilities. Thank you to Stefano Guzzini for his excellent comments on the theoretical basis for this argument and to Marc Williams and Roger Payne for their feedback. Thank you to Antje Wiener for her insights on norms in the international realm. I would also like to thank the following people who have stimulated my thinking on how IOs operate and how we can and should research them: Antje Vetterlein, Kate Weaver, Ralf Leiteritz, Bessma Momani, Diane Stone, Len Seabrooke, Michael Tierney and Jacqueline Best. Thank you to everyone who commented on this book at its various stages – you know who you are. This book would not have been completed without the financial assistance from Deakin University in the form of the International Studies Program Grant, the Priming Grant, and the New Staff Grant. Early research was conducted with assistance from the Department of Government and International Relations at the University of Sydney. Parts of chapter 3 appeared in 'Norm Diffusion within International Organisations: A Case Study of the World Bank', *Journal for International Relations and Development* 2005, 8 (2): 114–41. Parts of chapter 4 appeared in

'How Transnational Environmental Advocacy Networks Socialise IFIs: A Case Study of the International Finance Corporation', *Global Environmental Politics* 2005, 5 (4): 95–119. Parts of chapter 5 appeared in 'Socialisation, the World Bank Group and Global Environmental Governance', in *International Organisations in Global Environmental Governance* edited by Frank Biermann, Anna Schreyögg and Bernd Siebenhüner (2009, Routledge, London and New York): 91–109. These parts have been reprinted with the permission of Palgrave Macmillan, MIT Press, and Taylor and Francis. Lastly, I would like to thank my family for their faith, and especially my partner Matthew, for his continual love and support.

List of Abbreviations

AAA	American Anthropological Association
ACFOA	Australian Council for Overseas Aid
ACG	Arun Concerned Group
AFE	Alliance for Energy
BIC	Bank Information Center
BP	Bank Procedure
CAO	Compliance Advisor/Ombudsman for IFC and MIGA
CAS	Country Assistance Strategy, World Bank
CEA	Country Environmental Analysis, World Bank
CES	Environment and Social Development Department, IFC
CESIG	CES Investment Support Group, IFC
CIEL	Center for International Environmental Law
CMA	Compania Minera Antamina SA
CODE	Committee on Development Effectiveness, World Bank Group
CONADI	National Indigenous Development Board of Chile
CSA	Country systems approach, World Bank
DOTS	Development Outcome Tracking System, IFC
DPL	Development Policy Lending, World Bank (formerly structural adjustment)
EA	Environmental assessment
EAP	Environment Action Plan, MIGA
ED	Executive Director
EFIC	Export Finance and Insurance Corporation of Australia

EIA	Environmental impact assessment
EIR	Extractive Industries Review
EMS	Environment Management System, MIGA
ENRM	Environment and Natural Resource Management, World Bank
ENV	Environment Department, World Bank
ERRS	Environmental Risk Rating System, IFC
ERS	Environment Review Summary for Category B projects, IFC
ESD	Environmentally Sustainable Department, World Bank
ESE	Environmental and social effects indicator, IFC
ESIA	Environmental and Social Impact Assessment, for Category A projects MIGA
ESHS	Environmental, social, and health and safety requirements, IFC
ESRP	Environment and Social Review Procedure, IFC
ESRR	Environmental and Social Risk Rating, IFC
ESSD	Environment and Socially Sustainable Development Department, World Bank
EU	European Union
EVP	Executive Vice President, IFC
FDI	Direct foreign investment
FXC	Freeport McMoRan Copper and Gold Inc.
FY	Financial year
GABB	Grupo de Accion por el Bibio
GDP	Gross Domestic Product
GEF	Global Environment Facility
GP	Good Practice guideline
GWCPR	Greater Western China Poverty Reduction project, World Bank
IBRD	International Bank for Reconstruction and Development
ICSID	International Centre for the Settlement of Investment Disputes
ICRC	International Committee for the Red Cross
IDA	International Development Association
IEG	Independent Evaluation Group of the World Bank Group: includes the IEG-World Bank, IEG-IFC and IEG-MIGA replacing the OED, OEG and OEU (effective 15 December 2005)

IFC	International Finance Corporation
IFI	International Financial Institution
IMF	International Monetary Fund
INFID	International NGO Forum on Indonesian Development
INGO	International Non-government Organisation
IO	International organisation
IR	Internatonal Relations
IRN	International Rivers Network
IUCN	World Conservation Union
MDB	Multilateral Development Bank
MEA	Multilateral environmental agreement
MIC	Middle income country, World Bank Group
MIGA	Multilateral Investment Guarantee Agency
MIGPE	MIGA's Policy and Environment Department
MOR	Monthly Operation Report
NATO	North Atlantic Treaty Organisation
NGO	Non-government organisation
NRDC	Natural Resources Defense Council
NWF	National Wildlife Federation
OD	Operational Directive
ODA	Official development assistance
OEA	Office of Environmental Affairs, World Bank
OECD	Organisation for Economic Cooperation and Development
OED	Operations Evaluation Department, World Bank
OEG	Operations Evaluations Group, IFC
OEU	Operations Evaluation Unit, MIGA
OP	Operational Policy
OPIC	Overseas Private Insurance Corporation of the United States
OPM	Organisasi Papua Merderka
OSCE	Organisation for Security and Cooperation in Europe
P–A	Principal–Agent
PRSP	Poverty Reduction Strategy Paper
PTFI	PT Freeport Indonesia
QA	Quality Assurance team, IFC
QACU	Quality Assurance Compliance Unit, World Bank
QAG	Quality Assurance Group, World Bank

QPM	Quality Portfolio Management, IFC
SEA	Strategic Environmental Analysis, World Bank
SDN	Sustainable Development Network, World Bank
SPI	Summary of Project Information, renamed Summary of Proposed Information
TEAN	Transnational environmental advocacy network
UN	United Nations
UNCED	United Nations Conference on the Environment and Development
UNCTAD	United Nations Conference on Trade and Development
UNDP	United Nations Development Program
UNESCO	United Nations Education, Scientific and Cultural Organisation
UNEP	United Nations Environment Program
US-ED	United States Executive Director
US EPA	United States Environment Protection Agency
US AID	United States Agency for International Development
WALHI	Wahana Lingkungan Hidup Indonesia or Indonesian Forum for the Environment
WBG	World Bank Group
WCD	World Commission on Dams
WCED	World Commission on Environment and Development
WTO	World Trade Organization
WWF	World Wildlife Fund – now the World Wide Fund for Nature

1
Introduction

The World Bank Group (WBG) is a constellation of international organisations (IOs) with global reach.[1] Since the early 1980s, environmental groups have documented numerous cases where the World Bank (IBRD/IDA), the most well-known organisation, has contributed to environmental devastation and community dislocation through its development projects. In doing so, environmentalists challenge the perceived omnipotence of the World Bank in spreading globalisation and determining development agendas (George and Sabelli 1994; Goldman 2005; Woods 2006). The World Bank is viewed as such because it has financial autonomy through capital markets and bonds while it is financially underpinned by member states (Caufield 1996; Rich 1994). Traditionally, it has offered cheap loans to developing countries where private financing will not, and can mobilise and co-finance loans and projects with the private sector, thus providing a lifeline to credit-poor states.[2] Equally importantly, it provides technical experience and acts as a 'knowledge broker' to developing countries (Riggirozzi 2006; Stone 2003).

These practices mean that the World Bank wields significant material and ideational power over a large portion of the globe and has been the rallying point for critics of unsustainable economic development. From the 1980s, the WBG as a whole has advocated neoliberal economic policies through its research; structural adjustment programmes and projects; investments and guarantees. This is often described as the 'Washington Consensus' after John Williamson's coining of the term (Williamson 1990; Broad 2006; Nelson 1996: 606; Toye and Toye 2005). The World

Bank's subsequent incorporation of environmental and social issues sparked debates as to whether the World Bank promotes a 'Post-Washington Consensus' development agenda (Naim 2000; Vetterlein 2007; Williamson 2003), liberal environmentalism (Bernstein 2001), or even 'Green Neoliberalism' (Goldman 2005). In the 1990s environmental groups expanded their examination of the World Bank to look at the rest of the WBG. This book is devoted to examining the impact of the 'greening' process on the World Bank and two of its affiliates: the International Finance Corporation (IFC) and the Multilateral Investment Guarantee Agency (MIGA). To date, neither of these institutions has been examined in any detail. IFC is concerned with private sector lending and MIGA political risk insurance. Transnational environmental advocacy networks (TEANs) have been increasingly vocal in criticising their activities as private sources of capital grow and environmental protection over private sector development lags (on transnational advocacy networks, see Keck and Sikkink 1998).

Environmental changes within the World Bank are well documented in the scholarly literature: environmental activists in non-government organisations (NGOs) and TEANs more broadly campaigned against World Bank projects and pushed for institutional change using different strategies, while Bank member states established new policies and oversight mechanisms for the organisation (Caufield 1996; Fox and Brown 1998; Gutner 2002; Keck and Sikkink 1998; Miller-Adams 1999: 145; Nielson and Tierney 2003; Rich 1994). I argue that the cause of change within the World Bank and its affiliates IFC and MIGA cannot be simply reduced to the interest-based politics of member states or Bank management, although alternative accounts do precisely this (Nielson and Tierney 2003; Nielson, Tierney and Weaver 2006). Rather, TEANs *informed and helped shape* member states' decisions to implement new environmental standards (Bowles and Kormos 1999; Keck and Sikkink 1998).

Evidence of World Bank–NGO relations have been used to show how activists pressured the organisation to broaden its conception of development to include the environment, gender, social justice, human and indigenous rights (Fox and Brown 1998; Nelson 1997, 1995; Payne 1997, 1996; Rich 1994). Non-state actors like TEANs are driven by a 'principled idea or value that motivates their actions' (Keck and Sikkink 1998: 1). They include NGOs, activists, development practitioners, and others that collaborate on a particular idea (environment) organised into campaigns (project, policy or institutional change) and usually against someone or something (the WBG).[3] Often this work demonstrates antagonistic relations between non-state actors such as TEANs and development practitioners, and the Bank, culminating in a moral victory for NGOs (Fox and Brown 1998; Khagram 2004; Nelson 1995; Wade 1997). Alternatively, some argue that NGOs have been co-opted by the World Bank, thus undermining the ability of NGOs to green the organisation (Goldman 2005).

The book compares how the World Bank, IFC and MIGA have responded to sustainable development norms espoused by TEANs. In doing so, the book differs from previous work on the World Bank's environmental shift both theoretically and empirically. Theoretically, it brings the role of TEANs to the forefront of accounts of shifts within the World Bank Group in order to identify which processes lead to change within international organisations (IOs) (Checkel and Moravscik 2001: 225). Such an examination does not attempt to replicate studies of Bank–NGO relations that identify NGO strategies (see Fox and Brown 1998; Keck and Sikkink 1998). IO scholars have long recognised the influence of the external environment in shaping the agenda and actions of organisations (E. Haas 1990; Haas and Haas 1995; Le Prestre 1989). For organisational theory this was called the organisation's task environment or milieu (Le Prestre 1982: 5–6).

Scholarship on IOs examines how events and both state and non-state actors shape organisations, although only now are scholars distinguishing between the influence of material power and ideas (Chwieroth 2008; Leiteritz 2005; Momani 2005; Vetterlein 2007; Weaver 2007). Within International Relations (IR) two theorctical approaches attempt to explain IO change. A constructivist perspective, based on norms, culture and identity counter poses rationalist theoretical accounts of IO change. The latter includes neorealism, neoliberal institutionalism and the subsequent Principal–Agent (P–A) model, which are derived from micro-economics and assume that all actors are utility maximising egoists. Early constructivist scholarship posited that international norms were conveyed by IOs (and NGOs) to states, thus shaping state identities and behaviour. Both IOs and NGOs can be norm entrepreneurs or 'diffusers', spreading ideas and shaping state practices on human rights, the environment and security (Adler 1998; Checkel 2003, 2001; Finnemore 1996a, 1996b; Grigorescu 2002; P. Haas 1992; Ratner 2000). In demonstrating the role of ideas, constructivists argued that IOs have some autonomy from states and can diffuse norms to states through their operations (Barnett and Coleman 2005; Barnett and Finnemore 2004: 3–4, 1999). Constructivists refuted the one sided state–IO relationship assumed by rationalists, where states dictate IO behaviour. Yet constructivists were initially more concerned with articulating an independent role for IOs than identifying the genesis of IO ideas (Boli and Thomas 1999; Finnemore 1996a: 19, 1996c).

Rationalist theories such as neorealism and neoliberalism did not fare much better. Neither neorealism nor neoliberal institutionalism advanced a significant role for IOs, concentrating on state cooperation, competition and conflict; although the latter does view IOs as furthering states' interests (Keohane 1984; Mearsheimer 1994/5; Schweller and Priess 1997). As a result, an alternative rationalist hypothesis emerged to account for IO change based on the P–A model (Gutner 2005a, 2005b; Hawkins, Lake, Nielson and Tierney 2006; Nielson and Tierney 2005, 2003; Nielson, Tierney and Weaver 2006). The model advances IOs as agents, but gives primary explanatory power for IO actions to the interests of member states (principals). The P–A model seeks to explain the disjuncture between principal interests and IO (agent) actions or when and why IOs do not meet state demands (Gutner 2005a, 2005b; Nielson and Tierney 2005). Advocates of the P–A model point to the asymmetric information between principals and agents where the latter may conceal information from the principal that could be used against it to sanction 'deviant behaviour'. In this context, they examine how principals can establish or change incentive structures for the agent to meet principal demands (Nielson, Tierney and Weaver 2006: 6).

Although the P–A model is a plausible account of IO change, a close investigation of the evidence on the World Bank Group's greening points to the crucial role of TEANs in challenging WBG practices and in establishing appropriate behaviour for development institutions. Significant input from environmentalists determined that the Bank and its affiliates *should* change, including *how* they should do so, both through direct interactions with the World Bank Group and indirectly through powerful member states (Fox and Brown 1998; Keck and Sikkink 1998; Rich 1994). Attempts to analyse the Bank and its fellow institutions using the P–A model overlooks the role of non-state actors in framing environmental debates within development institutions, and in guiding their principals through interactions with key government agencies. Instead, the P–A model accounts for a narrow linear path of change within IOs from states to management to staff which overlook the contestation between IOs, states and non-state actors over the appropriate behaviour of IOs (Hawkins *et al.* 2006; Nielson, Tierney and Weaver 2006).

Both Gutner (2005a: 17) and Nielson and Tierney (2003: 241) do acknowledge the role of NGOs in influencing member principals but the focus for Gutner is on how the P–A model explains gaps between IO mandates and performance seemingly after NGOs have influenced IO 'mandates' (what the IO aims to achieve as prescribed by its policies and statements rather than a change in its Articles of Agreement or constitution). Nielson and Tierney, on the other hand, hypothesise that pressure from groups other than proximate principals will not have a significant influence on IOs (2003: 252). To ignore or downplay the role of TEANs in promoting norms of sustainable development fundamentally mischaracterises empirical accounts of change within the WBG.

I propose that IOs can and do internalise norms and ideas from non-state actors in order to spread them to (developing) states. Norms are defined as 'collective expectations about proper behaviour for a given identity' (Jepperson *et al.* 1996: 54; Finnemore and Sikkink 1998: 891). Norms are 'shared and social; they are not just subjective but *inter*subjective' (Finnemore 1996a: 22–3). The book examines how IOs are shaped by international norms through processes of socialisation by transnational environmental advocacy networks, rather than limiting the analysis to examine how member states impose change on IOs. That international norms are embodied by non-state actors like TEANs demonstrates that social structures may be constituted by a variety of sources and that non-state actors can shape world politics (Keck and Sikkink 1998; Price 1997,

1998). TEANs form campaigns which are 'activities that are combined to further an aim or goal which members from diffuse areas undertake collectively, usually based on a norm or principle and focused on policy change, and whose actions are often not based on rational interest explanations' (Keck and Sikkink, 1998: 8–9). I therefore propose that IOs are influenced by the social structure in which they exist. The social structure shared between actors is in the form of norms, rules and institutions. Norms, rules and institutions are social facts which result from the collective intentionality of groups within society (Searle 1995: 24–7). Social structures provide 'necessary conditions for intentional human action, and intentional human action is a necessary condition for it' (Bhaskar 1998: 36–7).

In providing a constructivist account of WBG change, the book is based on three ontological principles: that ideas as well as material factors matter; that identity influences agents' interests and actions; and that agents and structures are mutually constituted. The mutual constitution of IOs and international norms focuses the analysis on IO agency and processes of socialisation that lead to IO change. An IO's identity influences how it behaves according to its internal properties, while the social structure informs how it ought to behave. Examining processes of socialisation can demonstrate how IO identities shift to accord with new international norms. To examine the interaction between agents and structures, an interpretivist rather than either a positivist or scientific realist epistemology is used (Guzzini 2000: 156). Undertaking such an approach enables an analysis that captures the mutually constitutive dynamic between agents and structures; of interactions between the WBG and norms promoted by networks.

Importantly, the book demonstrates how IOs like the WBG organisations internalise norms such as sustainable development that are spread by TEANs, which IOs then attempt to diffuse throughout the international system. Arguing that IOs internalise norms from non-state actors is located within the international norms literature (Legro 1997). There are multitudinous and overlapping international norms that vary in strength and applicability. While it is important to examine how different norms (for example human rights, labour standards, gender and the environment) influence IOs, outside European studies there has been a relative lack of comparative analysis of how the same norm influences different actors. One exception is Finnemore's *National Interests in International Society* (1996a) although this does not analyse recipient states. European studies are awash with analyses mapping how regional IOs spread norms to influence European states or their officials (see the special edition of *International Organisation* 2005; Checkel 2005, 2001, 1999a; Flockhart 2006; Grigorescu 2002; Kelley 2004; Linden 2002; Schimmelfennig 2005). Yet there is little analysis on how IOs themselves are influenced, let alone comparisons of how the same norm shapes and is shaped by different IOs (an exception is Vetterlein 2007).

Empirically, the book goes *beyond* the World Bank to examine change within the WBG. The Group's activities extend across private sector project lending and the political risk insurance of direct foreign investment (FDI) that facilitates private investment in developing countries. The better-known World Bank is therefore compared to two of the WBG organisations: IFC, a private sector investor and venture project financier, and MIGA, a political risk insurer. Both IFC and MIGA have grown significantly within the past two decades with rapid private investment in developing countries outstripping Bank and broader official development assistance (ODA) lending. Direct foreign investment is the largest source of external funding for developing countries (World Bank 2006a). In 2007 $379 billion in FDI flowed to developing countries – the largest amount ever (UNCTAD 2007: xv). Private sector lending is triple that of official development assistance to developing states and the WBG is a major player in developing countries' rapidly expanding private sectors through its co-financing and guarantees (OECD 2007a; World Bank 2000).[4]

IFC is now the largest source of multilateral loan and equity financing for private sector projects and it continues to record growth (IFC 2007a, 2006a). It also facilitates private investment in the developing world and provides technical advice to developing states. MIGA has also grown, covering $2.1 billion in political risk insurance to international private lenders in 2008, with an overall portfolio of $6.5 billion guarantees. MIGA facilitates four dollars of FDI for every dollar guaranteed, and it is a central player in the international political risk insurance industry (MIGA 2008a: 3, 8). While they are less known they increasingly influence international development finance and have attracted the attention of TEANs.

Argument summarised: how TEANs socialise the WBG to be green

In accounting for environmental changes within the World Bank Group, it is first necessary to explore the cause of the WBG's incorporation of environmental concerns. The book traces the course of the struggle between environmental groups and the World Bank Group organisations. While change is evident within each of the organisations, less clear is the *cause* and *extent* of that change. In relation to the World Bank, the organisation initially ignored environmental groups before refuting their claims and then endorsing them. Each World Bank Group institution responded to the environmental challenge by following a similar pattern: they first ignored and then rejected environmental claims before engaging with the idea of sustainable development. However, each organisation varied its engagement with environmentalists and the extent that they subsequently incorporated environmental practices, from the 'rule based' environmentalism of the World Bank, to the 'market oriented' IFC, to the limited and belated 'market following' of MIGA.

Central to how IOs such as the WBG internalise norms is the process of socialisation. The book traces processes of socialisation from advocacy networks to the WBG and their principals in order to theorise how IOs' 'properties and preferences change as a result of social interaction' (Checkel and Moravscik 2001: 227, 220). Socialisation is defined here as a process whereby agents internalise norms that constitute the social structure in which they exist. For IOs, the socialisation process results from the mutual constitution of IOs and international norms advocated by TEANs. Socialisation is not a linear process but one of continuous interaction between agents and structures, or between the WBG and international norms promoted by TEANs. Socialisation can lead to fundamental shifts in an organisation's identity. To understand how IO identities are reconstituted, the emphasis is on how social structures socialise agents. However, the argument is grounded in the broader norm diffusion literature, which documents how IOs reproduce and reconstitute international norms by spreading ideas to states.

To map the process of IO change, socialisation is broken down into two distinct but simultaneous processes of direct and indirect socialisation. Within both direct and indirect socialisation, three micro-processes of socialisation are evident: persuasion, social influence (Checkel 1999b; Johnston 2001) and coercion (Risse, Ropp and Sikkink 1999; Wendt 1999).

Direct socialisation is where non-state actors, such as TEANs, interact with IOs to spread norms that constitute the social structure. The networks attempt to persuade IOs of the relevance of particular norms through ongoing campaigns. This includes meetings, letters, petitions, emails, faxes and phone calls. Persuasion is an ongoing, iterative process that involves 'changing attitudes about cause and affect in the absence of overt coercion' (Checkel and Moravcsik 2001: 221; Johnston 2001: 496, 499). TEANs also engage in social influence involving the distribution of punishments including 'shaming, shunning, excluding, and demeaning, or dissonance derived from actions inconsistent with role and identity' and rewards such as 'psychological well-being, status, a sense of belonging, and a sense of well-being derived from conformity with role expectations' (Johnston 2001: 499). Social influence is expressed through demonstrations, protests and petitions at the WBG project sites, offices or headquarters, and praise or condemnation through press releases, web posts and publicity stunts. However, IOs do not just conform to social structures but also mediate and recreate them through their responses.

Indirect socialisation is a process of socialisation in which member states are first influenced through persuasion, in order to then use coercion on the IO. TEANs influence the WBG through an indirect process of shaping powerful member states who then press for changes within the IO. This is part of the socialisation process because the very act of changing an IO's actions (establishing environmental policies) influences its interests (whether and how it approves projects) and ultimately its identity (what it believes its role to be) (Risse, Ropp and Sikkink 1999). In the case of the World Bank and IFC detailed in chapters 3 and 4, determining specific actions as unacceptable for leaders in international development, combined with social influence and persuasion, arguably lead to a rethink by these IOs about how to maintain leadership through other means; through identifying with, and then promoting, previously imposed sustainable development ideas.

Combined, direct and indirect socialisation involving persuasion, social influence and coercive pressure reconstitute IO identities. Thus, each micro-process of socialisation is important in shaping the identity of the World Bank and IFC, but as is argued below, the shift in identity comes from various combinations of the three processes rather than a single isolated one. These micro-processes mirror the three levels of internalisation established by Alexander Wendt (1999): coercion, calculation and belief. Yet I argue that micro-processes are enacted simultaneously as opposed to determining an overarching linear culture, for example Wendt's Hobbesian, Lockean or Kantian cultures that inform state actions in different periods (1999: 268). The micro-processes of persuasion, social influence and coercion are undertaken via avenues of direct and indirect socialisation. By promoting new shared meanings within world politics, TEANs can reconstitute the identity of IOs.

Socialisation is not just a one-way process. International norms influence states through the process of indirect socialisation. Key parts of powerful states, such as the US, can be and have been shaped by TEANs to reflect sustainable development norms. While the US response was initially instrumental, part of the state's interest shifted over time with the reconstitution of its identity. Ongoing US policy towards the WBG organisations has fundamentally shifted to focus on sustainable development rather than being adopted for instrumental means towards other state objectives. This is demonstrated throughout the chapters. Reversing the arrows, TEANs are in turn socialised by IOs. This includes how they are recognised and legitimated, how they respond to questions of their representation, effectiveness and knowledge, and how their operations change as a result of interaction with the WBG, although this is not the focus here.

Indirect socialisation may be considered a more successful means of influencing the WBG than direct socialisation although these processes occur simultaneously. While rationalists point to the role of powerful states in explaining IO change, there is much more than brute power involved as will become apparent throughout. Arguably, rationalist perspectives can only explain part of the process of change undertaken by the WBG and powerful member states such as the US. The socialisation process between two of the organisations (the Bank and IFC) and TEANs has changed over time from one of confrontation to one that is more receptive. The dynamics of the interaction between advocacy networks has shifted dramatically from the early 1980s to the present. This evokes an identity shift where the affiliates enact sustainable development norms.

Yet IOs are not passive recipients of ideas or dictates. Current IO scholarship examines IO autonomy to assess how, when and why IOs may choose to 'redesign' themselves independent of state interests (Barnett and Coleman 2005). The P–A model logic points to IO interests informing their actions yet they do not test this assumption. Contra rationalists, constructivists argue that actors' strategic interests are determined by their identity. In examining the extent and cause of environmental changes within the WBG, the book therefore examines the identity of the separate World Bank Group institutions in informing their actions. While organisational sociologists argue the culture of the organisation influences decision-making (Schein 2004; Weaver 2008, 2007), constructivists point to identity in mediating actors' responses to, and therefore reconstructing, international norms (Katzenstein 1996; Klotz 1995; Wendt 1999, 1992). In doing so, an IO's identity reconstitutes international norms, by mediating ideas thus helping to create newly shared understandings of IO behaviour between states, non-state actors and IOs. The argument proposed here provides both a holistic and a dynamic account of IO change that recognises the mutual constitution of IOs and international norms promoted by non-state actors.[5]

IOs have distinct identities that determine how they respond to the social structure within which they exist. The WBG organisations differ from other IOs and each other owing to their different mandates, professional base, organisational cultures and perceptions. States establish IOs, setting their mandate, scope and function, all of which establish their identity. Yet an IO's historical development (Cox and Jacobson 1973: 5) and culture based on the professional orientation of the majority of the staff (Finnemore 1996a: 25), create internal dynamics that influence how it acts and reacts to situations (Ascher 1983; Barnett and Finnemore 1999: 723; Kapur 2002: 65). Moreover, how the organisation's ideas and culture influence how the organisation's structure is interpreted is crucial to explaining how it fulfils its duties (Barnett and Finnemore 2004, 1999).

Identity is defined as an organisation's mandate and bureaucratic culture, and is both subjective and intersubjective. Thus, an IO has a mandate and a bureaucratic culture based on its dominant profession which influences how it undertakes its functions, but is also informed by how it perceives itself and is perceived by others. The subjective and intersubjective aspects of identity are essential in determining an identity shift in an IO, as opposed to tactical policy changes informed by instrumentalist decision-making propounded by rationalist approaches. A constructivist framework furthers the analysis of change by mapping the process, and by establishing that change is in fact much deeper than rationalist scholars of IOs would acknowledge, even though they now recognise culture as a variable in IO change (Nielson, Tierney and Weaver 2006).

Arguing that the World Bank's identity has shifted by internalising sustainable development does not mean the end of the World Bank–TEAN interactions. Environmental networks continue to oppose the actions of the Bank and dialogue between the two is part of an uneven process of change, characterised by intermittent conflict and cooperation. The WBG and TEANs both aim to further development, albeit in different ways, and continue to interact, producing and reproducing WBG organisation identities and norms of development. Thus, the mutual constitution of the WBG and international norms via TEANs means reciprocally shaping both the WBG identities *and* norms of development.

The focus on network–WBG interactions aims to demonstrate how particular norms are internalised by IOs. Non-state actors such as TEANs socialise IOs to diffuse and thereby reinforce and reproduce international norms. The WBG–TEAN interactions are examined through detailing the project, policy, and institutional changes undertaken by each organisation, and the subjective and intersubjective beliefs of the affiliates and TEANs regarding such changes. I argue that the World Bank is internalising sustainable development. In the case of IFC, I document how sustainable development norms have been diffused. The third case, MIGA, is an example of how an IO contests international norms. This is explained by each organisation's distinct identity and the strength of shared understandings of appropriate behaviour for lenders, investors and political risk insurers. The three cases therefore document the conditions for how international norms influence IOs: based on the strength of shared understandings of the new norm and how the identity of the IO enables the norm to be incorporated (Checkel 2005; Cortell and Davis 2001).

From here, the goal is to explore the *extent* of WBG change. The 'greening' debate currently focuses on how to measure the Bank's environmental operations in order to identify the extent that the organisation has become green (Gutner 2005a, 2002; Nielson and Tierney 2005, 2003). While this is important for determining how the environment is incorporated into Bank lending, how the Bank views and is viewed by state and non-state actors is also an important indicator of the Bank's ability to operationalise sustainable development. The book proposes that the shift within the Bank is both ongoing and much deeper than is currently recognised within the greening debate as a result of changing its internal properties as well as its external behaviour. Socialisation has occurred when the new norm becomes internalised to the point where each IO begins to see its role through the new norm. The WBG affiliates would thus see themselves as sustainable development lenders, investors, and guarantors respectively and would be recognised as such by TEANs and states.

The method used to describe and analyse these interactions is process tracing where 'one seeks to investigate and explain the decision process by which various initial conditions are translated into outcomes' (Checkel and Moravcsik 2001: 223). This means recovering the processes through which social agents change their properties and preferences (Checkel and Moravcsik 2001: 223). I conducted semi-structured interviews with WBG officials both within environment departments and operations and interviewed Washington-based TEAN activists in 2001, 2005, 2006 and 2007. I also examined official documents from the WBG and primary documents from TEANs to examine the motivations for action and the respective interpretation of IO and TEAN responses. This is backed by secondary literature to assess shifts in the IOs' identities.

Chapter outline

The book examines the process and extent of environmental change within three institutions of the WBG: the World Bank, IFC and MIGA. It argues that while lending patterns fluctuate, how the WBG promotes and practises development depends upon what they understand 'development' to mean. How the world's largest multilateral development bank and its affiliates react to changing lending patterns therefore has important ramifications on understanding international development norms. This analysis intends to show that, while sustainable development norms influenced each affiliate, each affiliate's identity ultimately determined *how* they interacted with, and the extent that they internalised and reproduced, the social structure in which they exist. Equally important is the strength of shared understandings of appropriate international financial institution behaviour. Following the rise of FDI to developing countries, TEAN attention has turned to less well-known financial institutions such as IFC, MIGA and export credit agencies. Opposition to these institutions by global civil society has led to both the 'politicisation of finance' (Evans, Goodman and Lansbury 2001: 37) and to a widening interest in global civil society interactions with international financial institutions (Higgott, Underhill and Bieler 2000; O'Brien *et al.* 2000; Scholte and Schnabel 2002). These events call for alternative, non-state-centric theoretical frameworks in which to analyse how IOs are situated within the international political economy and the complex inter-relationship between states, IOs and non-state actors.

Chapter 2 establishes the theoretical framework for the book. It provides an overview of the debates over causes of IO change in relation to constructivist and rationalist accounts. These differ over whether ideas or interests influence IOs and whether this emerges from inside or outside the organisation. The chapter posits that a constructivist account establishes a more comprehensive and dynamic analysis of IO and WBG change by examining how international norms shape IOs through interactions between IOs, states and non-state actors. It then unpacks the key concepts of socialisation and avenues of socialisation (direct and indirect) and outlines the concept of transnational environmental advocacy networks. Finally, the chapter places

TEANs as norm entrepreneurs within the context of development, thus providing the basis for examining each of the World Bank Group organisation's interactions with TEANs in the remaining chapters. There are many TEANs that overlap on different project, policy, and institutional campaigns and these are specified in each empirical chapter.

Chapter 3 analyses the 'World Bank' comprised of the International Bank for Reconstruction and Development (IBRD) and the International Development Association (IDA), a concessional lending facility for low-income states. The IBRD maintains IDA, although the latter has separate funds provided by voluntary member state contributions. Among other interactions, transnational environmental advocacy networks sought to limit IDA replenishment to halt the negative environmental impacts from World Bank loans. IDA replenishment has now become a political contest over power and purpose by member states (Weaver 2007). This is one of the interactions examined here between states, TEANs and the World Bank that contributed to the Bank's environmental shift.

The chapter traces how TEANs used campaigns to oppose the Bank's operations in order to prevent or mitigate the negative environmental impacts of Bank-backed projects. The chapter provides a history of the first high profile cases of Polonoroeste in Brazil and Narmada in India, where TEANs first challenged the WBG. Second, the chapter documents how TEANs tried to influence Bank policies in areas such as environmental and social safeguards, and information disclosure. Finally, the chapter assesses how the networks pressured for institutional mechanisms to ensure greater environmental accountability and adherence to strengthened safeguards. Throughout the process, the Bank was challenged to re-evaluate its ideas. By undertaking such practices repeatedly, it is argued that the Bank began to view itself as a sustainable development lender. The World Bank's implementation of environmental policies, project processes and institutional oversight mechanisms are well documented. Less obvious are the impacts of such changes on the organisation and its practices. I argue that a more fundamental shift has occurred, shaping not just the Bank's actions but also its identity. The book examines the ongoing process of identity change within the World Bank and its affiliates where the Bank continues to internalise sustainable development, as a result not only of state-based power politics, but from TEAN socialisation.

Chapter 4 then maps how IFC, like the Bank before it, became embroiled in environmental debates over its loans and guarantees. IFC operates separately although it has overlapping member states with similar power structures. It has a different role and function but espouses the same development norms of economic growth and poverty alleviation. Until recently IFC escaped scrutiny from the Bank's environmental critics. This is primarily because of the rapid growth in private sector financing and because private sector-oriented but still public international financial institutions have less overt connections to the development process than the Bank.[6] The chapter again views IFC through TEAN campaigns, examining IFC's first big project, the controversial Pangue dam in Chile. It then traces how TEANs pushed for IFC to have its own environmental and social safeguard policies and information disclosure. Finally, like the World Bank, the chapter examines how TEANs pushed for accountability mechanisms to lock these changes into place.

Chapter 5 then documents how MIGA then became the focus of TEAN criticism over its role as a political risk guarantor of private sector capital in developing countries that have a negative environmental impact. In each chapter, interactions between TEANs and the WBG are examined through each organisation's projects, policies, and institutions. TEANs have challenged all aspects of these IOs, thus questioning the very basis of IO practices (actions and ideas). The chapter documents how TEANs attempted to influence MIGA again through project campaigns, this time on the Freeport mine in West Papua. TEANs then attempted to ensure that MIGA would have its own environmental and social safeguard and information disclosure policies. Finally, TEANs also pressured for MIGA to have an accountability mechanism with IFC to ensure that private sector guarantors had the same oversight mechanisms as the rest of the WBG.

Analysing three cases enables us to compare how international norms influence IO identities. Moreover, by examining IFC and MIGA, neither of which has thus far received much attention, a more accurate picture can be drawn of the WBG's role, reach and, importantly, ability to change. This study therefore examines how identity shapes how IOs internalise international norms. That TEANs influence three of the WBG affiliates in exactly the same way, based on exactly the same arguments, with exactly the same member state power structure within each organisation, but resulting in differing responses, suggests that each case is particular and that each IO's identity influences such interaction. The cases seek to demonstrate how sustainable development norms espoused by TEANs increasingly shape private sector-oriented financial institutions with similar development goals but distinct professional identities. Chapter 6 concludes by assessing the broader implications of environmental shifts in the WBG organisation identities for the future of international development lending and environmental activism.

Notes

1 The World Bank Group includes the International Bank for Reconstruction and Development (IBRD; established 1944), the International Finance Corporation – IFC (1956), the International Development Association – IDA (1960), the International Center for the Settlement of Investment Disputes – ICSID (1966), and the Multilateral Investment Guarantee Agency – MIGA (1988). The 'World Bank' or 'Bank' refers to the IBRD and IDA. The Global Environment Facility (GEF – piloted in 1991 and established in 1994) is not part of the WBG because the Bank is merely an implementing agency for GEF funds. The ICSID is an arbitration board that does not interact with environmentalists and is not analysed.

2 In 1997–98 the World Bank increased its contractual loan spread to raise the costs of its loans, which was then passed on to borrowers, making it more expensive compared to favourable private sector loans (Mohammed 2005: 187). The Bank has recently tried to reduce the costs of its loans to make it more competitive (Birdsall 2006).

3 I do not include states or IOs in transnational advocacy networks as Keck and Sikkink do (1998: 8–10); this is detailed in chapter 2. IOs refer to intergovernmental organisations and do not include NGOs. Non-state actors refer to NGOs not IOs, as the latter are made up of states.

4 All currency values are in United States dollars.

5 That organisations respond to their environment based on their organisational 'identity' is sociologically inspired. The reflexivity of constructivism is often overlooked by rationalists who focus on

norms as structural rather than structural *and structured* (Guzzini 2000: 150).

6 Only the Bank influences broader government policy although both IFC and MIGA provide technical advice.

2
Changing IOs: identity and socialisation

As the largest and most well-known organisation within the WBG, the World Bank has received significant attention from policy-makers, activists and academia. Over time the Bank has expanded its operations to encompass a myriad of different ideas and agendas, a process often described as 'mission creep' (Einhorn 2001; Gutner 2005a). This chapter questions the origin of the norms that IOs such as the World Bank and its affiliates internalise. Where these ideas originate from is important because IOs play a prominent role in the process of norm diffusion, teaching states their interests. Yet constructivists have largely overlooked the origin of the norms that IOs diffuse while rationalists have either assumed that IOs merely enact the interests of their member states (principals) or that internal incentive structures established and maintained by principals can explain staff and therefore IO preferences. This chapter proposes that international norms can and do shape IOs such as the WBG organisations. It establishes a constructivist theoretical framework to examine how IOs consume or internalise norms via processes of direct and indirect socialisation from, in the case of the WBG, TEANs.[1]

In order to do so, it locates the World Bank Group within the social structure of development, where the WBG resisted broader understandings of 'development' to include environmental concerns. This dovetails with recent arguments that IOs may choose not to expand their operations from a fear of losing the ability to act autonomously (Barnett and Coleman 2005). As the remaining chapters indicate, World Bank, IFC and MIGA reluctance may have been based on maintaining their identity based on a fixed interpretation of their mandate which informs their ability to act independently without the constraining influence of either member state oversight of TEAN monitoring. First, however, the limitations of rationalist approaches (neorealism, neoliberal institutionalism and the P–A model) to IO change are identified.

States as determinants of IO change

States design IOs for a variety of purposes (Koromenos, Lipson and Snidal 2004). They delegate power to IOs to carry out set operations as defined in their Articles of Agreement or charter. State-centric approaches recently dominated analysis of IOs. Both neorealism and neoliberal institutionalism examined state cooperation in the international system, thus shaping our understanding of international institutions (Baldwin 1993). Neorealists' viewed IOs as arenas for states to achieve their interests. IOs were considered epiphenomenal to the structure of the international system with 'no independent effect on state behaviour' (Mearsheimer 1994/5: 7). As such, IOs were seen to provide 'little independent initiative' in their activities (Malik 1995: 226). This provided no insight into IO interests or actions that deviated from state dictates and bore little resemblance to many relatively autonomous IOs including the World Bank (Barnett and Finnemore 2004).[2] Schweller and Priess argued that neorealism's 'parsimony ... led to excesses such as Mearsheimer's stance on institutions that ... left realism without a well-developed model of institutional origins and effectiveness' (1997: 23). In comparison, neoliberal institutionalists view IOs as means for rational egoistic states to maximise their interests under anarchy (Fearon 1998: 269; Keohane 1984: 18–21, 1993: 273). Neoliberals point to the functional benefits of multilateralism for states: in reducing transaction costs, providing information, maximising utility payoffs, and promoting issue linkage amongst states leading to greater inter-state cooperation and collaboration (Lipson 1993; Martin and Simmons 1999; Ruggie 1993: 30).

While neorealism ignored the independent role of IOs, neoliberals emphasised how ideas determine which of the pre-existing exogenous preferences are chosen by states in order to achieve their pre-formed interests (Goldstein and Keohane 1993: 4;

Ruggie 1998: 866–9). Hug criticises rationalist explanations of states' preferences, arguing that a rationalist perspective has 'very little to say about where the fundamental preferences of actors come from' such that it 'can do little with individuals whose fundamental preferences change' (2003: 43–4). Some neoliberals go beyond the instrumental use of IOs by states to argue that states are not simply interest-driven but may be rule-driven under certain conditions. According to Jervis, IOs help states change their preferences over outcomes as an unanticipated result of cooperation within IOs. Institutions therefore take on a 'life of their own ... in not only binding the states more than the founders saw, but in changing their beliefs about what is possible and desirable: they shaped, as much as they reflected, interests' (1999: 46–7). While IOs do help facilitate inter-state cooperation through shaping interests, for the most part 'IOs tend to be of secondary importance and only in accounting for the creation and observance of ... rules' (Reinalda and Verbeek 1998: 2). Rules and norms may therefore have an impact on states' actions during cooperation, but neoliberalism retains the view of IOs serving states as rather than as agents with their own interests. Indeed Hug recognises that rational choice approaches apply specifically to individuals rather than to non-unitary actors such as IOs, where IOs may have their own interests (2003: 44).[3] Hug does not discount either constructivist socialisation or learning in explanations of IO preferences where non-unitary actor's (IO's) preference changes 'might be more common and because of multiple reasons' (2003: 44, 66).

In sum, neoliberals do not look inside the 'black box' of organisations and thus overlook IO actions and organisational change not determined by inter-state bargaining. As a result, Keohane noted that 'students of international affairs need a better theory of institutions' (1993: 293). Rationalist IO scholars therefore adopted the Principal–Agent (P–A) model to explain IO performance (Gutner 2005a: 11, 2005b; Hawkins *et al.* 2006; Nielson and Tierney 2005, 2003; Nielson, Tierney and Weaver 2006). The model analyses the relationship between principals (states) and the agent (IO) where 'the latter has been empowered to act on behalf of the former' (Hawkins *et al.* 2006: 7). Nielson and Tierney argue that the model extends neoliberalism's application to IOs where states give IOs 'real decision-making authority'

(2003: 242). The formulation accepts the relative autonomy of IOs in undertaking states' designated tasks. P–A model advocates test whether agent actions are commensurate with principal preferences.

In recognising IO autonomy, the model examines agent outcomes in light of principal expectations and their ability to oversee agents. The autonomy provided to the agent in the delegation process may mean that the principal is able to view the outcome but not the agent's actions (Miller 2005: 205). The delegation process entails side effects or 'agency losses' (Kiewiet and McCubbins 1991: 5). Essentially, agent autonomy provides room for 'agency slack' through slippage or shirking. Agency slack is 'independent action by an agent that is undesired by the principal' (Hawkins *et al.* 2006: 8; McCubbins, Noll and Weingast 1989: 246). Slippage occurs when 'an agent opportunistically shifts policy away from its principal's preferred outcome and towards its own preferences'. It may also shirk its delegated tasks by 'minimiz[ing] the effort it exerts on its principal's behalf' (Hawkins *et al.* 2006: 8).

Agents are therefore assumed to 'behave opportunistically, pursuing their own interests subject only to the constraints imposed by their relationship with the principal' (Kiewiet and McCubbins 1991: 5). Presumably, the IO's interests are to increase institutional autonomy, maintain or expand their budget and personnel, or to extend their power (Hug 2003: 66, n 31; Niskanen 1971: 36–9; Verbeek 1998: 22). Yet evidence suggests this may not always be the case (Barnett and Coleman 2005; Barnett and Finnemore 2004: 71). Within the rationalist research programme there have been detailed studies undertaken on state delegation to European Union agents (for example Garrett 1995; Pollack 1997; Tallberg 2000) including how and why European organisations such as the European Court of Justice extend their reach (Alter 1998; Mattli and Slaughter 1998). However, empirical research from both rationalists and constructivists is only just beginning on the interests and ideas of global organisations including the World Bank (see Barnett and Finnemore 2004; Best 2005; Chwieroth 2008; Gutner 2005b; Hawkins *et al.* 2006; Nielson and Tierney 2005, 2003; Nielson, Tierney and Weaver 2006).

The 'principal's problem' is how to retain control over its

agent: the principal has formal authority in its ability to provide incentives for the agent, but the latter has the informational advantage as an expert and authority in a given area (Barnett and Finnemore 2004: 25; Lupia and McCubbins 1994: 100; Miller 2005: 203–4). The agent's activities are constrained by how the principal devises its contract, determines how staff are selected and screened, and the imposition of monitoring, reporting and institutional checks designed to overcome agent slack (Kiewiet and McCubbins 1991: 26). The principals' choice of oversight mechanisms including rewards and punishments are determined by the costs of oversight and the tools available (McCubbins *et al.* 1987: 243, 249). McCubbins and Schwartz (1984) document two types of oversight strategies: police patrols and fire alarms. The first is costly, centralised, direct and active, based on constant surveillance of the agent. The second is less costly, decentralised, inactive and indirect. The latter establishes 'rules, procedures and informal practices' to enable others to raise the alarm in case of agent deviance. In other words, mechanisms are put in place to enable third parties (such as individuals and TEANs) to challenge agent violations of its goals and to seek redress (Lupia and McCubbins 1994; McCubbins and Schwartz 1984: 166). Recent analysis of IOs has focused on how principals can alter incentive systems to improve IO performances such as the World Bank's, a point returned to in the next chapter (Nielson and Tierney 2003; Nielson, Tierney and Weaver 2006).

The P–A model is rendered complex by the number of member states or 'multiple principals' IOs have. With a greater number of principals there is the potential for greater agency slippage. This results from a decline in individual principal control over the agent with an increase in the cost of convincing other principals to follow one's preferences (Vaubel, Dreher and Soylu 2003: 3). The P–A model research agenda thus examines IO performance in light of the preference heterogeneity of principals, which provide 'gaps' that allow greater agency slack (Gutner 2005a: 11; Hawkins *et al.* 2006: 35, 45; Weaver 2007: 496). Multiple principals also have varying degrees of power which influences the extent to which some principals' preferences are realised, including their ability to establish and enforce oversight mechanisms and to change incentive structures and procedures that favour principal interests (Miller 2005: 214–5; Nielson, Tierney and

Weaver 2006). Multiple principals may diverge in their preferences for IO action (and reform) which gives leverage to the agent to ignore or refuse to change its behaviour, thus undermining principals' credibility (Nielson and Tierney 2003: 249). The complexity of the P–A model is further compounded as principals are themselves 'collective principals' made up of a number of groups such as state executives, parliaments, bureaucracy, political parties and lobby groups with divergent interests and therefore preferences (Hawkins *et al.* 2006; Miller 2005: 211). For example, in the case of US relations with the World Bank, this includes US Congress, Treasury, the State department, the US Agency for International Development (US AID) and the US Environmental Protection Agency (US EPA).

The P–A model is useful in tracking states' delegation of tasks to IOs and IO performance. It can be used to explicate points in the delegation chain where IOs do not meet state demands. This may be based on principal preference heterogeneity and information asymmetry as outlined above, or may be the result of what Gutner has called 'antinomic delegation' where 'delegation consist[s] of conflicting or complex tasks that are difficult to institutionalize and implement' (2005a: 11). Gutner explicitly recognises the difficulty IOs such as the Bank face in attempting to reconcile its role as a Bank and as a development agency (2005a: 21). In this sense, IOs like the Bank are given the herculean task of attempting to reconcile potentially irreconcilable goals. Gutner thus identifies the complexity of current Bank operations. Yet the analysis remains centred on Bank–state relations (even extending this to include Bank–borrower delegation chains). As with all other P–A model analyses, this overlooks the role of ideas in shaping the identity of the IO and diminishes the role of non-state actors in doing so.

Theoretically, both neoliberals and P–A model advocates allow an independent role for ideas. Yet they continue to prioritise material over ideational structures: 'they prefer to explain International Relations as simple behavioural responses to the forces of physics that act on material objects from the outside' (Adler 1997: 321). Neoliberals add institutions as additional variables, thus adding a superstructure to the material base of neorealist assumptions (Adler 1997: 322; Risse 2000: 4; Wendt 1999: 95). For example, Goldstein and Keohane define ideas as 'beliefs held by individuals' using a 'rational choice approach to information processing [to] explain how individuals' beliefs can affect policy choices and outcomes' (1993: 3; Adler 1997: 322).

The P–A model of IO change is built on the same foundation. Hawkins *et al.* argue that the P–A model is not solely focused on the material interests of states but is 'equally consistent with theories that posit rational, egoistic, wealth maximising and those that assume boundedly-rational altruistic actors' (2006: 7). On this point, Guzzini states that rational choice approaches that argue that either egoism or altruism drive actor's behaviour risks indeterminacy. Specifically, he states that 'rational choice inspired theories then risk becoming mere taxonomies, a system of concepts which simply reformulate any behaviour into terms of rational action ... the biggest problem of rational choice inspired approaches would not be that they are wrong, *but that they can never be wrong*' (2000: 164, italics added; see for example Nielson, Tierney and Weaver 2006).

Rationalist accounts of IO change that incorporate the role of ideas and material factors do not see that power and interest are themselves effects of ideas and perception (Wendt 1999: 19). According to rationalist approaches, states' interests are *a priori*; they exist prior to inter-state interactions (Hobson 2000: 145). They prioritise actors' pre-existing preferences to explain events in specific circumstances, as opposed to recognising that material factors and individual beliefs are understood through intersubjectively held ideas or 'social facts' by actors, *and* that this shared understanding necessarily informs actors' interests and perceptions (Adler 1997: 323). Constructivist accounts, on the other hand, recognise that norms or 'social knowledge ... not only regulate behavior but also constitute the identity of actors' (Risse 2000: 5). As such, '[i]n rationalist models, interaction (including cooperation) does not affect actors' utility functions or identities ... Preferences help to explain interaction but not vice-versa' (Hasenclever *et al.* 1997: 25).

Neoliberal institutionalism and the P–A model can therefore explain part of the process of IO change. They can do so because principals have control mechanisms over IOs including adjusting budgets, changing constitutions and mandating new procedures in order to 'stack the deck' to favour their interests (Weaver 2007: 497). Yet this does not go far enough towards explaining IO behaviour for two reasons. First, as highlighted above, the P–A model like other rational accounts does not explain how actors such as states or IOs hold the interests and preferences that they do, irrespective of whether or not these are informed by either ideas or materiality. Second, the model does not take into account that ideas may also change the constitution of the actor, thus changing not only their actions but also their identity. Indeed, chapters 3 and 4 outline in detail how World Bank and IFC property effects were changed as a result of socialisation from TEANs, not just their behavioural effects, as rationalists would assume (see Alderson 2001; Atkinson 2006; Kelley 2004). This exemplifies the approach of rationalists who see rules as merely regulative in guiding behaviour, rather than as constitutive and shaping identities as constructivists contend (Kratochwil 1989: 26). A central constructivist insight is that identities (including IO identities) are reconstituted through interaction rather than enacting the adoption of practices to reflect state interests. The next section makes the case for a constructivist account of IO change that incorporates how ideas shape IO actions and identity.

IOs as norm diffusers and consumers

Challenging the neorealist/neoliberal focus on IOs furthering states' interests, constructivists first aimed to demonstrate that IOs shape state behaviour through spreading international norms (Adler 1998; Barnett and Finnemore 2004, 1999; Checkel 2003, 2001, 1999a; Finnemore 1996a; Flockhart 2006; Grigorescu 2002; Linden 2002; Ratner 2000; True and Mintrom 2001).[4] Constructivists therefore identified IOs as conveyers of norms rather exploring the origin of IO ideas. For example, Finnemore refuted a materialist account of state behaviour, documenting how states with divergent interests established similar policy objectives as a result of international norms spread by IOs (1996a). Yet Abbott and Snidal, who are influenced by constructivism, argued that IOs are established to legitimate and diffuse norms from powerful to less powerful states (1998: 18).

From a constructivist perspective, demonstrating the autonomy of IOs revealed a fundamental weakness in rationalist assumptions, which contributed to the rationalist adoption of the P–A model. IOs are important because they have extensive expertise in particular areas for which states often defer (Barnett and Finnemore 1999: 710, 2004; Verbeek 1998: 22). Technical expertise provides IOs with authority in the international realm. Such expertise and authority may 'significantly influence the capabilities, understandings, and interests of states' while 'promot[ing] certain norms and practices among states, often in unanticipated ways' (Abbott and Snidal 1998: 13). IOs do so through forming international agendas and regimes, defining discourses, enforcing rules and mediating conflict between states (Barnett and Finnemore 1999: 710). They are the 'glue' of the international state system that binds states together. In addition, IOs do not just determine which state interests are legitimate but also which non-state actors are legitimate. For example, an NGO requires official accredited status with the United Nations (UN). This legitimising role, along with their ability to shape international politics, makes IOs purposive actors (Barnett and Finnemore 2004, 1999; Finnemore 1996a). IO interests therefore need to be analysed independently of states as a result of their expertise, authority, diffusing and legitimising roles.

Recognisably however, many IOs do reflect unequal power relations between states through their structure and function (Gruber 2000; Thompson 2006), even if they also operate as actors in their own right. For constructivists it does not necessarily follow that an IO automatically reflects powerful states' interests, indeed, even the P–A model now aims to test this. If IOs do advocate the ideas and interests of powerful member states, a constructivist would question whether the IO was socialised to believe the ideas promoted by powerful principals: many IOs are made up of staff from (or educated in) powerful states, thus sharing the same ideas and therefore interests (Barnett and Finnemore 2004, 1999).

Such assumptions, however, need to be empirically examined. For example, scholars have examined the role of the organisational culture and internal norms of the International Monetary Fund (IMF) based on staff's neoclassical economist training in driving its emphasis on capital account liberalisation (Leiteritz 2005). This norm flowed up from staff to management and member states rather than the other way around (Chwieroth 2008: 130). Moreover, the IMF's organisational culture forestalled management reforms to its conditional lending measures which were pressed by member states (Momani 2005). Conversely Gould demonstrates how the instrumental power of private sector financiers shapes Fund conditionality for borrowers under certain conditions (2003) rather than being determined by principals. The current debate on the nature and change of IO behaviour now turns on whether ideas or interests shape IO decision-making and whether this comes from inside or outside the organisation (Weaver 2007).

As stated above, this book argues that ideas inform interests, thus demonstrating the simplicity of the either/or view of ideas versus interests, while proposing that international norms (external) can play a powerful role in changing not only IO behaviour but also their identity (internal). First, as previously mentioned, rationalists do not identify how IO preferences are formed in the first place, leaving much ground unexamined in analysing IO change (Chwieroth 2008: 133; Hawkins *et al.* 2006: 7). Explanations of IO stasis or change should therefore take ideas into account. Indeed, the constructivist literature has now moved to examine precisely this (discussed next). This book prioritises the role of ideas in shaping IO actions and identity. This is not to downplay the role of strategic action in accounting for IO decision-making either in relation to external actors, such as principals and non-state actors, or internal bargaining among staff and management (Bebbington *et al.* 2006; Hall 2007). Rather, international norms and the identity of the organisation locates, informs and shapes strategic action both within and outside the IO, including any internal 'battle of ideas' (Chwieroth 2008: 133; Johnston 2001; Schimmelfennig 2000).

Where this account differs from the current crop of constructivist theorising on IOs is that it demonstrates how international norms can shape IOs' actions and identity as a result of the socialisation from non-state actors such as TEANs. In this respect, ideas were not internally or professionally generated (as referred to above) and evidence shown throughout the book highlights World Bank Group resistance to new environmental ideas. This brings us to analyse how international norms and IO identity are mutually constituted. First however, we need to understand how the literature accounts for IO identity formation and where the ideas they hold originate. Finnemore has the most explicit analysis of the origin of IO norms within the literature on IOs as norm diffusers. She argued that the norms IOs convey emerge from within the IOs themselves as a result of either internal political conflict or from the embedded ideals of individual staff before joining IOs (1996a: 25, 53, 91).

Yet this is problematic in explaining the overall identity of IOs, especially global organisations with multinational staff and management. Notably, Grigorescu makes the connection between an IO's identity and the norms it conveys where he demonstrated that IOs may fail to transmit norms to states if they are not part of the IO's identity (2002: 468). Grigorescu points out that the pro-transparency norm advocated by member states did not accord with the identity of European IOs because it 'does not resonate with the norms on which these IOs were founded' (2002: 478, 468; Nielson, Tierney and Weaver 2006; Weaver and Leiteritz 2005). Grigorescu's argument establishes the need for further investigation into how IO identities influence their consumption of norms. A more convincing constructivist account of how norms emerge and shape an IO's identity is therefore needed to understand why IOs diffuse some norms over others.

Barnett and Finnemore's claim that IO actions are often based upon the dominant profession of the organisation, has been taken up by recent constructivist analysis of IO change (2004, 1999: 708–10; Chwieroth 2008). Often the dominant profession is integral to an IO's organisational or bureaucratic culture which may in turn shape its actions (Chwieroth 2008; Leiteritz 2005; Nielson, Tierney and Weaver 2006; Weaver 2008, 2007; Weaver and Leiteritz 2005). Most describe organisational or bureaucratic culture along similar lines. It may be defined as 'the deeply embedded ideologies, norms and routines that govern the expectations and behaviour of bureaucratic staff' (Weaver and Leiteritz 2005: 370; Leiteritz 2005: 6); or as 'internalised sets of norms, ideologies and cultures' (Momani 2005: 146); or the '"basic assumptions" or shared ideas about an organisational mission, routinised patterns of interaction, and standardised operating procedures' (Nielson, Tierney and Weaver 2006: 112); or finally, as a 'system of meaning that governs staff expectations and behaviour' (Chwieroth 2008: 133). Organisational culture can lead to IOs promoting norms from within rather than from management or principals (Chwieroth 2008; Leiteritz 2005), or may prevent IOs from consuming norms (Barnett and Coleman

2005; Grigorescu 2002; Momani 2005; Weaver and Leiteritz 2005). Recent attempts to bridge the rationalist–constructivist divide note that IO change is possible if principal determined reforms are 'adjacent to existing norms (i.e. they 'fit' within the existing culture)' (Nielson, Tierney and Weaver 2006: 110; Momani 2005).

Here organisational culture is understood as part of the organisation's identity. In examining what drives actors including IOs, constructivists argue that actors' social identities shape their interests and thus their actions. Identity 'makes a thing what it is' (Wendt 1999: 224). The collective or social identity of an actor is shaped through interaction and depends on its socio-historical context (Klotz 1995: 11; Wendt 1999: 229, n 108). IO identity is therefore defined as its mandate and bureaucratic culture, which is both subjective and intersubjective. To explain, an IO's social identity is not based upon the country of origin of individuals that make up the organisation, but the collective identity as a whole, which creates a bureaucratic culture in relation to its goals. Identity is more than just the sum of its parts (staff and management). This is in contradistinction to determining the identity of an IO based on individual staff members (Finnemore 1996a) or states and staff that comprise the organisation (for example, the P–A model and blended rationalist–constructivist models: see Nielson, Tierney and Weaver 2006). A collective identity does not presuppose methodological individualism. Indeed, Mercer argues that 'individuals make up bureaucracies, but we cannot understand the characteristics of bureaucracies (such as resistance to innovation) by examining only the beliefs of individuals' (1995: 238).

Wendt divided identity into corporate and social types; the latter developing through interaction (1999: 224–43). The corporate identity is intrinsic to the actor, existing prior to social interaction; it is a 'site' or platform for other identities. This creates difficulties in demonstrating how states' interests are constructed by the international system (Wendt 1999: 234). Zehfuss argues that Wendt's understanding of identity as partially given and constructed threatens his constructivism (2001) while Suganami argues that such distinctions demonstrate only a minor difference from rationalists (2002: 36). Rejecting this split in identity, I argue that collective identities are established in the

IO's foundation which is itself embedded in social interaction. This social, collective, organisational identity can be understood as 'a property of intentional actors that generates motivational and behavioural dispositions' meaning that an actor's identity is 'at base a subjective or unit-level quality, rooted in an actor's self-understanding'. Identities are therefore subjective and intersubjective (Wendt 1999: 224).

Recognising the subjective and intersubjective nature of identity is to examine how this identity is perceived and how this perception feeds back into its actions. An actor cannot base their identity purely on their own subjective analysis; others need to recognise them as such. The WBG organisations' identities are based on their bureaucratic culture premised on the dominant collective professional view about how to undertake their mandate and function, which itself was based on social interaction in its original formulation (the original creation of its mandate, constitution and staff). This evolves over time through interaction. For example, the World Bank has shifted from an engineer's bank to an economist's bank thus reshaping its understanding of its mandate and how it is perceived by others (Miller-Adams 1999; Wade 1997).

While some constructivists have viewed both IOs and NGOs as norm diffusers (Keck and Sikkink 1998; True and Mintrom 2001), the argument being put forward here is that these necessarily inform each other. As the evidence outlined throughout the remaining chapters will demonstrate, international norms promoted by non-state actors such as TEANs can be a driving force shaping IOs, often through states. This complicates the dominant constructivist position on two fronts: first, it shows that IOs may diffuse norms that do not emerge from within (contra Chwieroth 2008 and Leiteritz 2005); it also reveals that IOs may internalise norms that do not resonate with its identity (contra Barnett and Coleman 2005; Grigorescu 2002; Momani 2005; Nielson, Tierney and Weaver 2006; Weaver and Leiteritz 2005). Chapters 3 and 4 empirically detail how the World Bank and the IFC began to consume sustainable development norms that did not resonate with their views of development although the third case, MIGA, seems to fit the dominant pattern identified by constructivists so far.

Second, it highlights the role of international norms as

mutually constituting IO identities. Thus far, only Vetterlein (2007) emphasises the role of the external normative environment in fundamentally shaping IO change in the case of the World Bank and social policies, although many highlight the external environment as a trigger for change (see Nielson and Tierney 2003: 254; Nielson, Tierney and Weaver 2006; Weaver 2007; Weaver and Leiteritz 2005: 371–3). To date I have argued that identity determines how the IO sees itself, but this is also mediated by the social structure in which the IO exists. Identity is thus a

> key element of subjective reality, [and] stands in a dialectical relationship with society. Identity is formed by social processes. Once crystallized, it is maintained, modified or even reshaped by social relations. The social processes involved in both the formation and maintenance of identity are determined by the social structure. (Berger and Luckman 1987: 194)

The social structure shared between actors is in the form of norms, rules, and institutions. Norms, rules and institutions are social facts which result from the collective intentionality of groups within society (Searle 1995: 24–7). Social structures such as norms define expectations for behaviour. Norms shape interests (Finnemore 1996a: 27). If the norm is highly embedded then conforming to the norm produces no reaction from other actors (Finnemore and Sikkink 1998: 891). However, if an actor breaks a norm, then this action generates disapproval. While norms shape interests, repeated interaction between agents and structures means that over time, norms shape an actor's identity, which in turn reshapes norms. Norms inform actors' identities, such that 'collective norms and understandings constitute the social identities of actors and define the "basic rules of the game" in which actors find themselves in their interactions'. This includes when actors attempt to 'do the right thing' rather than 'maximising or optimizing their given preferences' (Risse 2000: 4–5).

Two caveats should be highlighted in the elucidation of how norms and IOs are mutually constituted. The first relates to the proposition that NGOs are diffusers of a world culture of international norms with Western and Weberian components as advocated by the new institutionalist school (Boli and Thomas 1999; Finnemore 1996a: 20–1, 1996c: 326, 1993; Meyer, Boli, Thomas and Ramirez 1997). The second relates to how norm diffusion compares to the process of policy diffusion throughout the world. There is a broad literature on the spread of policies across IR and comparative politics that examine the spread of globalisation and economic and political liberalisation (see for example the special edition of *International Organisation* 2006; Campbell and Pederson 2001; Streek and Thelen 2005). Like the institutionalists mentioned here this book explores how ideas shape the international system. Unlike the institutionalists, the aim here is limited to analysing specific cases that demonstrate that IOs are influenced by their social structure and that such interaction is mediated by their identity (Klotz 1995).

Although some of the mechanisms for spreading ideas may be similar, the conclusions that may be drawn from analysing the social world are variable and limited in time and place, rather than fixed and immutable as assumed in rationalist theorising (Ruggie 1998).[5] Agents are historically situated and this influences their identity. I argue that IOs are embedded in a social structure of international norms, denoted in the WBG cases by the presence of TEANs, which socialise IO behaviour and indirectly influence states during this process. What is therefore being proposed here is that change within IOs and indirectly states is a much deeper process, where IOs change their actions and identities as a result of international norms. This analysis therefore focuses on the position of the WBG organisations within the social structure in which they exist.

Constructivists aim to point out that actors 'internalise the roles and rules as scripts to which they conform, not out of conscious choice, but because they understand these behaviours to be appropriate'. This is important because the '[s]ocial structure of norms and rules govern the kinds of actions that will be contemplated and taken' (Finnemore 1996a: 29). Ideas therefore have structural characteristics in that norms 'are the medium and propellant of social action; they define the limits of what is cognitively possible and impossible for individuals' (Adler 1997: 325). Yet social structures 'are nothing more than routinised discursive and physical practices of social agents' that define the meaning and identity of the actor and its actions in any given context (Price and Reus-Smit 1998: 267).

As a result, both agents and structures are 'simultaneously involved in the production of social phenomena' (Wendt 1987:

361). For example, the WBG organisations act, and interpret norms of development, which are in turn constituted and reconstituted through a continual process of interaction with non-state actors. Constructivists argue that 'human agency creates, reproduces, and changes culture by way of daily practices'. Hence, social structures and agents are mutually constituted and 'cannot be reduced or collapsed into each other' (Risse 2000: 5; Reus-Smit 1996: 1). Alternatively, rationalists prioritise the nature and organisation of material forces such as power and interest.[6] Ruggie argues that ideas are constitutive and 'simply do not function causally in the same way as brutal facts or the agentive role that neo-utilitarianism attributes to interests' (1998: 869). While a positivist epistemology used by most rationalists establishes that 'human agents exist independently from their social environment and their collectively shared systems of meaning' (Risse 2000: 5), here it is recognised that these are mutually constituted. The meaning and effects of material power depend on the social structure in which agents exist. Material factors are thus understood and constituted by ideas. Put simply, material factors are accorded a function-status (Searle 1995: 19). Hence, power and interests are not unimportant 'but rather ... their meaning and effects depend on actors' ideas' (Wendt 1999: 24–5).

Actors cannot be divorced from the social structure in which they operate (Adler 1997: 325–30). Rationalist theories perceive that agents exist independently of the world and determine their own actions and what they can or cannot do (behavioural effects). Constructivists, on the other hand, argue that structure is deeper than is recognised by the methodological individualism of most rationalist theorising by stating that social structure constructs actors (property effects) through the collective intentionality of actors in creating common meaning (Searle 1995: 25). Constructivists thus argue that social structures constitute actors thus changing the properties of the actor. An IO identity shift is based on a demonstrable shift in IO practices (actions and ideas) which include IO and external (non-state and state) perceptions of change. The recursive nature of social life leads to the agent reinforcing new norms through such practices, which in turn influence how the IO sees itself. In turn, actors' identities and interests reconstitute norms, such that 'actors reproduce or alter systems through their actions'. As such '[f]undamental change of the international system occurs when actors, through their practices, change the rules and norms constitutive of international interaction' (Koslowski and Kratochwil 1994: 216). Norm change highlights the importance of actors' interpretations of their social world.

Constructivists use various analytic tools to understand intersubjective meanings (Ruggie 1998: 881). Searle argues that any account of social reality requires three elements: the assignment of function (status function referred to earlier), collective intentionality, and constitutive rules (1995: 13). The focus here is therefore to understand how IOs like the World Bank consume norms by their interaction with TEANs which leads to a change in social or institutional facts about the world, such as development norms including environmental sustainability. Methods used to establish this include gathering primary documents and secondary materials, and conducting interviews. This captures IO–norm entrepreneur (Florini 1996) interactions through examining their discussions, meetings and correspondence.

Collecting information on the social interaction between the IOs and norm entrepreneurs furthers understanding of IOs' responses to socialisation, indicating if their routinised discursive practices changed so that they began to view themselves in light of the new norm. Thus, how the organisations understand and interpret their own actions to accord with the norms espoused by norm entrepreneurs, leads to a change in their identities. The changing socio-linguistic routines determine that a change in the IO's identity has taken place. Positive reinforcement by norm entrepreneurs further entrench such identity changes (Elster 1989: ch 9).

Specifically, the WBG organisations operated within an orthodox economic development framework. With shifting perceptions of development the IOs interpreted their actions accordingly, first from conservative economic institutions to development lenders. I argue in chapters 3 and 4 that the Bank and IFC then became sustainable development lenders and investors, which informed their identities and reconstituted norms of development lending and investment (chapter 5 shows that this has not been the case with MIGA so far). The organisations' behaviour is not wholly based on the social structure within which they exist, nor do they exist entirely outside of social interaction. Rather, IO identities are informed by social interaction, and identity change results from socialisation, but how they change is distinct to each organisation's identity.

Regarding the WBG, understanding how norms of development alter identities requires analysis of how ideas emerge, as well as how IOs react to the social structure in which they exist. Put simply, international norms may be 'adapted' (superficially adhered to) or consumed or 'internalised' by the IO. This follows analyses that examine how organisations adopt, adapt, and learn from their environments (E. Haas 1990; Haas and Haas 1995). The result has been to argue that IOs learn through the adoption of ideas if internalisation or 'complex learning' occurs (Haas and Haas 1995). While Haas and Haas's learning model is not followed here, mapping the process of identity change within the WBG fits within this tradition.[7]

An IO's identity informs how it undertakes tasks and how it will behave in any given situation including how it reacts, consumes and diffuses international norms. Analysing how an IO has internalised new norms begins by tracing how this shift came about. In each of the following chapters, the identities of the WBG organisations are first examined. Then I document the rise of opposition against the WBG based on the WBG's own practices. The social structure of norms influences how IOs act, but these actions in turn reconstitute norms. In other words, the TEANs charged that WBG organisations' development was 'destructive' and 'unsustainable', which led to changed perceptions as to what appropriate development was. How sustainable development norms have in turn been reconstituted, needs to be analysed by then reversing the agent/structure role and by examining the structural properties of the IO and the agency of non-state actors that influence it.

This can be done by examining how TEANs established and effectively maintained interaction with the WBG organisations with regard to their projects, policies, and institutions through first opposing, then constraining, and finally reconstituting two of these IOs. This follows scholars working on transnational civil society (for example Price 1998; Wapner 1996) and social movements (O'Brien *et al.* 2000; Tarrow 2001), which view activists as agents, locating the source of ideational change with them. It is the process of interaction, whereby agents and structures are mutually constituted, that leads to shifts in both the WBG and norms of development. As is outlined throughout, the WBG organisations began to accord with the social structure within which it now exists through socialisation by TEANs. Detailing IO change through socialisation is examined next.

Processes of IO change: socialisation

Socialisation is a concept used to explain how an individual acquires the characteristics as a 'social being and participant' necessary for membership of society (Clausen 1968: 3). Socialisation is examined in terms of individuals, collectives or groups conforming to social norms and roles. Socialisation enables an understanding of how given contexts influence how agents behave based upon what is appropriate. The social structure therefore informs how agents behave but does not necessarily determine what they will do. Within international relations socialisation is increasingly recognised as a key concept in understanding how actors alter their behaviour and identity and embrace new ideas (Alderson 2001; Atkinson 2006; Bearce and Bondanella 2007; Checkel 2005, 2003, 2001, 1999a; Flockhart 2006; Johnston 2001; Kelley 2004; Kent 2002; Linden 2002; Schimmelfennig 2005, 2003, 2000; Thies 2003; Wang 2003). Yet there is no agreed-upon definition of socialisation nor any single understanding of what socialisation constitutes (Alderson 2001). Indeed, socialisation has been used by both rationalists and constructivists. Atkinson makes the useful distinction between rationalist use of socialisation based on examining behavioural change and constructivist accounts of a change in actors' internal characteristics or identity (2006: 511). Yet the rationalist/constructivist divide is not so clear cut.

Both rationalists and constructivists differ in their accounts of socialisation based not only on the impact of socialisation on the actor (behaviour versus identity change) but also on whether it is causal or constitutive, and the timing and connection between socialisation and rational action: from norms as the environment in which rational action is enacted (Johnston 2001; Schimmelfennig 2000); to normative influence occurring simultaneously with rational action (Kelley 2004; Schimmelfennig 2005, 2003, 2000); to a linear process of actors behaving strategically but changing over time towards an identity shift (Lewis 2003; Risse, Ropp and Sikkink 1999). First, the rationalist use of socialisation causing behavioural change is detailed before articulating blended rationalist-constructivist and then purely constructivist understandings of socialisation. These accounts demonstrate a shift from causal to constitutive understandings of socialisation leading to changes in either actors' behaviour or identity. Accepting that norms provide an environment for rational action to take place, the book demonstrates how norms shape material factors within processes of socialisation over time, such that actors may progress from enacting strategic responses towards an identity shift as a result of ongoing interaction.[8]

For rationalists, socialisation is an example of the use of both emulation and soft power. For example, neorealist Kenneth Waltz (1979) used socialisation 'to describe the homogenization of self-help balancing behavior among security-seeking states interacting among conditions of anarchy' (Johnston 2001: 489; Waltz 1979: 127–8). Waltz argues that socialisation 'is a process of selection and competition: states that do not emulate the self-help balancing behavior of the most successful actors in the system will be selected out of the system such that those remaining . . . will tend to share realpolitik behavioral traits' (Waltz 1979: 127–8; Johnston 2001: 489). Importantly, constructivists argue that this reasoning is dependent on bringing in implicit notions of social rules 'through which rational behavior becomes possible' (Dessler 1989: 460). Indeed Ruggie claims that

> [n]umerous critics have been puzzled by the presence of socialisation in a physicalist model that disclaims any sociality on part of its actors. But perhaps even more serious is the fact that Waltz . . . turns what is supposed to be a methodological principle into an ontological one: Waltz has actual states becoming socialised to his model of the international system, not to the more variegated world of actual international relations. (Ruggie 1998: 865)

Constructivists have therefore made the case that 'state governments are rational actors operating in a normatively institutionalized . . . environment' (Schimmelfennig 2000: 115–16, 119), and that IOs create social or normative environments for rational action to take place (Johnston 2001).

Other rationalists use socialisation to explain change in state behaviour through soft power (Atkinson 2006; Ikenberry and

Kupchan 1990; Wang 2003).[9] For example, Ikenberry and Kupchan argue that hegemonic US socialised secondary states 'at the level of substantive beliefs rather than material payoffs'.[10] For them, socialisation leads to elites in secondary states 'buying into' the hegemon's normative agenda (Ikenberry and Kupchan 1990: 283). Socialisation for Ikenberry and Kupchan occurs in three instances. First, socialisation occurs as a result of the external inducement of the hegemon. Compliance is underpinned by the threat of coercion which they argue leads to a substantive shift in beliefs by secondary state elites over time. This forces the secondary state to change their preferences, leading to a shift in long-term interests. Second, socialisation is where the hegemon induces normative compliance by appealing to the secondary state over what is the 'right' thing to do.[11] Third, socialisation occurs from the internal reconstruction of the secondary state by the hegemon such as Germany and Japan through US occupation and reconstruction (Ikenberry and Kupchan 1990: 290). Wang further argues that hegemonic states socialise not only secondary state elites but also public opinion (2003: 102–5).[12]

Unlike Ikenberry and Kupchan and Wang, Atkinson (2006) specifies the actual causal mechanisms of coercion, incentives and persuasion to demonstrate how the US socialises other states via inter-military interactions. Atkinson's argument is rooted in rationalist positivist theorising where the distinction between the international structure and individual states is causal even while she recognises the distinction between material coercion and incentives, and ideas (2006: 511). However, Atkinson's understanding of socialisation is based on methodological individualism and she follows Alderson (2001) in arguing that socialisation is a three-part process involving changing individual beliefs, political pressure and persuasion, and institutionalisation. Like neoliberal institutionalism, ideas through persuasion and institutionalisation are added to material pressure that is, at base, about changing individual action.

Attempts to blend rationalist-constructivist work on socialisation highlight the utility of the concept for explaining how ideas shape international politics. Alderson (2001) attempted to provide an overarching definition of socialisation for both rationalists and constructivists, defining socialisation as 'the process by which states internalise norms arising elsewhere in the international system' (2001: 416).[13] Significantly, Alderson's socialisation for both rationalists and constructivists remains grounded in methodological individualism based on individual belief change through causal mechanisms. Alderson also artificially delineates norm diffusion from socialisation arguing that they invoke different causal mechanisms where diffusion means an event in one place influences an event in another place, as opposed to socialisation where actors react in similar ways to different initial conditions (2001: 425). Even if you agree with this characterisation, this assumes that there is no overlap between the two. As Thies argues, both processes are contained in concepts of socialisation (2003: 548).

Rationalists therefore see socialisation as a *causal* rather than a constitutive process that changes actors' *behaviour*.[14] Some constructivists agree that socialisation 'is in part a causal process' but one 'of learning identities' where norms are causal because they regulate behaviour (Wendt 1999: 82). Yet many constructivists do not, arguing that socialisation is not casual in the sense than Actor A threatens Actor B to respond in a particular way (Adler 1997; Ruggie 1998). Rather the relations between agents such as IOs and structures like international norms inform and reconstitute one another. Processes here are constitutive rather than identifying causal mechanisms. According to Suganami 'constitutive relationships make something (or a particular description of something) logically or conceptually possible' (2002: 32). Harre, for example, argues that '[i]ntentionality (meaning) and normativity (conformity to rules and conventions), not cause and effect, need to be adopted as ... framing concepts' (2002: 614). Harre argues that

> [f]or nearly a century, psychologists [and social scientists generally] framed their theories, their methodologies and their interpretive and explanatory discourses exclusively in terms of cause and effect. For the most part this was not the concept of 'causality' as it is used in the natural sciences, but a philosophical innovation from the 18th century: causality as a regular concomitance ... The most important step in the move to a social constructionist point of view is to drop the Humean causal metaphysics of the positivist school in favor of normative explanations. (Harre 2002: 614)

For many constructivists socialisation is defined as the 'process by which principled ideas held by individuals [or agents] become norms in the sense of collective understandings about appropriate behaviour which then lead to changes in identities, interests and behaviour' (Risse, Ropp and Sikkink 1999: 11). Kent (2002: 344) endorses Schimmelfennig's definition of socialisation as 'the process that is directed towards a state's internalization of the constitutive beliefs and practices institutionalized in its international environment' (2000: 110–11). Internalisation means the adoption of social practices and beliefs where the agent practices the beliefs as its own and follows them autonomously. The socialisation process demonstrates how beliefs and practices are constitutive of the reproduction and diffusion of a social order (Schimmelfennig 2000: 112). In this regard, socialisation is both a process and an outcome. Socialisation is understood here as relational rather than causal and is defined as a process whereby agents internalise norms that constitute the social structure in which they exist. This analysis attempts to provide such a normative explanation of IO change based on ongoing interactions between actors and their social environments.

Beyond the causal debate most constructivists argue that socialisation changes actors' property effects or identity. While Schimmelfennig (2005, 2003, 2000) and Kelley (2004) look at rational action occurring simultaneous to suasion, a number of constructivists point to a progression from actors' strategic responses to changing normative environments towards an identity shift. For example, Risse, Ropp and Sikkink (1999) argue that human rights-violating states were socialised to become human rights advocates. They document a number of stages in this 'spiral' process. First, there was outright denial by states that they were violating human rights. After repeated pressure from transnational advocacy networks, the violating states recognised that human rights were important but maintained no wrongdoing. In response to continued pressure, violating states began to recognise their complicity in human rights abuses although no change in activities took place. In the final stage, states began to accord with human rights norms and 'habitualised' an identity of human rights defenders. This is an example whereby socialisation has been used to explain change in actors that goes beyond instrumental decision-making. Although Risse, Ropp and Sikkink do follow an initially instrumentalist argument about change within states' actions and interests, they argue that it goes further by demonstrating that habitualisation infers a shift in property effects or beliefs.

Alternatively, Kelley (2004) argues, in the case of European IOs, that material incentives clearly changed recipient behaviour where socialisation efforts had a lesser impact. Yet she also acknowledges that socialisation was present in shaping *how* states responded, particularly when normative European IOs were later given instrumental leverage (2004: 451). Kelley focuses on examining behavioural rather than property change, arguing that evidence is not available on states' degree of internalisation (2004: 428–9, 449–50). In addition, Kelley's argument propounds that socialisation can occur simultaneous to rational calculation.[15] Schimmelfennig also argues that rational action figures much more prominently than is suggested by the socialisation literature and any analysis of processes of socialisation must go beyond 'either/or' theorising (2000: 115–16, 119).

For Schimmelfennig (2005, 2003), European IOs succeeded in changing human rights and democracy norms in Central and Eastern Europe through membership incentives but have failed to produce compliance in illiberal regimes. This indicates that while material incentives are used to change states' behaviour simultaneously to suasion that identity does matter. Ideas and material factors both have explanatory power and are operating simultaneously but the impact is on an actor's property effects. Flockhart (2006) takes this further to argue that European IO attempts to socialise norms of the Euro-Atlantic community to Central and Eastern European states matter differently to recipients based on their social identity (2006: 91). Flockhart argues that states exist in social clusters characterised in terms of significant we and other groupings which shape how norms transferred by norm entrepreneurs are understood. Hence, socialisation incorporates both material and ideational influence, and affects both actors' behaviour and identity.

Clearly there are differences between rationalist and constructivist understandings of socialisation and different analyses distinguish separate aspects of the process. By breaking down the process into divisions or types, rationalists and constructivists alike are able to use socialisation to advance understandings of actor responses to changed environments. Lewis for example identifies three types of socialisation: thin, thick and deep (2003: 99, 104). Thin socialisation occurs within institutional environments. According to Lewis, socialisation 'in the rationalist image is characterized by instrumental adaptation ... and behavioural adjustments linked to, for example, concerns with reputation or trustworthiness'. In this instance agents 'make frequent or continuous cost–benefit calculations to determine normative compliance' (Lewis 2003: 105). That is, agents appeal to norms when it is in their interest to do so by way of rhetorical action (Schimmelfennig 2001: 63). This is observable through the response from those to whom the actor appeals. If the actor merely uses norm-based arguments in the pursuit of its self-interest over that of the community or group, then thin socialisation has taken place. This is akin to instrumental decision-making.

In Lewis's second instance, institutions have 'thick socialising effects on actors that go beyond the instrumental adaptation and the strategic conception of rules into self-interest calculation'. From there, thick socialisation can lead to the partial internalisation of norms 'resulting in the establishment of new collective rationalities and self-restraint in the articulation of national interests' (Lewis 2003: 99). According to Lewis, this challenges the rationalist assumption that states will always seek to maximise their interests. The final version of thick socialisation Lewis calls 'deep' socialisation. This is where 'internalisation takes on a holistic quality as norm compliance becomes taken for granted and near automatic' (Lewis 2003: 99; Hurd 1999: 396).

Lewis's types reproduce the spiral process identified by Risse, Ropp and Sikkink.[16] Risse, Ropp and Sikkink break down the process of socialisation into first, denial; second, strategic bargaining and tactical concessions; third, adherence; and lastly, the habitualisation of norms. Thus, thin socialisation equates with the steps of strategic bargaining and tactical concessions to particular norms. Partial thick socialisation is similar to Risse, Ropp and Sikkink's adherence of norms which influence national interests, while deep socialisation is the final stage of internalisation where norms become habitualised. Similarly Checkel distinguishes between type I and type II socialisation, the former equalling thin socialisation or instrumentalism and the latter internalised or habitualised behaviour of thick socialisation and 'possibly' deep socialisation based on an identity change (2005: 804). Checkel's strategic calculation, role playing and normative suasion fit within these categories. Within constructivism, analyses of socialisation by Kent (2002), Risse, Ropp and Sikkink (1999), and Lewis (2003) follow linear understandings of socialisation where agents initially reject new norms, then respond tactically, then accept the norm, and sometimes habitualise the norm within their practices.[17]

The argument made here makes two claims: first, that material pressure and normative suasion do take place at the same time as highlighted by Schimmelfennig and Kelley; but also like Risse, Ropp and Sikkink (1999: 15–17) and Lewis (2003) it argues that agents such as the WBG organisations may have initially become open to alternative norms for tactical reasons but the norm later became an entrenched aspect of the identities of the World Bank and IFC. Thus, the WBG initially accepted environmental aspects of development as part of its strategic interests but through ongoing interaction this led to changes in the World Bank and IFC's identity (but not MIGA's). Without unpacking where ideas come from, rationalist accounts only explain part of the picture in determining how decisions are made within the international system. Tracking when and how ideas inform how material incentives are understood on the one hand, and how actors' respond to moral suasion with or without material incentives on the other, can inform our analysis of the socialisation of IOs. Regarding the WBG, the socialisation process involves both thick conceptions of socialisation and thin simultaneously. How ideas and material factors simultaneously influence IOs, and how IOs progress from instrumental strategic calculation to an identity change is discussed next.

Avenues of IO change: direct and indirect socialisation

The previous section outlined how socialisation is used within IR and laid the basis for a constitutive analysis of identity change. The majority of both rationalist and constructivist analyses of socialisation above examined how states' behaviour and/or identity are shaped. This section pertains specifically to how *IOs* can be (and are) socialised. As we know, the very structure of IOs is unique. As organisations that are established to meet the interests of states yet which may be granted autonomy in terms of their everyday decision-making in areas of their expertise, their structure determines how they are socialised. This may be either through the delegation chain with IO principals promoting and enforcing norm change, or direct influence where international norms shape IO staff and management, or both. This section proposes that international norms influence IOs via norm entrepreneurs such as TEANs *directly* socialising management and staff and *indirectly* through socialising member states to enforce change.

Socialisation is the process whereby international norms influence IO behaviour by constituting and reconstituting their identities. International norms, embodied by norm entrepreneurs, appeal to IOs to change their practices to accord with new understandings of the 'right thing to do'. As highlighted earlier, this normative appeal may be met with denial of wrongdoing by the IO. Denying the legitimacy of the norm thus refutes any need to respond to the claims made. Following Risse and Sikkink's second stage of interaction or Lewis's thin socialisation, interaction between the social structure and IOs may result in instrumental adaptation or strategic bargaining by the IO if they are forced to make concessions to the new norm to ensure their funding as pressured by principals. Simultaneously, direct socialisation between the IO and norm entrepreneurs may lead to norm entrepreneurs constraining previously accepted activities, thus leading to an increasing recognition of the new norm (where for example, the IO's practices are no longer seen as legitimate, authoritative or effective). Ongoing normative pressure may lead to public acknowledgement of past wrongdoing by the IO and a promise to improve their performance. As with states, IOs may then vary in the extent to which new norms become internalised or 'habitualised' such that their identities are viewed through the prism of the new norm and reflect changes to their ideas and actions. This is based on the separate identities of IOs informing how they engage with international norms.

Direct socialisation may occur in three ways. First, through dialogue and influence at the international negotiation level: determining policies and influencing policy direction, for example through the World Commission on Dams or the Extractive Industries Review (although these are beyond the scope of this book). Second, direct socialisation may take the form of successful opposition at an IO's operational, programme or project level leading for instance to a re-evaluation and restructuring of the project or its abandonment. Third, direct socialisation may occur through influencing policy change, and internal IO reform through unofficial information sharing and dialogue with IO staff and management. Dialogue is important with IO staff as it is the most direct means of socialisation and has important ramifications in shaping ideas and influencing the direction and content of policies. Direct socialisation is 'thick' socialisation, where the interaction between norm entrepreneurs and the IOs leads to new understandings of the IOs' interests based on a shift in their identities. Examples of how direct socialisation (norm entrepreneur–IO interaction) leads to identity shifts in the WBG are examined in light of each WBG organisation's projects, policies, and institutions, including subjective and intersubjective understandings of these processes.

Indirect socialisation is where norm advocates influence member states to direct IOs to institutionalise new norms. Norm entrepreneurs attempt to reconstitute state interests and identities to direct IO actions to adhere to the new norm. The distinction between processes highlights how norm entrepreneurs influence the IOs through *direct* interaction, and *indirectly* through the principals to influence the IO, although in practice both processes take place simultaneously. The process of norm entrepreneurs influencing the IOs through their principals (using material force to press for IO change) is seen to be the most successful strategy within the literature on the World Bank (Bowles and Kormos 1999; Nielson and Tierney 2003). As previously mentioned, this shows that power does have some role to play where Executive Directors for the WBG were able to place these issues onto WBG organisations' agendas. Yet parts of governments such as Treasury in relation to the US (which supports the US Executive Director), were themselves engaged with TEANs. This represents thick socialisation from the network to parts of the US, and then thin socialisation (or instrumentalism) from the US to the WBG organisations, and is outlined in the next chapter.

Within both direct and indirect socialisation, three microprocesses of socialisation are evident: persuasion, social influence (Checkel 1999b; Johnston 2001) and coercion (Risse, Ropp and

Sikkink 1999; Wendt 1999). The norm entrepreneurs attempt to persuade IOs and their principals of the relevance of particular norms through ongoing campaigns. This includes meetings, letters, emails, faxes and phone calls. Persuasion is an ongoing, iterative process that involves 'changing attitudes about cause and effect in the absence of overt coercion' (Checkel and Moravcsik 2001: 221; Johnston 2001: 496, 499). Norm entrepreneurs also engage in social influence involving the distribution of punishments including 'shaming, shunning, excluding, and demeaning, or dissonance derived from actions inconsistent with role and identity' and rewards such as 'psychological well-being, status, a sense of belonging, and a sense of well-being derived from conformity with role expectations' (Johnston 2001: 499). Social influence is expressed through demonstrations, protests and petitions at operation or project sites, offices or headquarters, and praise or condemnation through press releases, web posts and publicity stunts. However, IOs do not just conform to social structures but also mediate and recreate them through their responses.

Norm entrepreneurs may also attempt to persuade principals to then use coercion on the IO. For example, TEANs influence the WBG through an indirect process of shaping powerful member states who then press for changes within the IO. This is part of the socialisation process because the very act of changing an IO's actions (establishing new policies) influences its interests (whether and how it undertakes its operations) and ultimately its identity (what it believes its role to be) (Risse, Ropp and Sikkink 1999). In the case of the World Bank and IFC detailed in chapters 3 and 4 (but not MIGA as examined in chapter 5), determining specific actions as unacceptable for leaders in international development through social influence and persuasion, arguably led to a rethink by these IOs about how to maintain leadership through other means; through identifying with, and then promoting, previously imposed sustainable development norms.

Combined, direct and indirect socialisation involving persuasion, social influence and coercion reconstitute IO identities. Thus, each micro-process of socialisation is important in shaping the identity of IOs, but as is argued below, the shift in identity comes from various combinations of the three processes rather than a single isolated one. As noted in the introduction, these micro-processes mirror the three levels of internalisation established by Alexander Wendt (1999): coercion, calculation and belief. Yet I argue that micro-processes are enacted simultaneously as opposed to determining an overarching linear culture (Wendt 1999: 268). The micro-processes of persuasion, social influence and coercion are undertaken via avenues of direct and indirect socialisation.

By promoting new shared meanings within world politics, materially weak non-state actors can reconstitute the identity of IOs. Non-state actors both independently and through states may socialise IOs to internalise norms that constitute the social structure. While NGOs 'may not typically serve as sites of socialization for state actors' (Bearce and Bondanella 2007: 707, n 20), within transnational advocacy networks they may constitute the normative environment within which IOs such as the WBG organisations operate. That transnational advocacy networks influence the World Bank has been detailed extensively (Fox and Brown 1998: 511; Keck and Sikkink 1998: 13; Nelson 1996; Paul and Israel 1991; Wade 1997). This process is rooted in the inability of civil society within developing countries to negotiate the terms of development projects agreed to between developing states and IOs. As a result, local NGOs attempt to bring about change through forming TEANs with northern NGOs to pressure northern states to then influence the WBG. The concern here is how such processes shape the WBG organisations. The mutual constitution between TEANs and the WBG affiliates is exemplified by direct and indirect socialisation between the IO and the social structure of TEANs that influence the organisations' identities.

Empirically, direct and indirect socialisation cannot be separated from each other in terms of their success, although the literature on the World Bank prioritises indirect socialisation as being measurable, observable and causal compared with direct socialisation (TEANs directly shaping the WBG). This is so for two reasons. First, it is considered easier to document why change came about in IOs as a result of the material pressure from principals. Second, rationalists would argue that it is difficult to measure the level of influence of direct socialisation placed on IOs through unofficial and official discussion and suasion, from letter writing, protests, media coverage, and information flows between norm entrepreneurs and IOs. Often, direct socialisation is not given explanatory power in accounts of Bank change because it is hard to ascertain the extent to which it helped shift the WBG's stance on environmental issues. This remains a critical methodological concern for rationalists because their research agenda often focuses on pattern finding rather than process tracing (Marsh and Sharman 2007), although evidence uncovered during interviews, reinforced by primary and secondary literature on WBG interactions with TEANs, attest its importance.

Indeed, there is evidence to suggest that direct socialisation played an important role in influencing the direction of change within these IOs, particularly when TEANs positively reinforce WBG responses to calls for change (Caufield 1996; Elster 1989: ch 9; Rich 1994; Wade 1997). The evidence provided in the following chapters substantiates the constitutive effects of the interaction between non-state actors, states and IOs. Thus, indirect socialisation involves both thick socialisation and instrumental decision-making. Initial instrumental pressure placed by the US, foremost among principals, on the Bank led to tactical changes by the IO. However, while the IO resisted these overtures as a threat to its identity at the beginning, over the long term it began to see sustainable development as part of its role as a leader in development. Thus, the IO began to view sustainable development as a norm to champion as a result of its perception of itself as a development leader. Thus, both normative influence on the principal, as well as the principal's material power shape the IO. This process occurs at the same time as direct socialisation of the IO. Both processes lead to a shift in an IO's identity, rather than either the brute force of states or the moral authority of TEANs independently. The next section situates the WBG within its development context and explores the rise of TEANs.

Norms of development, TEANs and the World Bank

The World Bank Group plays an important role in international development through setting development agendas, prioritising economic reforms, identifying loan requirements and recognising and legitimising other actors. Yet the WBG organisations are situated within a social structure. A brief history of international development is provided before recounting the rise of environmental NGOs and the formation of TEANs that emerged to challenge the WBG's understanding of what constitutes international development. Norms of development are based upon differing conceptions of what constitutes progress and how it ought to be achieved. Shared assumptions about how to achieve development through modernisation, determined by economic indicators, dominate the international system. TEANs challenge this by persistently calling attention to the negative impact of economic development on the biosphere. After outlining the wider context of shifting development norms, how TEANs exemplify the changing social structure through socialisation is elaborated.

Development practices have undergone significant shifts since the 1950s, although development remains focused on economic growth through modernisation and industrialisation. In international development the state was seen as the primary means of development up to the 1970s. By the late 1970s, methods of development through official development assistance to the state had not produced economic 'take-off'.[18] In the 1980s, neoliberal lending practices came to the fore. As developing states reduced the role of the state under structural adjustment programmes, many, social services became the domain of development NGOs. The weaknesses of the private sector within developing countries also led donors to 'explore the alternatives of working through non-profit, voluntary institutions' (Bratton 1989: 570). As the role, numbers and strength of NGOs increased so did their influence in international development, broadening the focus to include issues such as poverty, inequality, the role of women, and local participation. The size and scope of NGO activity has increased dramatically over the last four decades (Marcussen 1996: 406; Princen and Finger 1994: 1–4). During this period, environmental NGOs also rose to prominence.

Numerous studies show the increasing power of environmental groups in world politics (Keck and Sikkink 1998; Lipshutz 1996; O'Brien *et al.* 2000). The environment became a major international issue in the early 1960s and 1970s. Environmentalists questioned the assumptions of orthodox economic systems that externalise environmental damage. Prior to the 1960s, multilateral environmental agreements (MEAs) were based upon wildlife and conservation issues, maritime pollution, and environmental threat from the spread of nuclear weaponry (Caldwell 1991: 5–6). Between 1921 and 1959, 20 MEAs were signed. By the 1970s the number had reached 49 (Brenton 1994: 89). More than 500 MEAs now exist. Early MEAs were state-driven 'with rather less attention paid to political, economic or social impacts', and much of the debate was 'absent a high degree of public concern or interest' (Elliot 1998: 7–8).

The rise of public awareness of environmental degradation emerged in the 1960s and 1970s, as a result of a number of defining incidents which brought the natural environment into public purview. Major events included: the first sight of the planet as a single biosphere from space; increased scientific understanding of environmental damage such as biodiversity loss, deforestation, ozone depletion and climate change; the dissemination of ecological literature such as *The Silent Spring* (Carson 1962); and intellectual debates over population growth and finite resources such as Paul Erlich's book *The Population Bomb* (1968) and the Club of Rome's *Limits to Growth* Report (1972) (Brenton 1994: 18, 22–3). These events combined to produce an emerging awareness throughout global civil society, resulting in substantial increases in the membership of environmental NGOs. Initially the Sierra Club (one of the earliest and most influential American environmental organisations) had a few tens of thousands of members, but by the early 1970s the numbers had risen to 140,000. Similarly, the national Audubon Society, one of the oldest environmental NGOs, had increased to 200,000 members by this period (Brenton 1994: 19). The first international environmental NGOs focusing on advocacy included the World Wide Fund for Nature, Greenpeace International and Friends of the Earth. A further surge in environmental NGO membership occurred in the US in the early 1980s as new environmental problems came to light: from four million in 1981, to seven million in 1988, to eleven million in 1990 (Bramble and Porter 1992: 317; Brenton 1994: 125). The rise and strength of NGO influence is attributed to three main NGO functions. These are,

> [First] expert knowledge and innovative thinking about global environmental issues, acquired from specializing in issues under negotiation; second their dedication to goals that transcend narrow national or sectoral interests; and third, their representation of substantial constituencies within their own countries that command attention and that sometimes influence tight electoral contests. (Porter and Welsh Brown 1996: 51)

Environmental NGOs have been at the forefront of normative change in the international system. NGOs undertake different processes to influence actors including: shaming campaigns; lobbying; consumer boycotts; monitoring environmental issues, actors and agreements; and acting as environmental watchdogs. They are examined here as part of TEANs which constitute the social structure within which the WBG organisations act because change within the WBG cannot be solely attributed to the role of environmental NGOs in challenging dominant development norms. Activists, indigenous peoples, the media, academia, trade unions and religious groups are also vital for a better understanding of this process. Varying compositions of the TEANs are provided in each of the following chapters.

TEANs are fluid, loosely based connections of non-state actors that organise around issue-based campaigns and may include epistemic communities.[19] Transnational environmental advocacy networks may therefore include: research and advocacy NGOs, activists, local social movements, foundations, the media, churches, trade unions, consumer organisations and intellectuals (Keck and Sikkink 1998: 9). Keck and Sikkink's formulation of transnational advocacy networks also include 'parts of regional and international intergovernmental organizations; and ... parts of the executive and/or parliamentary branches of government' (1998: 9). Yet these are excluded from the TEANs herein, in order to maintain the theoretical distinction between agents such as the WBG and the social structure or norms of sustainable development propounded by TEANs. The distinction is important with regard to examining WBG/TEAN interaction at the policy, project, and institutional levels. While Finnemore (1996a), True and Mintrom (2001), and arguably Grigorescu (2002), conflate the aims and identities of IOs and NGOs, this is because both types of organisation transform state policies in their cases. Moreover, this is derived from Keck and Sikkink's conceptualisation of transnational advocacy networks which are based around campaigns or 'activities that are combined to further an aim or goal which members from diffuse areas undertake collectively, usually based on a norm or principle and focused on policy change, and whose actions are often not based on rational interest explanations' (1998: 8–9).[20]

The distinction between governmental and non-governmental

organisations is maintained because non-state actors aim to reshape and reconstitute actors and practices to accord with their shared principled ideas compared with states and IOs that are bureaucratically driven. In effect, this means that the two types of organisations act according to different impulses. For example, transnational advocacy networks made up of NGOs, foundations, activists, alternative media and grassroots organisations, aim to influence agents including IOs and states based on advocacy. IOs, on the other hand, respond to normative suasion by non-state actors as determined by their identity, which is bound by their mandate and bureaucratic culture, and is subjective and intersubjective. It would be illuminating to uncover *when* non-state actor norms coincide with IO norms where the norms IOs espouse were not initially adopted as a result of non-state actor pressure. Further, the differences between governmental and non-governmental actors need to be kept distinct theoretically. This is based on a holistic position that the identity of the organisation drives its behaviour as determined by its collective identity rather than individually shared interpretations. As such, changes within states and within IOs come from changes in the organisation's overall understanding of norms and appropriate behaviour as opposed to individual reform efforts, although these do ultimately contribute to reconstituting IO identities in the long term. The role of powerful states is also kept distinct from transnational advocacy networks because it is integral to the process of indirect socialisation discussed earlier (see also Figure 2.1, page 54).

How the pieces to the puzzle of WBG change fit together is thus: the WBG promotes the dominant economic development norm, which necessarily impacts on the environment. Increasing knowledge about the impacts of WBG loans, investments and guarantees uncovered by TEANs led to the recognition that WBG development was environmentally destructive. TEANs are therefore agents diffusing critical information about WBG activities, challenging both the WBG's perception of itself and how it is generally perceived. Through sending alternative information from WBG-funded project sites to the WBG in Washington, DC, the networks question the WBG's authority. As such, TEANs exist to reconstitute the WBG organisations' identities through first exposing their practices. These networks then lobby,

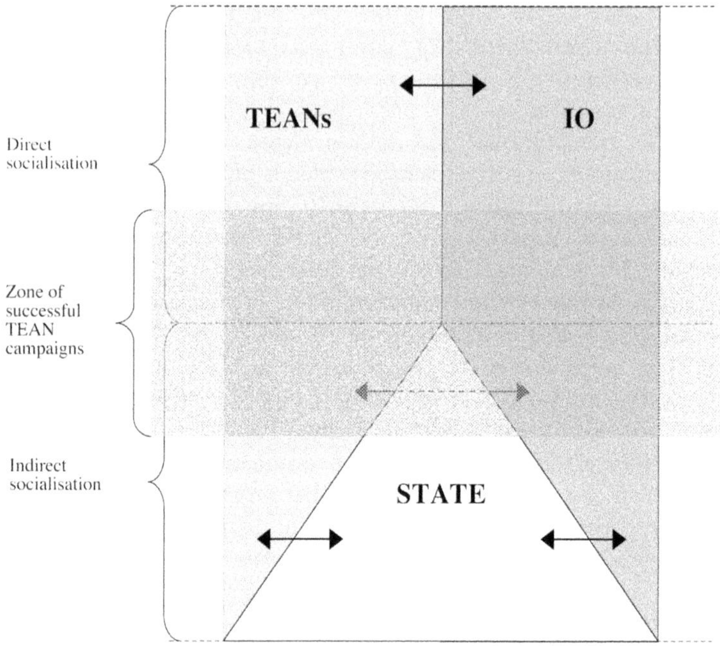

Figure 2.1 *Direct and indirect socialisation between Transnational Environmental Advocacy Networks and IOs.*

persuade, and engage in dialogue with the affiliates and their principals based on alternative conceptions of development.

Overall however, the nature of TEANs, emerging as they have in light of WBG interests and continued practices, lend these networks to be analysed as a social structure influencing states and IOs to internalise sustainable development. Sustainable development aims 'to ensure that it meets the needs of the present without compromising the ability of future generations to meet their own needs' (World Commission on Environment and Development 1987: 8).[21] TEANs therefore challenge the WBG's orthodox economic development, and act to oppose the WBG's actions and reconstitute its understanding of development. TEANs emerged in response to Bank-funded environmentally and socially damaging projects. How the WBG organisations reproduce sustainable development norms depends upon their identities and their creation of shared understandings of sustainable development with TEANs. Sustainable development norms are thus transformed through their reproduction.

Throughout the following chapters the processes whereby TEANs influence the identity of the affiliates to incorporate norms of sustainable development as the 'right thing to do', rather than from instrumental pressure to internalise sustainable development, are traced. Socialisation processes occur directly from the TEANs to the WBG. Indirect socialisation incorporates how states pressed for environmental changes within the WBG as a result of the norm entrepreneurship of TEANs. This shaped states' interests and in turn influenced the WBG organisations, reconstituting their identities to reflect sustainable development norms in the case of the World Bank and IFC (but not MIGA).

States are not the main proponents of ideas, yet they provide the capacity to enforce change. It is only when TEANs are able to link their ideas for change with that of the state that indirect socialisation ensues. Recall that both direct and indirect socialisation processes occur simultaneously. Both are needed for successfully influencing the WBGs and ultimately changing their identities because, as with the analysis by Risse, Ropp and Sikkink (1999), material pressure led to instrumental reactions from the WBG, which then led to an opening up to alternative ideas from TEANs. Figure 2.1 depicts how TEANs, states and the WBG interact and how norms are diffused and consumed. TEANs and the WBG organisations interact with each other directly, spreading norms from the networks to the affiliates, as seen in the top half of the diagram. Meanwhile, in the bottom half of the diagram, indirect socialisation is depicted as the TEANs spread norms through member states, where the state then pressures the WBG organisations to adopt new norms. The WBG organisations consume norms from TEANs when both direct and indirect socialisation occurs. This is depicted in the middle of the diagram by the zone of successful socialisation from TEANs to the WBG organisations, where both direct and indirect socialisation occurs simultaneously. Within the avenues of socialisation the microprocess of social influence, persuasion and coercion through lobbying are played out. The remaining chapters demonstrate how this occurs.

Notes

1 Norm consumption and internalisation are used interchangeably throughout.
2 IO autonomy has been defined as 'the range of potential independent action available to an agent after the principal has established mechanisms for control' (Hawkins *et al.* 2006: 8). Relatively autonomous IOs have independent scope for action outside member state directives. For example the World Bank has a strong president (management) that organises the day-to-day affairs of the organisation.
3 This criticism also pertains to states.
4 IOs and NGOs are analysed separately here. For a review of the constructivist literature on norm diffusion see Park 2006.
5 Further research is clearly warranted to assess if and how the mechanisms of policy diffusion such as coercion, competition, emulation and mimicry differ from the mechanisms of norm diffusion such as social influence, persuasion and coercion (see *International Organisation*, Special Edition on the International Diffusion of Liberalism, 2006). There is some overlap between these terms but this is beyond the scope of this analysis.
6 Rationalists adhere to an empirical realist ontology that is generally accompanied by a positivist philosophy and a deductive method (Bhaskar 1998: 19–20; Fleetwood 2002: 30).
7 'Learning' is also used to understand how actors respond to changing social structures (Alderson 2001; Thies 2003; Wendt 1999: 326–36).
8 While seeming to accept the 'linear' progression towards an identity shift, the argument here is reflexive such that shifts are not fixed because ideas and actors are constantly constituted and reconstituted through ongoing interaction.
9 Wang views Ikenberry and Kupchan as constructivists for their use of socialisation (2003: 101).
10 Presumably this is in addition to material incentives or the threat of coercion.
11 Note that this is based on a rationalist (positivist) epistemology as discussed earlier.
12 Logically, Ikenberry and Kupchan's second and third processes of socialisation could lead to an identity shift although this is not explicitly tested.
13 Although this raises questions of how and why states internalise norms arising 'elsewhere' (Thies 2003: 546).
14 This follows a Wendtian perspective on the causality of ideas (2000) which most constructivists reject (for example Hollis and Smith

1991; Smith 2000b; Suganami 2002; Zehfuss 2001). On behaviour versus identity shifts: the continuum from strategic action to identity change is discussed next. However, scholars who argue that identity shifts occur are constructivists not rationalists, even if logically socialisation *could* end with a shift in identity in the rationalist accounts of socialisation (for example see Bearce and Bondanella 2007; Ikenberry and Kupchan 1990; Kelley 2004).

15 For the flow of the argument Kelley is discussed in the constructivist section although the argument accords more with a rationalist understanding of socialisation as per the previous section.

16 Lewis attributes these degrees of socialisation to Risse (2003: 99).

17 Rationalists limit their analysis to thin socialisation or the convergence of actor interests through interaction (Bearce and Bondanella 2007).

18 For the history of development theory see Leys (1996: Chs 1–4).

19 An epistemic community is a 'network of professionals with recognised expertise and competence in a particular domain and an authoritative claim to policy-relevant knowledge within that domain or issue-area' (P. Haas 1992: 3).

20 For the distinction between transnational advocacy networks and social movements see Tarrow 2001. NGOs' collaboration with each other and other actors drove the campaigns against the WBG and led to this analysis of them as transnational advocacy networks. Again, these are detailed throughout the chapters.

21 There is a cottage industry devoted to defining sustainable development but the proposition here is that sustainable development is determined through shared understandings of appropriate behaviour between development practioners such as the WBG organisations, states and TEANs. Further discussion of definitions of sustainable development and the World Bank can be found in Bernstein 2001 and the World Bank 1997.

3

The World Bank and new norms of development

Introduction

The previous chapter outlined how international norms constitute and reconstitute IO identities through processes of direct and indirect socialisation. Demonstrating that IOs consume norms from their social structure and reproduce them explains how and why IOs diffuse the norms they do. Building on this framework, this chapter analyses how direct and indirect socialisation from TEANs led to an identity shift within the World Bank via persuasion, social influence and coercion. Each of these three micro-processes of direct and indirect socialisation is evident in analysing three core components of the World Bank: its projects, policies and institutions. Taken together, they provide a comprehensive account of how the Bank's identity has changed over the past thirty years to become a 'rule-based' sustainable development lender (discussed below). Bearing in mind that the Bank's sustainable development identity is neither fixed nor stable, and is continuously (re)negotiated by states, TEANs and the World Bank, section one describes the World Bank's environmental identity. The Bank's project, policy and institutional changes compare markedly with previous token environmental changes in the 1970s, demonstrating that the Bank has changed in more than just rhetoric.

The Bank's identity shift is then unpacked by tracing the rise of TEANs in the early 1980s as they emerged to challenge the Bank's 'problem projects'. Specifically, two of the earliest, largest and most influential TEAN campaigns are outlined – Polonoroeste in

Brazil and Narmada in India – as are two subsequent projects cancelled because of mass opposition – Arun III and the Greater Western China Poverty Reduction project. These cases are important in creating significant and ongoing changes within the World Bank and for highlighting how the Bank began to understand the importance of environmental considerations in its project operations and the impact of the social influence of TEANs. Following on from these project campaigns, TEANs engaged in direct and indirect socialisation of the Bank (via member states) to establish environmental and social safeguard and information disclosure policies. The Bank's far-reaching response would shape its practices, making it a norm setter of environmental and social policies for international development and finance lenders (Civic 1997–8; Hunter 2008: 459; Kingsbury 1999). Finally, TEANs then engaged in persuasion, social influence and coercion through member states for the establishment of an Inspection Panel to uphold sustainability as a norm within the Bank. The Inspection Panel set a precedent in providing a means of recourse for peoples adversely affected by IOs. As documented throughout, these three components demonstrate how TEANs drastically changed the direction of the Bank to the extent of altering its identity.

The World Bank's identity

World Bank loans were originally economically conservative in order to guarantee support for floating Bank bonds on Wall Street (Mason and Asher 1973: 73). While the trend away from lending conservatism began under President Black in 1958, it was not until President McNamara in 1968 that the size and scope of lending increased substantially (Kraske 1991: 161; Mason and Asher 1973: 491). This included traditional sectors such as industry and agriculture, and new sectors such as export-oriented industrialisation, population planning, unemployment and urbanisation (Le Prestre 1989: 17). In increasing lending 'McNamara … further broadened the range of activities eligible for Bank financing, deepened the Bank's concern with development strategy, doubled the lending, and almost doubled its staff' (Mason and Asher 1973: 697; van de Laar 1980: 14). Changing World Bank operations to 'development' lending broadened the Bank's scope to include poverty alleviation (Ayers 1983; van de

Laar 1980). McNamara expanded the Bank's development repertoire whilst retaining its original premise of sound economic lending (Maddux 1981: 45). Thus, the Bank incorporated broader development concerns yet its banking mandate remained unaltered. Environmental issues were added to the development agenda in the 1970s, although this did not lead to fundamental changes within the Bank as discussed below.

The World Bank established an Office of Environmental Affairs (OEA) in 1970. Around this time the institution introduced environmentally aware criteria into its practices. It was the first multilateral development lender to do so (Stein and Johnson 1979: 13–14). Le Prestre argues that there were three reasons why the Bank established an environmental office: economic, political and intellectual (1989: 19). Economic motivations came from the realisation that environmental damage (from pollution for example) was financially costly to mitigate. Political factors influencing the Bank's adoption of environmental concerns stemmed from states establishing both domestic and international responses to environmental issues, as evidenced by the US National Environmental Policy Act in 1969 and the United Nations Conference on the Human Environment in Stockholm in 1972. The Bank's response to the impending 1972 conference pre-empted the emergence of an environmental organisation that might impinge on its development mandate. Le Prestre argues that the Bank felt threatened and thus sought to expand its own influence. This fits with the view that securing turf is central to IOs' material interests (Verbeek 1998: 22). Other scholars point to member states such as the US endorsing environmental activities within the Bank (Kay and Jacobson 1983).

Finally, Le Prestre argues that the Bank was open to intellectual circles or epistemic communities that promoted broader understandings of environment and development issues. This epistemic community included Barbara Ward, an influential environmental economist and a leading figure at the Stockholm conference and in the environmental debate at large (Kraske 1991: 169). Arguably, it was Ward who influenced McNamara's decision to adopt environmental issues under the rubric of development (Le Prestre 1989: 22–3). Thus, the combining factors of economic costs, purported IO fear, and normative influence prompted the establishment of the OEA.[1]

From the 1970s, the World Bank defined the 'environment' along the same lines as the United States Environment Protection Agency (US EPA) to encompass a wide array of issues, including the impact of projects on people and the intersection of environmental degradation and human welfare (Wade 1997: 621, 631). The 'environment' became a broad umbrella under which a number of sectors including public health and later indigenous peoples were included, along with issues that did not 'fit clearly within any existing unit or ... [were] barely accepted as legitimate' within the Bank (Le Prestre 1989: 31). The Bank initially conceptualised the environment as having three main areas: public health, the natural and urban environment, and a social dimension. Early environmental work focused on health and 'brown' issues such as pollution, industrial activity and energy utilisation.

Throughout the 1970s McNamara made numerous claims about the Bank's environmental work. According to McNamara, in 1972 the Bank had each project evaluated by the OEA, although there was only one environment professional on staff at the time. He also claimed that there were guidelines for correlating effective ecological protection with development, yet there were only fragments of such guidelines until 1975, and only for industrial pollution and occupational health and safety, with rudimentary checklists for other sectors (Wade 1997: 636). Compounding this piecemeal approach was internal factionalism between environment and project staff, and an incentive system that prioritised lending money before environmental considerations. Before the 1980s there was no consistent overall strategy for environmental issues in the Bank's lending activities (Reed 1997: 229).

> All through the 1970s and into the 1980s the Bank was considered a leading advocate of environmental protection among those concerned with such issues. Yet having acquired the mantle of leadership, the Bank downplayed environmental issues in the years that followed, both to the outside world and still more to itself. (Wade 1997: 623)

In the aftermath of the 1972 UN conference, President McNamara made no mention of the environment in his annual report to the Board of Directors indicating his next five year plan.

McNamara's 1973 annual report had a short section on environmental impacts but it would be another six years before another heading on the environment was included (the 1979 report) and then another six years after that (1985). As a result, there were eleven annual reports between 1974 and 1985, but only one had a separate section on the Bank's environmental work (Le Prestre 1989: 24). Soon after the announcement by McNamara in 1970 of the Bank's inclusion of environmental concerns into its development agenda, environmental considerations lapsed without being integrated into actual Bank practice. As a result, during this period environmental issues were not given much attention at the project design stage resulting in their omission from the project cycle – the principle vehicle for World Bank operations (Wade 1997: 617). This did not portend a major change within the World Bank's identity. As a result, the Bank's claims of environmental awareness became increasingly questioned.

The emergence of TEANs challenged the prioritisation of economic development over the environment, epitomising normative conflict. Arguably, the World Bank had not envisaged that environmental ideas might be antithetical to its understanding of development, thus threatening its identity as a leader in development lending (Wade 1997: 624). The Bank initially dismissed this challenge, sidelining environmental ideas through a 'business as usual' approach, but the prominence of non-state actors continued to grow (Rich 1994: ch 5). As detailed below, TEANs would increasingly influence the Bank through direct and indirect socialisation. Ongoing TEAN scrutiny led to a shift from the Bank's 'business as usual' approach to one of 'do no harm' in the late 1980s progressing to 'do good' in the 1990s. Further decisive Bank activities in the early 1990s constitute what I characterise as a 'rule-based' environmental identity shift within the World Bank, from the 'environment as exception' in the mid-1970s to the 'environment as routine'.

By 'rule-based' environmental shift, I mean that the Bank's environmental shift was spearheaded by the explicit introduction of internal environmental procedures, policies and standards as a result of direct and indirect socialisation by TEANs. These standards may be considered 'rules' which are prescriptions or proscriptions for its behaviour (Krasner 1983: 186; Kratochwil 1989: 59). They delimit what is and is not appropriate behaviour for international development lenders. The Bank tacitly and then explicitly accepted these rules for its development practices. Scholars argue that these standards now constitute customary or administrative international law (Holder 2004; Hunter 2008). The Bank's environmental shift is bound to its environmental standards which have been seen as regulatory or 'compliance-driven' compared to IFC's increasingly flexible-market driven environmental shift (Wright 2006a).

The distinction between rule- and market-driven shifts is not to indicate that rules are separable from norms or that rules are absent from the market. Rather rules are determined by their function within interactions between the Bank, TEANs and member states, which reconstitute norms of appropriate environmental behaviour (Kratochwil 1989: 55).[2] In this case, the Bank's shift is designated as 'rule-driven' because it has over time come to explicitly express its intentions and has made clear its commitment to these rules (Kratochwil 1989: 56). This may be compared to IFC's post-2006 shift (and MIGA's 2007 activities) towards explicitly articulating new standards that it has tacitly committed to, with an as yet unclear understanding with TEANs as to how this strengthens sustainable development.

The World Bank's environmental shift is evident through the dramatic increase in environmental staff and environmental project funding (both stand-alone and component lending); the implementation of a Bank-wide Environment Strategy in 2001; the creation of environmental and social safeguard policies; devising and expanding ongoing environmental monitoring and evaluation; and the establishment of an environmental and social accountability mechanism. Additional activities include the following: becoming an implementing agency for the Global Environment Facility (GEF) in 1991, and for the Montreal Protocol on Substances that Deplete the Ozone Layer's Multilateral Fund in 1992, as well as introducing partnerships and programme funding for global and regional environmental public goods including but not limited to carbon financing mechanisms to reduce greenhouse gas emissions from 1999.[3] The Bank is now the largest 'multilateral source of environment-related financing' (World Bank 2008a: xvi).

Socialisation has occurred when alternate development norms become internalised to the point where the Bank views itself as a sustainable development lender thus demonstrating an identity shift that is recognised by others. While there remains substantial need for the consolidation of the Bank's environmental identity through further 'mainstreaming' and 'upstreaming' environmental norms in the Bank's diagnostic tools such as its Country Assistance Strategies (CAS), the changes detailed next effectively establish the identity of the Bank as being based on three pillars: economic development, poverty alleviation *and the environment*.[4] The next section elaborates how TEANs first began to influence the World Bank to internalise sustainable development norms.

The World Bank's 'problem projects'

Having briefly outlined the evidence of the Bank's environmental identity, this section establishes the initial processes of direct and indirect socialisation which led to that shift.[5] When 'environmental NGOs began to attack the Bank, they did so especially for its neglect of ... green or natural resource issues, which had been driving the growth of environmental consciousness in the West for the previous two decades' (Brenton 1994: 125). It was this surge of environmental concern, combined with an increasing awareness of the complexity and depth of environmental problems, which led to the intensity of NGO scrutiny of Bank practices (Bramble and Porter 1992: 314). Opposition to the Bank gained momentum in 1983 with the influential 'Multilateral Development Bank' reform campaign (Wade 1997: 637). Northern NGOs formed transnational environmental advocacy networks with activists and southern NGOs as the campaign intensified, coalescing around projects as the best way to demonstrate the ill-effects of Bank policies and practices.

Initially, a coalition of environmental NGOs operating in the US, particularly in Washington, DC where the Bank is located, began focusing on the World Bank. This included the following NGOs: the Natural Resources Defense Council (NRDC), the Environment Defense Fund (EDF, now Environment Defense), Environment Policy Institute (EPI, now Friends of the Earth – US), National Wildlife Federation (NWF), and the Sierra Club (Gutner 2002: 55; Wirth 1991: 2645). These groups were joined by NGOs such as the Bank Information Center (BIC), which was formed in 1987 to provide strategic information and assistance to

NGOs on 'projects, policies and practices of the World Bank and other multilateral development banks' (BIC 2001).

These groups linked to southern NGOs and activists on specific campaigns such as Polonoroeste, thus creating TEANs. Transnational environmental advocacy networks also formed in later campaigns such as Narmada through a conjoining of northern and southern NGOs and other groups.[6] Many southern NGOs were unable to influence their governments on the environmental impact of World Bank-funded projects. As a result, they joined forces with northern NGOs to directly pressure powerful Bank principals such as the US, Western European states and Japan (Hunter 2008: 452). Powerful states in turn used coercive pressure on the Bank, which then tried to pressure the country undertaking the project. Focusing here on the indirect socialisation of the World Bank from member states and TEANs, this 'boomerang pattern' (Fox and Brown 1998: 511; Keck and Sikkink 1998: 12–14) aimed to explain how southern NGOs and activists could affect change in developing countries.[7]

Using a 'case study approach' allowed TEANs to challenge the Bank on its actions through social influence, persuasion and coercion via lobbying rather than on ideological grounds (Wirth 1998: 52). The Polonoroeste campaign would establish processes of direct and indirect socialisation used by environmental networks thereafter. The methods used to expose and influence World Bank operations included,

> publicizing case studies of World Bank-financed ecological disasters in Brazil, India and Indonesia, [as well as bringing Bank practices to the attention of] congressional and parliamentary hearings in the United States and a number of European nations, and the mobilization of media attention in both the developed and the developing world. (Rich 1995b: 189)

As this 'partnership advocacy' emerged, it widened to a network of more than just southern and northern NGOs to include the media, church groups, and some government bodies both in the north and south (Wirth 1998). Formation of the networks centred on project campaigns that overlapped in their use of direct and indirect processes to socialise the World Bank. The two most influential campaigns significantly overlapped in terms of both the actors involved and the processes used in indirectly pressuring the Bank through US Congress to halt projects in Brazil and India. Meanwhile, a host of other 'problem projects' were also detailed in Congress to add to the seriousness of the Bank's lack of environmental oversight.

It should be noted that an NGO–World Bank Committee had been established in 1981 (Paul and Israel 1991: 5). Initially, made up of World Bank staff and operation/development northern NGOs rather than environmental advocacy NGOs, it was perceived by some to be a public relations exercise. The committee now reflects a more diverse range of southern and advocacy NGOs. However, the committee was limited by the differing expectations of both the Bank and NGOs, regarding the broad headings under which issues such as structural adjustment and debt relief were raised. TEANs perceived the committee to be a 'non-player' because it was not involved in the 1983 Multilateral Development Bank reform campaign, although TEANs now invite the NGO working group of the committee to support their position on issues such as information disclosure (Covey 1998: 100–3).

TEANs established a process of indirect socialisation via the US Congress. The focus of the campaign became centred on US Congressional hearings relating to the International Development Association (IDA) soft loan programme of the Bank (Nielson and Tierney 2003: 257). IDA was created in 1960, principally to provide soft loans at concessional rates to developing countries. This was initially designed as a means of lending to developing countries with limited resources and credit rating. IDA is a separate fund administered by the World Bank with different terms and articles of agreement, although the same Bank staff handle IDA credits in conjunction with IBRD loans (often theses are blended in the same operations). IDA funds are currently lent to seventy-eight of the 185 members of the IBRD.

To raise funds for IDA, rather than asking for an increase of Bank members' capital, states voluntarily became members of IDA through an initial subscription, accompanied by periodic replenishments (Shihata 1991: 11). IDA members are divided into contributor and borrower countries. IDA proved to be a sticking point for the largest IBRD/IDA contributor, the US, which had been late or refused to make agreed contributions in the past (Mason and Asher 1973: 419). This is linked to the difficult task of approving funding for IOs through US Congress, which is where TEANs found the chink in the World Bank's armour. By persuading US Congress via its Foreign Assistance Appropriations Committee on the environmentally and socially destructive nature of Bank lending through IDA, TEANs were able to influence the Bank by threatening to have its funding cut (Rich 1994: 125; Woods 2000: 827). Thus, indirect socialisation – or influencing parts of the US to pressure the Bank – enabled advocacy networks to harness the material power of states to change the actions and subsequent identity of the World Bank.[8] As IDA credits are blended with IBRD loans, shaping the former would also influence the latter. The networks persuaded states to use their material power to instigate change. This initially led to the Bank making limited concessions to the US and TEANs, and as argued throughout, led the Bank to become increasingly aware of the sustainable development norms promoted by TEANs. Bowles and Kormos state that

> [i]n the early 1980s, these environmental NGOs detailed the ecological impacts of several prominent Bank projects. They provided a steady stream of data gathered in the field to Congress, and Congress, in turn, acted as a megaphone, amplifying calls for reform and bringing to bear its considerable financial leverage. (Bowles and Kormos 1999: 222)

Between 1983 and 1987, there were more than twenty hearings on the environmental and social performance of Multilateral Development Banks before six sub-committees of US Congress (Bowles and Kormos 1999: 213; Gutner 2002: 56; Wade 1997: 656). Initially, the Bank did not respond to the campaign against it led by the NRDC, the EPI (Friends of the Earth) and the NWF in 1983–4. They would be joined soon after in a TEAN by other players including US NGOs and campaign-specific southern NGOs with indigenous activists testifying to the committee. Northern-based environmental advocacy NGOs became linked to project campaigns in Brazil, India, and elsewhere to pressure member states to implement environmental reforms within the Bank.

The network was able to convince the sub-committees to hold hearings before voting on legislation. These hearings would be a focal point of their campaign and would feature environmental

NGOs and indigenous peoples from Brazil and India affected by Bank-financed projects. In 1984, the sub-committees issued nineteen recommendations via US Congress to the US Executive Director of the World Bank (Rich 1995a: 5).

> The demands were devised, developed, and successfully advanced in a skilful campaign by Non-governmental organisations. They worked through Congress to force the administration to take up environmental protection and allied themselves with like-minded groups in other countries to build an international consensus on the greening of the World Bank. (Gwin 1994: 49)

The recommendations included: increasing the number of environmental staff; consulting national environmental and health ministries regarding projects; sharing information with environmental NGOs; and financing more small-scale projects (Wade 1997: 661). The World Bank, however, did not respond to the claims being made by TEANs. Social influence through media attention to the hearings increased, as did public opposition, with the Polonoroeste project prominent. Within the US Congress, the Democrats opposed environmental destruction while Republican Senator Kasten opposed the amount of aid flowing to Multilateral Development Banks (MDBs). This led to an agreement by Bank President Clausen for a meeting between Bank representatives, Senator Kasten and environmental NGOs in 1985 (Nielson and Tierney 2003: 257). This was unprecedented as the World Bank maintained that its relations should only be with member states' treasuries as stated in its Articles of Agreement.

By 1986, the campaign had become stronger and larger and was redirected towards persuading the US Treasury to then use coercive pressure on the Bank. This coincided with the Latin American debt crisis; the US Treasury was pursuing a greater role for the Bank in debt relief through the Baker Plan. This was a separate issue as loans under the Baker plan would be disbursed under the IBRD and not IDA where TEANs were focusing their attention, although the IBRD and IDA cannot easily be disassociated. However, to increase the Bank's activities in debt relief the World Bank would need another general capital increase of membership funds. For this, the Bank needed congressional approval for the IBRD increase, relying on Senator Kasten for approval (Nielson and Tierney 2003: 258; Wade 1997: 667–8).

Thus, in 1987, US Congress was to vote on an increase in IBRD funds as well as vote on replenishing the eighth contribution to IDA.

The combination of the debt crisis and the massive advocacy campaign thus culminated in the 'partial victory' for the network when in 1986, US Secretary Baker ordered the US Executive Director (US-ED) to oppose a power sector loan (for an initial twenty-five dams, leading to approximately 136 dams) to Brazil on environmental grounds. Although this loan was approved, it was the first time an Executive Director had opposed a loan on purely environmental considerations (Wade 1997: 670–1).[9] This signified a major shift at the executive level of the World Bank, amply showing how TEANs had managed to make environmental issues an item on the agenda of powerful states. While environmental concerns coincided with US attempts to increase IBRD funds for other purposes, the ability of environmental groups to influence Congress is significant in showing their ability to shape political outcomes. This influence would establish the beginning of influencing key parts of the US government, further documented in the following sections on policies and institutions. Moreover, other World Bank principals, particularly Germany, Japan, Sweden, the Netherlands and Australia began to raise questions about the role of the World Bank in environmentally disastrous projects (Gwin 1994: 51; Khagram 2004: 120, 124–5).

Previous statements by the World Bank assured members and critics that the destruction would have been worse without the Bank's involvement (Caufield 1996: 177). Yet by 1987, the Bank began to take an alternative approach to TEANs than the perceived indifference and arrogance of previous years (Le Prestre 1989: 193, 198). As will be demonstrated, the Bank moved from explicitly ignoring, then rejecting, TEAN claims, to engaging and responding to issues with more comprehensive measures. The next sections outline in more detail the process of direct socialisation by TEANs within specific problem project campaigns, in order to demonstrate how IOs consume norms from TEANs.

The Polonoroeste campaign

Beginning in 1982, Polonoroeste was a World Bank- (and Inter-American Development Bank-) funded project that aimed to open up the Amazon forest for farming, cattle ranching and settlement through a road-building and colonisation programme in northwestern Brazil (Auferheide and Rich 1988: 301). Bank ecologist Robert Goodland drafted the Bank's Indigenous People Policy during Polonoroeste but it would not be adopted until after Polonoroeste was approved; the protection of indigenous Amerindian reserves would be included only in later loans to Brazil.[10] Meanwhile, the Polonoroeste project would come to epitomise the worst aspects of Bank lending. The project pushed local inhabitants off their traditional land, severing their sustainable livelihoods.[11] Concurrently, the project opened up the forest to unsustainable practices of logging, ranching and using unsustainable farming methods on unsuitable soil, while creating opportunities for pork-barrel corrupt political processes that contributed to stripping the land. Other spill-over effects included: rapid deforestation at unprecedented levels; widespread malaria; the encroachment of colonists onto protected reserves; and mercury pollution from gold mining into the rivers – all of which contributed to Polonoroeste becoming the first case to illustrate environmentally degrading Bank practices (Auferheide and Rich 1988: 301; Keck 1998: 185). This was highlighted by the murder in 1988 of one of the principal activists, Francisco 'Chico' Mendes, a local rubber tapper and trade unionist fighting the project, which was well documented by the media in the US and Europe (for more details see Caufield 1996; Cowell 1991; Le Prestre, 1989; Revkin 1990; Rich 1989, 1994; Wade 1997).

Environmental NGOs mounting the World Bank reform campaign in Washington, DC needed evidence to convince US Congress of the negative impacts of Bank projects. The Polonoroeste campaign began at the Washington level when NGOs heard rumours, confirmed by leaked World Bank reports, that Polonoroeste might be environmentally destructive on a large scale. It was only later that links to local people adversely affected by the project became a central element in their campaign (Keck 1998: 187), although personal networks between Washington NGOs and Brazilian environmentalists contributed to making Polonoroeste the first case of the World Bank reform campaign (Rodrigues 2000: 134).[12]

Initial opposition to World Bank operations in the Brazilian state of Rondonia came from David Price, a regional specialist and consultant for the World Bank. Price advised against the project because of 'grossly deficient' information regarding 'the location of isolated tribal groups, the suitability of the soils for agriculture, and even the distribution of land tenure arrangements' (Rich 1994: 115). Price claimed that his report was distorted but the project went ahead regardless. In fact, there were also internal Bank reservations about the environmental impacts of the project (Le Prestre 1989: 179). Yet it was not until the opposition of TEANs had garnered media attention that the inadequacies of the project were acknowledged. TEANs' social influence included an exposé of the environmental degradation in a segment of the widely broadcast current affairs programme *60 Minutes* in 1987 (Rich 1994: 139, 141–5).

With regard to the Brazilian component of the TEAN, the Polonoroeste campaign exemplifies the issues inherent in two aspects of environmental advocacy: establishing transnational networks and empowering domestic activists. First, the campaign was a precedent to oppose the World Bank and other MDBs using a case study approach. As a result, it took some time before links were established between northern NGOs and southern activists and peoples adversely affected by the project. Brazilian opposition became linked to northern NGOs through foreign and Brazilian anthropologists, such as Steve Schwartzman of Survival International and Carlos Alberto Ricardo of the Ecumenical Center for Documentation and Information, as well as journalists and academics (Keck and Sikkink 1998: 138). As such, the TEAN was just beginning to emerge. The first Brazilian witness in the US Congressional hearings on Polonoroeste was environmentalist Jose Lutzenburger, although he had only a 'sketchy knowledge of Rondonia' (Keck 1998: 187).[13] None of the Brazilian activists initially engaged in the Polonoroeste campaign were from either Rondonia or the Amazon region. Contact with the Acre rubber tappers under union leader Chico Mendes was established in 1985, resulting in the establishment of a National Council of Rubber Tappers thus linking the local to the national, and then to the international network with northern NGOs.

Second, Brazilian activism was emboldened by international attention on the global impact of deforestation, a subject of environmental attention since the 1970s, and was intricately linked to World Bank-led development in the Amazon. The mobilisation of peoples adversely affected by the Polonoroeste project, Amerindians, local rubber tappers, and national Brazilian environmental groups, signified a strong Brazilian coalition against the project. The campaign used direct socialisation via social influence to spread knowledge about the destruction of the Amazon in a documentary titled *Decades of Destruction* by Adrian Cowell, who was involved in the TEAN. The documentary was shown in a dozen countries including the US in 1990 (Rich 1994: 139).

The result of the campaign on Polonoroeste was the suspension of the Bank's remaining loan disbursements (a quarter of a billion dollars) until the Brazilian government prepared and undertook emergency environmental and Amerindian land protection measures (Rich 1994: 126). The Bank then undertook another project in the area. Planoflora aimed to rectify the social and ecological damage created by Polonoroeste and would again attract mass opposition by TEANs made up of most of the same actors involved in the Polonoroeste campaign. In 1995, TEANs filed a claim with the World Bank's Inspection Panel over violations of World Bank environmental and social safeguards in the Planoflora project (Keck 1998: 201; Rich 1994: 166–9; Rodrigues 2004). Thus, Polonoroeste set three precedents. It was the first time that a project had spawned a subsequent project aimed to meet the environmental and social safeguards not met in the original project. Second, TEANs emerged to oppose World Bank projects over their environmental impacts, which grabbed the attention of the international media, states and Bank management. And most importantly, it was the first time a project's lending had been suspended as a result of environmental opposition. The subsequent Narmada campaign shows that this would not be the last.

The Narmada Sardar Sarovar campaign

Following on the heels of Polonoroeste, another project, the Narmada Sardar Sarovar Scheme in India, also erupted into a major campaign and public relations disaster for the World Bank. The Narmada dam scheme was designed to be the biggest hydroelectric project in history, and involved two separate loans from the Bank. These were the Narmada River Development (Gujarat) Sardar Sarovar Dam and Power Project, and the Narmada Development (Gujarat) Water Delivery and Drainage Project. The projects were agreed to in 1985 and 1986 respectively (Shihata 1994: 10). The related projects were designed to run through three provinces and supply irrigation to farmers and electricity to the greater population. The scheme involved the construction of thirty major dams, 135 medium-sized dams and another 3,000 small dams over a 40- to 50-year period. Yet the project became the focus of one of the largest civil protests within India since its independence. Indeed, '[f]rom the beginning of project implementation, local and international non-governmental organisations had criticized both the environmental assessment and the resettlement/rehabilitation component of the Narmada projects' (Shihata 1994: 10).

Narmada was considered a 'paradigm project campaign' (Wirth 1998: 61) because it was not only the first campaign to actively stop Bank lending to a country on environmental and social grounds, but also because the campaign was coordinated simultaneously from both the project affected area in India and Washington, DC. While there were numerous other projects in India with resettlement issues, Narmada became internationally known because of the 'remarkable alliance of determined villagers, local activists, and international groups that fought it' under the banner of the Narmada Bachao Andolan – Save the Narmada (Caufield 1996: 24). Direct socialisation from 1989–1990 included social influence via acts of civil disobedience, mass protests (including one of up to 60,000 protesters from 250 organisations in the state of Madhya Pradesh), rallies, petitions and marches, and included high-profile Indian celebrities and clergy, culminating in a hunger strike (Caufield, 1996: 14–15; Khagram 2004: 123).[14] Indirect socialisation took place simultaneously with TEANs engaging in dialogue and persuasion directly with European principals such as Sweden, and indirectly through the European Parliament (Khagram 2004: 124–5).

In response to widespread opposition and conflicting claims over Narmada the World Bank President commissioned its first ever independent review in 1992, led by Bradford Morse, a former US Congressman and later head of the United Nations Development Program (Gutner 2002: 30). Both the reviewers and TEANs demanded that the reviewers have complete autonomy and full access to Bank files, which the Bank accepted (Wade 1997: 702). The Morse report estimated that the dam and associated canals would affect an estimated 240,000 people. Moreover, the activists claimed that not only would this destroy people's livelihoods, but that there were no adequate environmental or resettlement plans in the project, a fact that the Morse report supported (Morse and Berger 1992). The Morse report was the first time that the World Bank had allowed, let alone commissioned, an independent review of one of its projects.[15] The report discovered that no environmental impact assessment of the project had been undertaken and that impacts on people downstream of the project had not been analysed. Negative impacts from the project included: salinity, reduced irrigation, and the establishment of breeding grounds for water-borne diseases. Moreover, the Morse Commission discovered that there was no comprehensive resettlement plan, nor any data, to resettle villagers to be displaced by the project. Deadlines for India set by the World Bank in 1985, 1988, and two in 1989 to provide resettlement plans were not met. In 1990 the World Bank then asked for partial plans from India which were not forthcoming.

In addition, the Commission discovered ample evidence that these concerns had already been detailed in earlier World Bank reports on the project and had been ignored (Caufield 1996: 25–7; Khagram 2004: 89). The Bank had asked the Morse Commission to recommend improvements to the project – the report recommended that the Bank step back and review its approach (Payne 1996: 134). The World Bank's response to the Morse report was to release a document entitled *Narmada: Next Steps* ten weeks after the release of the Morse report. *Next Steps* claimed that the Indian government was moving towards adherence to World Bank policies, arguing that there was no need to halt the project. The authors of the Morse report claimed their report had been ignored and misrepresented, a fact which they conveyed to the Executive Directors.[16] Similar outrage manifested within the TEAN; they intensified direct socialisation through social influence by advertising their opposition in the *Financial Times* and the *New York Times*.[17] As a result, indirect socialisation via coercive pressure by the Bank's principals increased. By October 1992, Executive Directors from the US, Canada, Japan, Germany, Australia and Scandinavia called for a suspension of disbursements, but the Board was split between industrial and developing Executive Directors with the former in favour of cancelling the loan (Khagram 2004: 130). The Board however, voted to give India until 1 April 1993 to meet the terms of the loan. On 31 March 1993 India asked the World Bank to cancel the rest of the Narmada Sardar Sarovar loan, which it would have had to do the next day due to Indian non-compliance (Caufield 1996: 27–8). *This was the first case where a loan had been stopped completely due to non-compliance with environmental and social stipulations.*

Both the Narmada Dam and the Polonoroeste project were large debacles which tarnished the image of the Bank. Its history of funding mega-loans for mega-projects became synonymous with lax environmental stipulations and the forcible movement of people. The World Bank became the target of environmental and human rights groups the world over. The emergence of TEANs through the alliance of southern NGOs, activists, and northern NGOs enabled social influence through protests and marches at both the individual project level as well as persuasion through dialogue at the policy level in Washington, DC. In the wake of Polonoroeste and Narmada, President Conable introduced stand-alone environmental projects, a move pressured for by environmental networks (Rich 1994: 146). From 1989, the amount of money lent for environmental stand-alone projects and the number of environmental projects increased cumulatively. Initial lending began in 1989 with approximately \$100 million for a handful of environmental projects. In the 1990s, environmental project lending increased from \$564 million in 1993 for seven projects, to \$1,072 million in 1996 for sixteen projects. Lending hovered at \$514 million in 2000 for thirteen projects, and \$516 million in 2001 for seven projects (World Bank 2001c: 8).

Overall the Bank's environmental project and programme spending then declined from \$3.3 billion in 1993 to \$0.7 billion in 2002, its lowest ebb (World Bank 2003a: 13). Since then however, the Bank has increased lending levels to \$1.3 billion in 2004; \$2.5 billion in 2005; \$1.4 billion in 2006; \$2 billion in 2007; and \$2.6 billion in 2008 (World Bank 2008d). The resumption of higher funding levels demonstrates a renewed commitment to environmental lending.[18] Significantly, the increase in environmental lending became more prominent after the mid-1990s (Nielson and Tierney 2003: 271), supporting the claim that the

World Bank is internalising sustainable development norms as a result of ongoing socialisation from TEANs. This occurred while overall Bank lending declined between 1980 and 2000 in traditional high environmental impact sectors such as energy; industry; oil, gas and mining; transport; and urban development (Nielson and Tierney 2003: 267). Yet from the early 2000s the Bank has renewed its commitment to infrastructure lending (Khagram 2004: 198; World Bank 2008b). This return to large infrastructure projects is discussed in the concluding section in this chapter.

Polonoroeste and Narmada were not the only projects in the 1980s that advocacy networks campaigned against. Others such as the Indonesian Transmigration Plan were high on the list of Bank environmental disasters (Le Prestre 1989: 174–7) as well as coal-fired power plants in Singrauli, India and the Itarparica dam in Brazil.[19] Suffice to say that the overarching 'Multilateral Development Bank' campaign had ample reason to pressure the Bank on environmental and social grounds, although the impact of the Polonoroeste and Narmada campaigns had the largest effect on the World Bank. Narmada was a paradigm case not only for advocacy networks to perfect links between local activists, villagers and northern NGOs, but also a benchmark for the World Bank on limits to its carte blanche implementation of orthodox economic development norms. While subsequent searching within the development community led to calls for an accountability mechanism to monitor the World Bank, the lesson of Narmada would be repeated soon after in the Arun III project in Nepal.

Further 'problem project' campaigns: 1990–2000

While opposition to Polonoroeste and Narmada challenged the activities of the Bank, more 'problem projects' were continuously coming to light. The Arun III project in Nepal was a standard mega-project for the World Bank. It was a \$1 billion investment project with \$175 million borrowed from the Bank. The hydroelectric dam, reservoir and attendant road construction involved private sector investment and aimed to provide cheap electricity to Nepal to use for export to India. The project had provoked widespread criticism in the early 1990s from the international/Nepali advocacy network on social, environmental and economic grounds (Udall 1995). The network comprised two

Nepali NGOs, the Arun Concerned Group (ACG) focusing on human rights, and the Alliance for Energy (AFE) concerned with environmental and economic issues.

Yet the Arun III dam and reservoir scheme did not have the highly controversial problems that Narmada had.[20] It did not require the flooding of surrounding areas that Narmada did, nor massive forced resettlement issues, although it potentially threatened indigenous communities and the fragile ecosystem with the opening up of the region from isolation. Arun III, it seems, was as environmentally friendly as a large project can be (Fox and Brown 1998: 487). Yet critics argued the cost of the project was beyond Nepal's capacity, challenging the World Bank's commitment to large infrastructure projects over cheaper, smaller alternatives (Payne 1996: 134). The TEAN and US AID persuaded the US Executive Director to oppose the project. The TEAN swayed other Executive Directors: they convinced the German Executive Director to oppose the project, while the Japanese representative wavered although both governments had funds invested in the project.

There was also internal Bank opposition to the project, with a high-ranking Bank staff member opposing the project, and then resigning, due to the unbalanced use of funds in Nepal, arguing that it would crowd out investment for other social sectors (Fox and Brown 1998: 487). While opposition intensified, the project went to the new Inspection Panel in February 1995 – its first case – to see if the Bank had followed its own resettlement policies (Payne 1996: 134). According to Fox and Brown, advocates for the dam had clearly overlooked the social, environmental, and economic considerations, so that moderate project critics, citing a lack of mitigatory measures to offset the negative effects of the project, soon joined the TEAN in opposition (Fox and Brown 1998: 487). Irrespective of all this, Bank management took the loan to the Board for approval.

Before the differing views of the Inspection Panel and that of the Bank's management could reach a climax, the new Bank President James Wolfensohn overruled management, cancelling the project outright (Gutner 2002: 30). The 'August 1995 cancellation of the proposed loan showed that an emerging international "alarm system" had gained growing capacity to block questionable development projects before they were built'

(Fox and Brown 1998: 486–7). Moreover, the combination of increasing TEAN criticism following on the heels of the Narmada project, internal opposition and the emergence of an Inspection Panel, all opposing or seeking changes to the project, led to a decisive move by Wolfensohn to halt the cycle of environmental destruction and advocacy network opposition.[21] While the Arun III dam project had reached the stage of approval, changes instituted by Wolfensohn (detailed below) further relate to the 'new' Bank's attempt to change. Wolfensohn's Bank was projecting itself to be more environmentally and socially accountable in order to differentiate from the old ways of doing development.

Soon after, the Greater Western China Poverty Reduction (GWCPR) project became another example of a mega-project that reached the Inspection Panel for analysis on environmental and social grounds before the normative pressure from TEANs became too great to ignore. The GWCPR project was designed to reduce poverty in three provinces in Western China: the Inner Mongolian Autonomous Region, Gansu, and Qinghai. The latter region attracted significant controversy through the opposition of a TEAN on combined social and environmental grounds. According to TEANs the proposal for Qinghai was to resettle 57,775 poor farmers into traditional Tibetan lands and included a forty-metre dam, irrigation, and a land-levelling component that would lead to pervasive soil erosion and increased salinity.[22] The World Bank received a request for an inspection of the proposed project on 18 June 1999 from the International Campaign for Tibet on behalf of peoples affected by this project (Reynolds 2000: 20).[23] Six days later, the Board approved a $100 million IDA loan and a $60 million IBRD loan for the $334 million project.

On 9 September 1999 the Board authorised an Inspection Panel review of the project. Loan disbursements were predicated upon the Inspection Panel's findings of the Qinghai component. The combined issues of Tibetan rights, dam construction, and potential forced resettlement issues led to a massive campaign by TEANs including social influence via demonstrations and persuasion by swamping the Executive Directors with letters. The Panel's report was presented to the Executive Directors in April 2000. In July 2000, the Board rejected the Bank management's support for the project after the Inspection Panel found that the

Bank had violated seven of the ten relevant safeguard policies.[24] Soon after, China pledged to continue to finance the project itself without Bank funding. This project testified to the continuation of mega-projects being designed without proper environmental assessment and environmental classification (it was classified as a less environmentally risky 'B' rather than an 'A' project even though it included resettlement; the classification system is discussed further below).[25]

Popular opposition to World Bank projects has shown how advocacy networks are increasingly having a *direct* influence on the Bank, with campaigns addressed to the President and the Executive Directors, as seen in the Arun III and the GWCPR case, rather than indirectly through states, such as Narmada and Polonoroeste. However, the Bank has not just been reactive to TEANs, but has instituted both stand-alone environmental projects as well as a number of environmental policies (discussed next). In this regard, the Bank moved beyond the immediate instrumentalist response to the US funding cut threats that characterised Polonoroeste and Narmada. Instead, these later cases demonstrate how the Bank had begun responding to direct socialisation regarding problem projects. This signified a shift from reacting only to material pressure, to reacting to the normative influence of the networks, where the Bank tried to distance itself from old ways of 'doing development'. This interaction demonstrates that the Bank had begun to reassess what the appropriate behaviour was for a sustainable development lender. It also testifies to TEANs successfully applying normative pressure to IOs, while the earlier campaigns show how the networks influence how states exercise material power.

Assessing the impact of problem projects

In the early 1990s TEANs were highly influential as the full implications of the Bank's involvement in the Narmada scheme were being publicised and both direct and indirect socialisation processes were at their peak. TEANs prompted the US to threaten to cut funds to the Bank completely unless an independent review of the Narmada project was undertaken. The Bank acquiesced, releasing the Morse report in 1992, after increasing its consultation and project information disclosure policies, which are discussed below (Nielson and Tierney 2003: 261). However, these changes did not halt TEAN activities, as the full implications of projects previously approved and in the process of being implemented were coming to light. While Polonoroeste was the focus of the initial 1983 campaign helping to bring about the mandatory implementation of environmental assessment, the Narmada dam scheme in India in the mid-1980s cemented the need for rigorous guidelines to ensure detailed responses to potential environmental disasters. The Narmada campaign and TEAN socialisation were influential in establishing an independent Inspection Panel within the Bank (outlined further in the chapter), in light of the Morse report attesting to the legitimacy of TEAN complaints. The Panel would allow peoples affected by the implementation of Bank projects to protest if the Bank had not enforced its own environmental or social goals to ensure their safety and livelihood (Wade 1997: 687–9).

Controversy over TEAN campaigns dovetailed with the leak of an internal Bank review of project quality requested by President Preston in 1991 and undertaken by a Task Force on Portfolio Management. The Wapenhans report, named after Bank Vice President Willi Wapenhans who led the investigation, was leaked soon after the Morse report on Narmada in 1992 (Hunter 1994: 2). The Wapenhans report claimed that over a third of World Bank projects completed in 1991 were 'complete failures as judged by the Bank's own staff' with a 'dramatic increase of 150 per cent rise in failures over the previous ten years'. As such, 37.5 per cent of projects completed in 1991 were deemed failures (only fifteen per cent were deemed so in 1981) with a fifty per cent increase in cancellations of loan programmes between 1989 and 1991 (Wapenhans *et al.*1992: 9; Weaver and Leiteritz 2005: 373). Moreover, staff claimed that thirty per cent of projects in their fourth or fifth year of implementation had major problems (Chatterjee and Finger 1994: 146). The report further noted that borrowers only complied with twenty-two per cent of loan conditions (Wapenhans *et al.* 1992: 9; Weaver and Leiteritz 2005: 373). Wapenhans detailed that internal Bank procedures had caused the deteriorating portfolio performance including: over-optimistic expectations at the time of project approval; a culture of approving loans over realistic project performance; and prioritising new commitments over continuing projects (Caufield 1996: 259; Rich 1994: 255; Wapenhans *et al.* 1992: 30–1). The report was leaked to TEANs who used social influence to highlight the report as a scathing indictment on the Bank's use of orthodox economic development norms that do not accurately reflect development problems. The monitoring and evaluation of Bank projects would be strengthened, but only after TEANs had furthered norm diffusion within the Bank through processes of direct and indirect socialisation on the need for mandatory environmental rules.

The World Bank's environmental safeguard and information disclosure policies

While the previous section focused on direct and indirect socialisation of the World Bank through high profile project campaigns mounted by TEANs, this section analyses how the networks then attempted to socialise the Bank to create a suite of environmental and social protection and transparency rules. First, the impacts on the organisation during the 1980s from direct and indirect socialisation are outlined, before specifically detailing interactions between the Bank and TEANs on environmental and social safeguard and transparency policies. This section again demonstrates how ongoing engagement between the Bank and TEANs led to substantial policy changes within the Bank.

As pointed out previously, in 1986–7 there was a marked shift in World Bank–TEAN relations. In 1986, then Bank President Clausen attempted to reconcile the Bank with TEANs by asking for 'fruitful dialogue in which we [the Bank] could take advantage of the expertise on these critical policy areas accumulated over the years by your [NGO] organisations' (cited in Wade 1997: 670–1). President Conable, who took the helm in 1986, furthered the rapprochement between the Bank and the networks by seeking dialogue with NGOs.[26] This signalled that TEANs and norms of sustainable development were increasingly recognised by the Bank. Some scholars viewed this as tactical, yet it had a profound influence on the way in which the Bank would approach environmental issues in the future (Wade 1997: 673).

During this period an internal Bank restructure in 1987 integrated environmental issues more firmly into the Bank's structure (Le Prestre 1989: 34). President Conable aimed to assist its borrowers achieve sustainable development by 'integrating environmental considerations into the mainstream of the Bank's country programs' (Piddington 1992: 216). As a result, a central Environmentally Sustainable Department (ESD) replaced the ineffective OEA in mid-1987 (Nielson and Tierney 2003: 259). It was located in the policy and research section of the Bank, in order to act as a 'monitor and mentor' to the vice presidents of the then four regional offices (Shihata 1991: 142). Within each of the regional offices a small environmental unit was established in the Technical Department with five to ten staff (Piddington 1992: 216). These changes attempted to move the Bank from the 'environment as exception' to 'environment as routine' (Wade 1997: 675). President Conable specifically referred to the negative environmental consequences of Polonoroeste when proposing the new Environment Department (World Bank 2008a: 150, n 6). Rich notes that the sweeping environmental changes introduced by President Conable had long been advocated by TEANs (1994: 146).

However, the Environmentally Sustainable Department did not initially function as planned, with the central departments unsure of their relationship to policy or operations. It had no direction, no leadership, a small staff of fifty, which was much larger than five staff in the OEA in 1986, yet it was still overwhelmed by the volume of projects it faced – and it was constantly criticised by TEANs. ESD focused on ecological issues in response to NGO criticism, but the lack of 'brown' (pollution) specialists and environmental economists meant that there was little integration between the different organisational cultures of the Environment Department and the rest of the Bank (Nielson and Tierney 2003: 260). Operations staff opposed the Environmentally Sustainable Department because it lacked 'monitorable objectives' and the means to integrate the environment into decision-making processes. TEANs thought ESD ineffective.

This was offset by ESD's attempt to integrate environmental criteria into the rest of the Bank's work by recruiting environmental specialists, launching training courses on environmental analysis, and preparing environmental projects (Wade 1997: 680). The Bank was responding to TEAN claims and the subsequent policy demands made by the US on their behalf (the US made its replenishment for the eighth round of IDA funding contingent on these conditions). These changes were significantly different from the token changes introduced by the Bank in 1970, demonstrating an ongoing shift in Bank thinking that reveals more than a superficial understanding of sustainable development.[27] How the specific processes of direct and indirect socialisation shaped the Bank's environmental policies are examined next.

Environmental and social policies

After 1987, there was increased pressure on the Bank to introduce procedural guidelines already being used by other agencies (such as the United Nations Environment Program (UNEP)) on when and how to use environmental assessments (EAs). The Bank's main focus turned towards implementing measurable environmental criteria, emerging in the form of EAs and environmental impact assessments (EIAs). Although EAs were established voluntarily in 1984, they were only used for projects certain to have an impact on the environment. As a result of the reorganisation, regional offices were given the right to review and clear projects, but were unsure as to how to do so regarding projects' environmental and social aspects.

Indirect socialisation ensured that a steering committee within the Bank was established to produce Bank-wide procedures by 1988. Coercive pressure on the Bank came from the US Treasury, who advocated that the the US Executive Director ascertain that sufficient guidelines were in place to ensure the systematic environmental assessment of all projects. This occurred when US Congress, strongly influenced by TEANs, prepared to pass a law to ensure that all MDBs adopt EA principles and guidelines espoused by UNEP which would determine US conditions for funding the ninth round of IDA replenishments (Bowles and Kormos 1999: 217).

> In contrast to the general policy demands the United States had made in previous replenishment talks [on other issues], its environmental demands included specific policy and operational reforms: environmental impact assessments of proposed projects, environmental action plans for borrower countries, and disclosure of assessments and plans to local Non-governmental organisations and other concerned groups in advance of loan approvals by the Bank Board. (Gwin 1994: 49)

TEANs therefore managed to ensure that environmental concerns were becoming the norm for Bank project practices through indirect socialisation. Wade argues that 'Undoubtedly the campaign led by US environmental NGOs was a major factor in driving the Bank to change its ways' (1997: 655). From inside the Bank, Shihata agreed that it was due to mounting international awareness, from the Brundtland Commission and the development community that 'the Bank made ecology a priority in its activities *since the late eighties*' (1991: 31; emphasis added).[28] The culmination of events demonstrates how TEANs socialise IOs indirectly by first influencing powerful member states.

Bank ecologist Robert Goodland states that US pressure 'certainly helped' the Bank adopt the EA policy that he had drafted but failed to persuade the Bank to adopt. President Conable's sign-off on the policy at the end of his tenure, Goodland argues, was 'influenced by the US'.[29] The policy was Operational Directive (OD) 4.00 on environment assessment – later revised to OD4.01 to accede to TEAN and US demands – which would set out the procedures and conditions of use of EAs throughout the Bank. The revised Operational Directive in 1991 included compulsory borrower information to be circulated to communities and local NGOs prior to consultations regarding the project, and again after an EA has been undertaken, and the release of the EA to the Executive Directors (Wade 1997: 682, 686–7). OD4.01 classifies projects for environmental assessment into categories A, B and C, which are determined by their anticipated impact on the environment. Category A projects have the potential to cause significant environmental harm and require detailed EAs and public consultation by the borrower. Category B projects may have less environmental impact than A, such that the safeguard policies may mitigate any negative effects. Category C projects are deemed to have no environmental impact, such as structural adjustment programme- (now development policy-) based lending and roll-over project disbursements.[30] This classificatory system would be emulated by the other MDBs and export credit agencies (ECAs) (Kohn 2002: 288–9).

OD4.01 is an umbrella policy that applies to all projects to determine their environmental category. The remaining environmental and social safeguards may be triggered depending on the specific project. The full suite of environmental and social safeguards established by the Bank came into effect throughout the late 1980s and 1990s with ongoing TEAN engagement, and was revised in the 2000s.[31] The number of groups in the TEAN involved in reforming the World Bank's policies expanded during this period (Hunter 2008: 453). The updating of policies such as forestry, indigenous peoples, and involuntary resettlement, for example, took five years of engagement (Davis 2004: 26; Flejzor 2007; Kingsbury 1999: 324).[32] One environmental law scholar involved in the policy reform process argued that TEANs 'essentially set the environmental and social policy agenda of the FIs [financial institutions]' where TEAN 'concerns over impacts on indigenous rights and the environment in Brazil, and internally displaced people in Narmada, for example, led more or less directly to reforms in World Bank policies relating to environmental assessment, resettlement and indigenous peoples' (Hunter 2008: 457).[33] The Bank's environmental and social safeguards are detailed in the box below.

Box 3.1 *The World Bank's safeguard policies*

OP4.01 Environmental Assessment (1989, revised 1991, 1999, 2004, 2007)
OP4.04 Natural Habitats (1995, updated 2001)
OP4.09 Pest Management (1996, updated 1998)
OP4.30 Involuntary Resettlement (1990, updated 2001)
OD4.20 Indigenous Peoples (1991, updated 2005)
OP4.36 Forests (1993, updated 2002)
OP4.37 Safety of Dams (1996, updated 2001)
OPN 11.03/OP4.11 Cultural Property (1986)/
OP4.11 Physical Cultural Property (2006)
OP7.50 Projects on International Waterways (1994, updated 2001)
OP7.60 Projects in Disputed Areas (1994, updated 2001)
OP4.00 Piloting the Use of Borrower Systems to Address Environmental and Social Safeguard Issues in Bank Supported Projects (2005)

Source: World Bank 2006c.
Note: Operational Policy Notes (OPN) provide guidance for staff, but most were upgraded to mandatory Operational Directives (OD) in the 1990s. In the 2000s the majority of Operational Directives were converted into operational Policies (OPs) as discussed further in the text. The type of policy in place from 2006 is given in the box.

TEANs continued to use persuasion and social influence on the Bank to improve its environmental and social safeguards and their implementation. As a result the Bank was engaged in updating and tightening the safeguards throughout the 1990s and 2000s with consultations with TEANs and other stakeholders. On dams, the intractability of discussions would lead to the creation of the World Commission on Dams in the late 1990s (WCD 2000), while the Bank's activities in oil, gas and mining operations led to the Extractive Industries Review (EIR 2003). Both processes would attempt to create shared understandings of how to approach sectoral development sustainably. Overall, TEANs are now perceived as legitimate influences on Bank practices although pushback remains.[34] During this period Bank lending in sectors known for their high environmental impact such as infrastructure, high dams and forestry declined in some cases from the 'chilling effect' of potential TEAN opposition (World Bank 2001a: 22).

From 1998, the Bank undertook a conversion of its safeguard policies into mandatory Operational Policies (OP), mandatory Bank Procedures (BP), and non-mandatory Good Practice guidelines (GP). The aim was to make the safeguards clearer for staff to apply (Civic 1997–8: 246; Green and Raphael 2002: 3; Miller-Adams 1999: 22). The conversion process was vehemently opposed by TEANs and led to renewed efforts to examine the Bank's overall environmental agenda (Lawrence 2005b). TEANs saw this as a retreat of the Bank from the environmental leadership it displayed in establishing the safeguards, and questioned whether this would diminish the role of the Inspection Panel in upholding the integrity of the safeguards (Civic 1997–8: 247). Others argue that policies such as Indigenous Peoples were made clearer (Kingsbury 1999). The Bank's environmental specialists maintain that the conversion process is to make the policies clearer and more operational, although TEANs note that specific provisions have been removed in policies such as indigenous peoples, involuntary resettlement and forestry (IRN 2004).[35]

The 1990s demonstrated how TEANs were socialising the Bank directly and indirectly to establish, strengthen and routinise its environmental and social safeguards. However, in the late 1990s and 2000s, the increasing wealth of the Bank's 'middle income country' (MIC) borrowers such as Argentina, China,

India, Mexico and Turkey raised new concerns within the Bank about the financial viability of the institution (Birdsall 2006; Weaver 2007: 17–18). Middle income countries became increasingly eligible for alternative funding from private capital markets.[36] The leverage of developing countries has led the Bank to streamline its operations and policies to become more competitive, flexible and user-friendly in the areas of procurement, financial management and the environmental and social safeguards. The Bank argued that it had a 'compliance dilemma' as it was squeezed between its financial viability and the pressure from stakeholders and shareholders to uphold 'costly' compliance (World Bank 2001b: v), although argument is not based on calculating non-compliance or later clean-up costs.

TEANs challenge the Bank's assessment that safeguard compliance costs are to blame for a decline of MIC borrowing, when it was the Bank's policy in the 1990s to leave high demand sectors such as infrastructure lending to the private sector (IRN 2004; Miller-Adams 1999) – although fear of TEAN opposition did affect staff decisions to avoid high environmental impact projects during this period (Fox 2000). The Bank however argued that an 'excessively legalistic interpretation of Bank policies may be affecting the demand for Bank lending', even though a Bank review of compliance costs did not involve interviewing borrowers (World Bank 2001b: vii, 2).[37] The review also demonstrated that fiduciary rather than environmental and social safeguards increased loan costs for borrowers dramatically. For example, the Bank estimates that increased compliance for environmental and social safeguards will cost borrowers between $42 and $55 million compared to procurement and financial management costs of between $79 and $149 million (World Bank 2001b: 2, 15). Nonetheless, TEANs argue that the Bank has focused on reducing the role of the safeguards in Bank lending (IRN 2004).

Based on these arguments, the Bank began to discuss a *Middle Income Strategy* for MICs in the early 2000s. Aiming to reduce the cost and 'hassle' of its loans based on declining income, the Bank began to re-engage in infrastructure lending (World Bank 2006a: 21) and proposed the use of national environmental and social standards for Bank loans. This dovetailed with powerful member states' interests in improving borrower capacity and putting borrowers in the 'driver's seat' and the increasing desire by MICs for greater policy autonomy (Pincus and Winters 2002). Draft proposals for a country systems approach (CSA), allowing MICs to use their own national policies in relation to environmental and social issues, were floated in 2002 (World Bank 2005b: 1). A World Bank memorandum argued that the CSA would be applicable in countries that have policies 'equivalent to the Bank's policy framework applicable to the operation, and where relevant country implementation practices, capacity, and track record are acceptable' (World Bank 2005b: 2). The CSA would further contribute to the harmonisation of official development assistance (ODA) that powerful member states agreed to under the 2005 Paris Declaration on Aid Effectiveness because all loans to the borrower would have to meet a single national standard rather than multiple donor standards.[38]

The Bank's Committee on Development Effectiveness (CODE) agreed to the CSA if it did not compromise 'the objectives and operational principles of its safeguard policies'. CODE recommended testing the CSA's feasibility through a 'program of safeguard pilots' (World Bank 2005b: 5). On 18 March 2005 the Bank approved the new OP/BP4.00 *Piloting the Use of Borrower Systems to Address Environmental and Social Safeguard Issues in Bank Supported Projects*. The CSA was strongly opposed by TEANs who saw this as a move by the Bank to weaken its environmental and social policies by shifting responsibility to client countries whilst undermining the scope of the Inspection Panel (IRN 2004).[39] The Center for International Environmental Law (CIEL), for instance, noted that OP/BP4.00 effectively reduced requirements for the safeguards from sixty-five pages to three. In doing so, OP/BP4.00 does not define key terms, removes explicit requirements for each of the safeguards, and does not specify what role Bank staff would play in the safeguard application process (CIEL 2004).

Seven Category B pilot projects are active at time of writing in Bhutan, Egypt, Ghana, Jamaica, Romania (two projects) and Tunisia. The Bank envisages fourteen countries taking part in the pilot, with seven more projects being prepared (World Bank 2005a: 18). However, Bank staff admit that borrower country EA quality and management plans are 'variable' and that borrower compliance needs to be 'reinforced' (quoted in Marschinski and Berhle 2007: 11). On the basis of the low-risk pilot projects being conducted, in 2007 the Bank recommended to the Board of Executive Directors a scaling-up of the national equivalent process from project-level to country-level lending. The Board declined pending a formal evaluation (World Bank 2008c).

The report recommended extending the use of the CSA and argued that the pilots demonstrated positive use of EA and national equivalence for physical cultural resources. The use of equivalent standards for other environmental (but not social) safeguards, the Bank argued, were 'encouraging' although they required the Bank to fill the gaps where country system measures were lacking (World Bank 2008c: 2). One notable outcome of the review is the recognition of the significant cost of ensuring that national equivalent standards meet the Bank's safeguards through the Safeguard Diagnostic Review, although the Bank argues this will decline over time with repeat projects and sector loans (World Bank 2008c: 2). Thus far the US remains cautiously in favour of up-scaling the pilot to the country level but argues for extending the pilot 'in order for a more robust set of findings and conclusions to emerge' rather than scaling-up based on scant evidence. Most importantly, the US remains an environmental advocate; it has opposed a Bank recommendation to *not* fill gaps where there are Bank safeguards but not country standards. The US states that,

> [t]he World Bank's safeguard policies represent a model of international good practice, and that specific provisions exist not just to protect the Bank from reputational risk but because they promote sustainable development. We are concerned that such flexibility in gapfilling would undermine the UCS [use of country systems] goal of strengthening country capacity. (US Treasury 2008)

That the Bank argues that the costs of environmental compliance may undermine its ability to attract loans points to a reinterpretation towards sustainable development being borrower-driven rather than meeting Bank–TEAN rules. By the 1990s the Bank had established the most comprehensive and wide-ranging environmental and social safeguards as a result of direct and indirect socialisation from TEANs. The Bank routinised these policies, making them compulsory throughout its operations. The Bank grappled with how to operationalise sustainable development norms throughout its operations through mainstreaming and monitoring and evaluation efforts (discussed below). Bank perceptions of its declining relevance led the Bank to reinterpret sustainable development norms by incorporating them into a country-led development approach. Recognisably the Bank's identity is neither fixed nor stable. While its safeguard policies are central to the Bank's environmental shift, the CSA demonstrates an attempt by the Bank to move beyond its rules-based sustainable development towards a market-based sustainability. Meanwhile TEANs continue to advocate that the Bank's environmental and social rules should be 'the floor, rather than the ceiling, for other MDBs and ECAs' (Kohn 2002: 300; Hunter 2008). The evolution of the Bank's information disclosure policy is discussed next.

Environmental transparency

In the 1990s TEANs aimed to further diffuse sustainable development norms within the Bank by promoting transparency through direct and indirect socialisation. Direct socialisation of the Bank, begun through persuasion and social influence over Polonoroeste and Narmada, continued with demands for vital information on the environmental and social impacts of Bank lending to prevent future problem projects. Moreover, transparency is the most significant example of TEANs successfully undertaking indirect socialisation; influencing states such as the US to further instruct the Bank. It is worth reinforcing that US material power was informed by a shift in interests of US Treasury and Congress, which resulted from persuasion by advocacy networks towards ensuring the Bank's social and environmental accountability. This compares with the US using coercive pressure to further its broader foreign policy goals through the Bank as it had with debt relief in the mid-1980s (Bowles and Kormos 1999: 224). Indeed, Pincus and Winters claim that the US has become somewhat ambivalent towards large-scale Bank projects to further foreign policy aspirations as a result of 'the growing role of Congress and nongovernmental organisations ... in setting the terms of the Bank–US relationship' (2002: 6). The strength of TEANs in shaping the Bank's information disclosure policies resulted from advocacy networks discussing, informing, and as a result, influencing key members of the US Congress over internal World Bank decisions (Bowles and

Kormos 1999: 213). TEANs were aware that the 'secrecy' of the Bank, based on borrower confidentiality, meant that peoples affected by problem projects were unable to effectively mitigate or oppose them.

TEAN persuasion of members of US Congress resulted in the 1989 Pelosi amendment for information disclosure within MDBs. The Pelosi amendment, presented by Congressional member Nancy Pelosi and authored largely by the Sierra Club, placed conditions on the US Financial Institutions Act (Keck and Sikkink 1998: 149).[40] This required the US Treasury to instruct US Executive Directors of MDBs, such as the World Bank, to oppose any environmentally significant project that had not had an environmental assessment (Nelson 2001: 1839; Shihata 1994: 28). Moreover, the US-ED was to oppose the project if the EA had not been made available to the Board at least 120 days prior to the Board meeting to approve the project (Keck and Sikkink 1998: 149). This has since been adopted by other MDBs.

The Pelosi amendment meant that TEANs could use social influence such as shaming and shunning the Bank to greater effect by accessing more information on Bank projects. TEANs could help disseminate information to peoples affected by Bank projects. By monitoring the Bank, environmental networks attempted to enforce the environmental accountability of the organisation. Indirect socialisation of the Bank, via states, was reinforced by the subsequent establishment of the Working Group on Multilateral Aid, otherwise known as the 'Tuesday Group' (Hunter 2008: 464, n 113; Keck and Sikkink 1998: 149). The Tuesday Group began in 1989, as a direct result of the Pelosi amendment and the role of US AID in overseeing the environmental aspects of MDB operations. The group, meeting regularly, was made up of the US EPA, US AID, US Treasury and environmental advocacy network NGOs such as the Bank Information Center, Friends of the Earth, Greenpeace, and WWF (all with sister organisations and networks in Europe) totalling between 15 and 25 NGOs at any one time (BIC 2003). The aim was (and remains) for environmental NGOs and the US government to come to common agreement on the environmental projects and policies of MDBs. TEANs were maintained by a constant communication of ideas to and from environmental NGOs within the Tuesday Group. Establishing a common normative conception of development between parts of the state and environmental NGOs within advocacy networks is the most concrete example of how the networks influence the Bank – indirectly through the US – by repeated interaction and socialisation.

The Tuesday Group established an institutional mechanism for indirect socialisation whereby environmental NGOs communicate with different US government agencies, including the powerful US Treasury, to determine the position of the US-ED on the Bank's Board to further norms of sustainable development. The institutionalisation of this interaction demonstrates the normative shift towards sustainable development. Such a combination of groups, from US Treasury to environmental networks, has enabled a stronger sustainable development stance by the US-ED, thus cementing the position that TEANs strongly shape the US. The Tuesday Group continued throughout the Bush administration. Even with a less committed US Executive Director the Pelosi amendment 'restricts the discretion of US officials overseeing the MDBs' (Hunter 2008: 466).

Subsequent information disclosure concessions were heavily linked to the allocation of IDA 10 replenishment, with environmental NGOs testifying to US Congress in 1993 that the money for IDA should be redirected to other more accountable organisations if changes to information disclosure were not made by mid-1994 (Nelson 2001: 1839; Nielson and Tierney 2003: 261). The Bank's information policy of 1994 was not the extensive document that TEANs wanted, although it was the first real substantial policy on information disclosure. The disparity between the demands of TEANs and Bank policies meant that Congress used coercive pressure to up the ante by lending only two years' funding for IDA 10 instead of the usual three, withholding the third on further policy improvements. The Bank has since implemented such changes, including establishing public information centres, thus making project documents widely available. A large amount of information is now available on the internet, a medium it used extensively in the 1990s, notably from 1998 to 2000, to revise its information disclosure policy with open fora for public comment. Further concessions in August and May 2001 for even greater transparency were linked heavily to the pressure of the Tuesday Group and TEANs spearheaded by NGOs, such as the BIC and including over 550 NGOs from over

100 countries (BIC 2001). A new information disclosure policy was implemented in 2002 and in 2005 the World Bank began to disclose Executive Director Board meeting minutes, signalling a distinct shift in stance in favour of transparency.

The World Bank's information disclosure policy is the most transparent and inclusive of all MDBs, demonstrating that indirect socialisation has been effective in influencing the World Bank to alter its behaviour. Yet constant direct socialisation, through emails, letters, meetings and consultation, has also been integral to changing the identity of MDBs to become more transparent and accountable (Nelson 2001: 1845). Public consultation has been an area where the Bank has improved dramatically (Green and Raphael 2002: 65). As one commentator notes, the World Bank now has 'the highest disclosure standards generally – [which is] no small testament to the focused campaigns on the Bank' (Blanton 2007: 263).[41] As such, TEANs influenced the Bank to establish Bank-wide procedures on environmental policies and information disclosure through continuous processes of direct and indirect socialisation characterised by persuasion, social influence, and coercive pressure from lobbying via the Tuesday Group.[42] These processes demonstrate how IOs consume norms from TEANs. The next section examines how processes of direct and indirect socialisation influenced the Bank with regard to implementing mechanisms to uphold sustainable development practices.

The World Bank's institutional mechanisms

Having detailed how TEANs used direct and indirect socialisation to influence the World Bank to establish environmental, social and transparency rules, this section documents how creating those rules led to the Bank's institutionalisation of evaluation, monitoring and accountability procedures to uphold them (the latter through direct and indirect socialisation as detailed below). The section demonstrates how these three procedures represent ongoing efforts by the Bank to further institutionalise, habitualise and internalise environmental norms into its operations beyond TEAN socialisation. The vehicles for doing so include organisational changes, the creation of a Bank-wide Environmental Strategy in 2001, and ongoing internal investigations into the

Bank's environmental practices. Organisationally, environmental norms and rules were prioritised within the Bank restructure begun under President Wolfensohn in 1996. When TEANs first began to pressure the Bank in the mid-1980s, the number of environmental specialists within the Bank was five, but by 2000 this had risen to 300, later levelling at a lower 250 (Nielson and Tierney 2003: 264).[43] Significant increases in environmental staff, compared to other parts of the Bank, took place in the late 1990s (Weaver 2008: 281).

In the aftermath of Arun III, Wolfensohn created a new central Vice Presidency to further integrate the environment into the Bank's work, elevating the old ESD into the Environmentally and Socially Sustainable Development (ESSD) Network (Wade 1997: 710–12). ESSD comprised three departments: Environment (ENV), Agricultural and Rural Development, and Social Development, with cross-cutting teams for forestry, sustainable land and natural resource management, water, and project quality and compliance; later adding teams for air quality and the urban environment (Green and Raphael 2002: 5; World Bank 2003a: 20). Wolfensohn created a matrix system dividing the Bank into regional departments and networks. The networks would sell their services to the regions to provide advice on specific projects and programmes. The networks included the ESSD, Human Development (HD), Poverty Reduction and Management (PREM), and Finance, Private Sector and Infrastructure (FPSI).[44] Each of the (now) six regions have a Regional Environment Unit to provide technical advice and review safeguard compliance for the project task teams. While giving the environment structural prominence, the matrix system created two unintended outcomes. Devolution to the regions undermined the momentum on cross-cutting environmental themes in ESSD at the centre (Liebenthal 2002: 4; World Bank 2001a: 43). Second, Country Directors were given greater control in the 'internal market' because environmental staff competed against other specialists for 'slots' in country lending programmes and to sell their services to project task teams (Gutner 2005a: 20; Liebenthal 2002: viii, xi, 17; Weaver 2008: 271).

Environmental evaluation and monitoring in the World Bank

How the Bank instigated internal learning within the organisation initially came from the main World Bank evaluation mechanism, the Operations Evaluation Department (OED). OED evaluates roughly 40 per cent of Bank projects after funds have been disbursed.[45] Renamed the Independent Evaluation Group (IEG) in 2005, the OED/IEG was established in 1970 at the behest of US Congress (Gwin 1994: 21).[46] The OED's reports are distributed to the rest of Bank staff in order to learn from previous lessons, although these documents are rarely read (Weaver 2008: 159). Nevertheless, OED evaluations are quite critical of the Bank's environmental performance (Rich 1994: 170). As Wapenhans notes '[I]f it appears that lessons of experience have not been learned, it is not because it has been inaccurately recorded' (2000: 231). Indeed, TEANs have used internal documents such as OED evaluations as evidence to justify their claims (Rich 1994).

In 2001 the OED undertook an evaluation of the Bank's overall environmental effectiveness (World Bank 2001c). The report stated that the Bank was partially successful in its efforts. Notably, the Bank's EAs were the most comprehensive EAs in the world and were being emulated by other aid agencies (Hunter 2008: 442; World Bank 2001c). Yet shortfalls remained. The evaluation noted that staff questioned the value of the EA process, viewing it as time consuming, irrelevant, and often undertaken by staff with little environmental experience. Yet senior environment staff argue that Bank staff no longer question the use of EAs as they have become a mandatory part of the project preparation process for Category A projects and are recognised best practice (World Bank 2001a: 21).[47] For the Bank's environmental compliance specialists, the question became how best to ensure consistent EA use.[48] The OED report stated that there was a lack of environmental integration in projects, particularly in the design phase, and identified as much as twenty per cent of project mitigation and monitoring as inadequate (World Bank 2001c: 10; also noted earlier by Wade 1997: 714–15). This indicated the need to internalise environmental norms.

Immediately after, the OED released an overall review of the Bank's environmental performance (Liebenthal 2002). This 'forthright' report (Wade 2003: 759) highlighted that the Bank had improved its environmental performance substantially since 1987 with an increase of environmental staff, environmental lending, and introducing safeguards but that 'these achievements have fallen short of the expectations of many stakeholders'. Although the Bank had introduced sustainable development norms into projects and policies, the report stated that it had not incorporated the environment into its strategic level of operations; had failed to integrate environmental issues into the Bank's core activities such as its Country Assistance Strategies (CAS) and its Poverty Reduction Strategy Papers (PRSPs); and lacked precise goals and performance monitoring.[49] It noted that the extent of mainstreaming of environmental concerns was 'disturbing'; lagging behind the Bank's compliance efforts (Liebenthal 2002: vii, 8, 13, 19–20). While the report reiterates the Bank's strengths and weaknesses in practising sustainable development noted elsewhere (Green and Raphael 2002; World Bank 2001c; World Bank 2001a: 23, 43), it specifically blamed the Bank's 'culture and structure' as producing 'an unnecessarily adversarial relationship between compliance with safeguards and the promotion of environmental sustainability' (Liebenthal 2002: xvi). Reinforcing the 1992 Wapenhans report, it identified a 'consistent lack of management commitment to the environment, coupled with a lack of ... accountability' reinforced by a 'lack of staff incentives and resource allocations' (Liebenthal 2002: vii–viii, xi, 12).

For example, the 2002 report detailed that the Bank handled Category A projects well, but that projects were being misidentified because staff face 'ongoing disincentives to categorise a project as A' based on time and cost (Liebenthal 2002: 34, 55). The report also highlighted the need for greater EA specialist involvement throughout the project cycle particularly for Category A projects, again noting cost as a factor (Liebenthal 2002: xiv). Five years earlier Robert Wade had written that environment staff received no incentive to fulfil their job requirements and disincentives to object to projects in the preparation phase (1997: 716–17). Evidently this remained an ongoing issue as environmental specialists had to ensure safeguard compliance while simultaneously trying to sell their services to the same project staff (Liebenthal 2002: 21). Further, operations staff remained unaccountable for the projects they design and implement. As a result, staff continued to be rewarded for getting projects completed rather than for preventing environmental damage (Gutner 2005a; Shihata 1995: 19; World Bank 2005c: 8, 12, 24).

Both the OED's 2001 evaluation and drafts of the 2002 environmental performance review contributed to the creation of a Bank-wide environment strategy in 2001 called *Making Sustainable Commitments: an Environment Strategy for the World Bank* along with regional environment strategies (World Bank 2001a). The Bank-wide strategy was developed through formal and informal consultation with donors, borrowers, and civil society including TEANs. Indeed, NGOs and governments were the largest percentage of respondents at thirty per cent each (World Bank 2001a: 200–5). The strategy set the direction of the Bank's environmental work for the next decade. Its stated goals were to integrate the environment into the Bank's economic development and poverty reduction goals; to improve the quality of life and growth; and to protect the regional and global commons (World Bank 2001a: 6–13; on the latter see Park 2007a).

The strategy noted that the 'scope of coverage and quality of application of the safeguard policies at the project level has gradually improved over the last two decades' but that weaknesses existed in their systematic application (World Bank 2001a: 20, 23). This was thought to be linked to 'perceptions, by staff and management, of ambiguities in the scope, intent and requirements of the policies'. Overall, the strategy identified the need to improve the Bank's cross-sectoral environmental work as well as its accountability, staff incentives, skills mix, resources, and transparency in environmental monitoring (World Bank 2001a: 24, 65, 68). The strategy recognised three impediments to improving the Bank's environmental practices: that the Bank's environmental commitments often outpaced their ability to deliver; that environmental practices have yet to be mainstreamed throughout the organisation; and that the importance of sustainable development is 'still evolving' in borrowers (World Bank 2001a: xix). The strategy envisaged 'mainstreaming' environmental issues throughout the Bank's work through using not only EAs but other diagnostic tools such as country and strategic environmental analyses (CEA and SEA respectively). These would be 'upstreamed' into the Bank's policy tools such as the CAS and its PRSPs. The strategy further outlined the need to improve the safeguard system, and programme and project design (World Bank 2001a).

More specifically, the World Bank undertook three Bank-wide safeguard evaluation reviews in 1992, 1997 and 2002. The first assessed Bank efforts after introducing OD4.00 EA in 1989 and updating it in 1991. The second assessment review in 1997 reported a remarkable improvement in the Bank's activities but that environmental screening, public consultation and EA supervision were insufficient (World Bank 1997: xv). It also highlighted that projects were being rated above average by the project team for their environmental ratings, yet ratings were lower if an environmental specialist was involved (Green and Raphael 2002: 8; World Bank 1997). The third safeguard assessment reviewed projects from 1996 to 2000. It reported that Bank management 'has progressively strengthened the process of safeguard compliance' while improving reporting and accounting lines from the regions to the centre to ensure consistency (Green and Raphael 2002: 13). Improvements were also evident in public consultation during the EA process and in Bank training and knowledge dissemination on safeguard use.

To improve the use of the safeguards within the Bank, the Quality Assurance and Compliance Unit (QACU) was established within ESSD in 2000. In order to create an integrated safeguard review system, QACU aimed to provide safeguard clarity, guidance on safeguard use, and to review and clear safeguards throughout the project cycle (Green and Raphael 2002: 139). To improve clarity, QACU took over the conversion of the safeguards and devised criteria for safeguard use. This included creating the Integrated Safeguards Data Sheet that makes publicly available which specific safeguards apply to each project (Green and Raphael 2002: 144; Treakle, Fox and Clark 2003: 270). Guidance included safeguard information materials, while new review and clearance procedures aimed to ensure consistency in QACU and the regional safeguard units' decision-making (a multi-departmental team was assembled to implement this: the Safeguard Management and Review Team) (World Bank 2003a: 20).[50] Senior World Bank environment staff repeated the need for the World Bank to consolidate the changes it has made to its polices, projects, and institutions to further internalise norms of sustainable development.[51]

Established much earlier than QACU in 1996 was the World Bank's Quality Assurance Group (QAG). QAG was established to monitor and evaluate *overall* Bank lending quality. Part of this push was to create 'Bank-wide systems to track operations with safeguard requirements' and monitor compliance costs (Green and Raphael 2002: 18). Early QAG reviews from 1998 to 2000 report two trends: first that compliance was higher for high-risk Category A projects than for other project categories. Second, more recent projects perform better environmentally than older projects (World Bank 2003a). A 2008 IEG evaluation of the Bank's environmental record between 1990 and 2007 now reports that over time projects of all environmental categories performed similarly, while projects' environmental performance has 'a better record' from the mid-1990s to 2007 than in the pre-1995 period (World Bank 2003a, 2008a: 28, 155, n 32). For the Bank, this is evidence that it is internalising environmental norms.

Part of the Bank's learning processes are QAG assessments. Two are now routinely undertaken: one on the basis of a project loan's 'quality-at-entry' (QEA) after Board approval, and one on the 'quality-of-supervision' (QSA) during loan disbursement. Through these and QAG annual reports, two indicators could be used to assess the Bank's internalisation of environmental norms: the quality of environmental projects (coded as environmental and natural resource management or ENRM from 2001), and the Bank's overall project compliance with its environmental rules or safeguards.

First, bank projects are variously codified by network and theme (for example ESSD versus ENRM).[52] Approximately fifteen per cent of all Bank loans between 1990 and 2007 were for ENRM (World Bank 2008a: 22). Early QAG reviews evaluating projects between 1995 and 1998 report that only fifty-eight per cent of environmental projects were ranked 'satisfactory' compared with the seventy-one per cent of the Bank's project portfolio average. Yet assessments of the 1999–2000 period ranked seventy-five per cent of environmental projects as satisfactory compared with the seventy-three per cent Bank average. QAG then began reporting dramatic improvements in environmental project ratings. In 1999 and 2000 QEA assessments returned ninety-four per cent success for environmental projects for quality-at-entry, although project supervision levels were lower than the Bank average and declining (World Bank 2001a: 28). In 2004 and 2005 environmental projects at quality-at-entry ratings remained high at eighty-five and eighty-seven per cent respectively, this time for their environmental aspects (World Bank 2006b: 52).[53] Environmental projects during supervision also improved throughout this period: in 2003–4 environmental projects rated eighty-six per cent and then ninety-four per cent in 2005–6 (World Bank 2007a: 24). In contrast, IEG's 2008 evaluation of completed ENRM projects reveals that they performed at the same rate of satisfaction as the Bank average of seventy-six per cent between 1990 and 2005, although this was still higher than pre-1990 levels (World Bank 2008a: 26, 28).

The second indicator, overall safeguard compliance, also improved dramatically in QAG assessments. By 1999–2000, QAG reports indicated that the EA process had been largely mainstreamed for investment lending, returning high levels of satisfaction with safeguard compliance for all Bank projects (World Bank 2001a: 21). In 2001 the Bank's compliance with environmental safeguards achieved a ninety per cent satisfactory rating. In 2002 overall environmental safeguard compliance slipped to eighty-seven per cent but with a ninety-three per cent satisfactory rating on environmental assessment, the umbrella safeguard (World Bank 2003a: 41). On average, Bank projects' quality-at-entry achieved eighty-nine per cent satisfactory environmental compliance throughout all QEA assessments, with the latest ratings indicating high compliance per safeguard triggered (World Bank 2006b: 83–4). In stark contrast however, safeguard compliance during project supervision throughout the Bank's entire portfolio remains much lower with seventy per cent in 2003–4 and sixty-eight per cent compliance in 2005–6, indicating weak safeguard supervision particularly for Category B projects (World Bank 2007b: 35, 37, 39–40).

The dramatic increase in the Bank's environmental project and overall portfolio performance in QAG assessments has not gone unnoticed. Critics questioned how the ratings could have improved so immediately and on what basis they were derived (Lerrick 2006: 4; Rich 2002: 49). According to Weaver, the World Bank's shift under Wolfensohn towards a results-oriented development framework meant that staff were increasingly under pressure to show improved loan performances. As a result, staff self-evaluations on project performance were, and remain, overly optimistic. This is reinforced by project team managers under-reporting risks by failing to 'flag' projects at risk of not meeting their development outcomes and even actively avoiding doing so through overriding repeatedly 'flagged' risky projects (2008: 274).[54]

The basis for over-optimism and under-reporting that inflate QAG assessments are recognised by a 2004 IEG report that states that staff incentives continue to impede improvements in monitoring and evaluation by rewarding staff for 'delivering projects through the approval system' rather than aiming to improve results on the ground (World Bank 2005c: 24). Notably, current project team evaluations during a project's implementation are more critical but remain confidential, while projects' final implementation reports 'highlight successful project components and hide failures' as project managers are under pressure to deliver good ratings (Weaver 2008: 160). More recently, QAG's 2007 annual report recognises that under-reporting remains a problem: less than half of risky projects are being identified by staff with frequent failures to flag a project's potential risk throughout the project cycle. As a result of staff over-optimism, QAG states that up to twenty-five per cent of the Bank's overall project portfolio may face serious issues in not meeting their development outcomes. In this regard, even QAG assessments direct attention to staff perceptions that 'formal and informal incentives were primarily focused on getting projects to the Board, with quality, safeguards and supervision being secondary' (World Bank 2007a: 27–8).

While QAG is currently reviewing its evaluation system, over-optimism and under-reporting undermine QAG indicators as evidence that sustainable development norms have been internalised within the World Bank. Indeed, the 2008 IEG evaluation of the Bank's overall environmental sustainability states that the Bank's performance in implementing the safeguards has been mixed and that shortcomings persist (World Bank 2008a: 25, 155). This remains a key concern for the full internalisation of the Bank's environmental identity. Under Wolfensohn the Bank devoted considerable attention to improving its environmental record but the incentive and approval process continues to undermine the Bank's environmental potential. Interviews with Bank staff suggest that the approval process is still occurring but that it is less pronounced than it was, while staff training and incentives such as 'Green Awards' which promote sustainable development have been ramped up (World Bank 2003a: 21).[55] Some NGOs and scholars have continued to argue that until the Bank changes its fundamental operating structure it will never truly be green (Gutner 2005a; Rich 2002; Seymour 2004).

Overall these environmental monitoring and evaluation efforts were instigated to further the Bank's 2001 Environmental Strategy. Evaluating the specific goals of the strategy in relation to the Bank's environmental practices reveals that the Bank has institutionalised detailed monitoring and evaluation procedures to habitualise the integration of environmental norms and rules within its operations. It is also clear that there are persistent weaknesses in internalising environmental norms. Supervision of safeguard compliance warrants management action. Management is well aware of the lack of staff incentives and resources, and impediments to cross-sectoral work need to be overcome to further mainstream sustainable development norms and rules throughout the organisation (World Bank 2008a: 30–1). For some, this represents a failure by the Bank to adequately mainstream sustainable development (Gutner 2005a).

In upstreaming sustainable development norms into the policy tools, the CAS and the PRSP also face challenges. For example, the 2002 EA assessment review acknowledged that environmental issues were not mainstreamed into either the CAS or the PRSP (Green and Raphael 2002: xvi, 130). A 2003 interim report evaluating the environment strategy's implementation states that the Bank was meeting it targets in improving staff training on the environment; rolling out of the new CEA and SEA tools; increasing advisory work for borrowers on environmental issues; and introducing environmental issues in the CAS and PRSPs (World Bank 2003a: 17). However, a detailed 1999 review of thirty-seven CASs acknowledges significant regional disparities on the treatment of environmental issues and that they fail to connect to the Bank's poverty agenda (World Bank 2003a, 2008a: 19). For example, the CAS has been an effective vehicle to examine Brazil and China's environmental needs, while Russia's CAS shows no environmental improvement (World Bank 2008a: 33). A further Bank study of forty interim and full PRSPs revealed that environmental concerns ranked 0.9 on a zero to three ranking scale from no mention of the environment at all (zero) to good practice (three), although the full PRSPs fared better than the interim papers (World Bank 2002, 2003a: 3).

The most recent IEG evaluation of the World Bank's (and IFC and MIGA's) environmental sustainability in 2008 concurs that the organisation 'had not been able to integrate environmental stewardship centrally or integrally into country programs, incorporate them as requirements for sustainable growth, and provide lending for environmental priorities' which the report suggests is often because of borrowers' 'lukewarm interest' and the predilections of regional vice presidents, country directors, project teams and borrowers (World Bank 2008a: xi, 19). Borrower disinterest is repeated throughout the environment reviews (World Bank 2001a, 2008a). For some this points to externalising the blame in order to explain poor performance (Weaver 2007: 507; 2008). Where the Bank can make a difference is through further shaping conditions for senior Bank management to integrate sustainable development options for their borrowers. In order to do so, the Bank must overcome its pressure to lend process. It will soon become apparent how the Bank will tackle this: the environment strategy is currently under review (2007 to 2009) with a new *WBG* environment strategy to be released in 2010.

In sum, the Bank has undertaken widespread assessment and reporting of its environmental practices. Indeed, it has been a 'pioneer in evaluating and reporting development outcomes of projects and programs' (World Bank 2007a: 22). Under Wolfensohn, the Bank institutionalised environmental norms into the structure of the Bank through the creation of the ESSD Vice Presidency, the creation of a Bank-wide environment strategy in 2001, and the creation of QACU to further improve the use of environmental rules. The Bank has undertaken repeated, detailed and in many cases frank assessments of its environmental practices through the OED/IEG and QAG (Nielson, Tierney and Weaver 2006: 117). Persistent problems remain in terms of improving staff incentives to meet and accurately report safeguard compliance and to further 'upstream' environmental norms into the Bank's policy sector work. Yet as the 2008 IEG evaluation concludes, the Bank has improved its environmental performance over time. The Bank has institutionalised and habitualised environmental norms, although it has not fully internalised them. These issues will be returned to in the final section of this chapter, on the overall identity changes evident in the World Bank. For now however, it is important to remember that TEANs have been highly successful in instigating such changes through diffusing sustainable development norms when they combine direct and indirect pressure on the Bank, typically through project case studies and shaping Bank policies and the institutions that underpin them. As such, TEANs have engaged with the Bank on problem project campaigns, on using socialisation to push for environmental rules, and by aiming to make the Bank uphold them. Returning to the early 1990s, the next section examines how this led to the creation of the Inspection Panel, again as a result of direct and indirect socialisation.

Environmental accountability in the World Bank: the Inspection Panel

TEANs furthered the norm diffusion process within the World Bank through pressing for an accountability mechanism to uphold its environmental rules. Establishing a credible accountability mechanism to ensure the Bank meets its environmental and social rules was an important and unprecedented step for an IO. The World Bank was the first IO to have a mechanism that made it directly accountable to private citizens affected by its operations (Bradlow 2005: 409; Udall 1997). This had a 'ripple effect' on the other MDBs, who would establish their own accountability mechanisms modelled on the Bank's soon after (Suzuki and Nanwani 2006: 188–9, 206). As detailed below, the creation of the Inspection Panel is a result of direct and indirect socialisation. This is further evidence that the Bank has constituted and reconstituted international norms of sustainable development; making accountability to affected peoples central to appropriate development behaviour.

In the early 1990s the Bank's history of non-compliance with its environmental and social guidelines came to a head with the high-profile project campaigns detailed earlier in the chapter. After the Bank institutionalised the suite of environmental and social safeguards, direct interactions between TEANs and the Bank then began to focus on how to stop or mitigate environmentally and socially damaging Bank projects already in the lending pipeline. The Inspection Panel was created by the World Bank in response to persuasion, social influence and coercion by

TEANs to improve the Bank's accountability to project-affected peoples; a fact the Bank readily acknowledges (Fox 2000: 279; Hunter 1994: 2; Kapur 2002: 72; Shihata 1994: 9–13; Umana 1998: 1; World Bank 2003b: 2).

Direct socialisation emerged through TEANs attempting to persuade the Bank of the need for an inspection-type function. TEANs drafted a number of proposals for a panel during this period (Udall 1997: 5–6). Social influence continued from the high-profile Narmada dam project campaign feeding directly into the accountability debate. The Morse report's revelations regarding the Bank's oversight of environmental and social considerations regarding Narmada lent impetus to TEAN and US Congress support for an accountability mechanism to ensure the Bank's ecological sustainability (Clark 2003: 7; Udall 1997). Indirect socialisation therefore emerged when advocacy networks, US Treasury and US Congress coalesced around this issue, which came to a head in 1993 when US Congress again threatened to withhold IDA 10 replenishment funds should the Bank not establish such a mechanism (Bowles and Kormos 1999: 220). Fox argues that 'transnational campaigns put the issue on the agenda, but the Inspection Panel's creation was made possible by leverage politics based on conjunctural domestic state-society coalitions within the United States' (2000: 289). Direct socialisation was again evident when the Panel was then established in consultation with Washington-based environmental NGOs (Clark 2003: 7; Kapur 2002: 72).

The Panel began operating in 1994 to investigate claims made by a group of people adversely or potentially affected by a World Bank-funded project. The Panel is therefore unique in 'combining the possibility of access of individuals and private groups to rights under international law, with the opportunity to question the activities of international organisations' (Bissell 1997: 741; Former Inspection Panel Member). The Panel's mandate is to:

> help resolve major differences in cases where it is asserted that rights and interests of the parties are adversely affected because the Bank has failed to follow its operating policies and procedures in the design, appraisal and/or implementation of Bank lending operations. (Bank President memorandum, cited in Shihata 1994: 36)

As such, the Panel may only investigate claims against its own actions, or inaction, rather than against borrower states, and claimants must be directly affected or potentially affected by the project to be considered legitimate.

The Panel is made up of three members who are appointed by the Bank's Board of Executive Directors for five-year non-renewable terms, with a small staff and secretariat. Its role is investigative and advisory, not judicial (Nelson 2001: 1843; Suzuki and Nanwani 2006: 206). The Panel process is triggered when it receives a claim and determines its validity. Initially, the Panel had twenty-one days from receiving the claim to recommend the Board accept or reject the claim for a full investigation. Within the same period Bank management had to provide evidence that it had complied or intended to comply with Bank rules. In its 1994 operating procedures, the Panel determined that it would conduct a preliminary investigation to determine the merit of the claim prior to making its recommendation (Udall 1997). If the Board agreed to a full investigation the Panel could find that the Bank had violated its own policies. If that proved to be the case then Bank management had six weeks to respond to the Panel's findings detailing remedial actions to resolve the problem. The Bank would then be required to ensure that all complaints, findings and recommendations of the Panel and the Executive Directors' decisions were made public.

However, this process was circumvented from the very beginning. Bank management began presenting remedial action plans on how it would address claims of non-compliance 'just prior to the meeting, or at the same meeting at which the Board addresses the Panel's recommendation'. As a result, last-minute remedial plans by management gave the Panel no time to assess whether or not they would address claimant concerns (Umana 1998, cited in Suzuki and Nanwani 2006: 207). Many saw this as interference from Bank management in attempting to pre-empt the independence of the Panel. The highly politicised nature of the process was also apparent, with borrower principals voting to oppose investigations on the basis of having their sovereignty undermined (Clark 2003: 12–13; Udall 1997: 64). However, full Board support for the Inspection Panel was evident in an internal review of the Panel in 1996. The review clarified the Panel's operating procedures by affirming the Panel's conduct of preliminary investigations prior to presenting recommendations to the Board while extending their scope (Nelson 2001: 1843; Udall 1997: 63; World Bank 2003b: 10).

Between 1994 and mid-April 1999 the Board authorised only one full Panel investigation: its first claim in 1994, Arun III. Of the fourteen claims in this period, eight (fifty-seven per cent) were not recommended by the Panel for investigation. Of the five remaining claims that were recommended by the Panel (after Arun III), the Board denied investigations for three and restricted the Panel's ability to investigate two more (Clark 2003; World Bank 2003b). These decisions were made irrespective of TEAN allegations of serious environmental and social abuses by the Bank and high-profile project campaigns including, in the case of a power generation project in Singrauli India, where Bank management admitted safeguard violations (Udall 1997; World Bank 2003b: 12). Increased tensions and the inability to find consensus on Panel claims led to a Board working group being established in 1997 to improve the Panel process. TEANs, US Treasury and the US Executive Director then persuaded the Board to make the Panel revisions transparent. They succeeded in establishing a public comment period for reviewing the Panel and brought in project-affected peoples to speak to the Board (Clark 2003: 16).

On 20 April 1999 the Board approved a further clarification of the Panel's role and scope. The clarification restricted Bank management from presenting its remedial action plans to the Board; they were to be direct to the Panel instead (Suzuki and Nanwani 2006: 216). While the 1999 clarification institutionalised intervention by Bank management in the Inspection Panel process, the clarification also restricted the Board's ability to reject the Panel's recommendation for investigation to five technical grounds based on the original Bank resolution establishing the Panel (Bradlow 2005: 416; World Bank 2003b). Two months later, the Board accepted the Panel's recommendation to investigate the GWCPR project leading the Chinese government to withdraw the project in 2000. Since the clarification the Board has approved all recommendations 'on a non-objection basis' (Bradlow 2005: 419). As a result, Fox argues that the Panel has been remarkably autonomous in its investigations (2003: xxii). The Inspection Panel is now widely accepted as a legitimate body (for a rejection of this view see Wade 2009).

The Panel is also a means of upholding the accountability of the World Bank as a sustainable development lender. As of October 2007, the Inspection Panel has received forty-nine requests for investigation, sixty-five per cent of which have included concerns over EA compliance (World Bank 2008a: 25). Environmental assessment and project supervision are the most often requested policies for investigation (Bradlow 2005: 417; World Bank 2007c: 126). Although the Panel has no enforcement mechanism to ensure the Bank meets Panel recommendations, the Panel has 'heightened the debate about the bank's commitment to, and effectiveness in, promoting environmentally sustainable development' (Treakle, Fox and Clark 2003: 247). This is because requests for inspection have successfully put the 'safeguard policies on the map' within the Bank (Fox 2002: 154; Green and Raphael 2002: 55–7). Initially Bank management noted that staff were avoiding high-risk projects like high dams and logging in order to prevent or 'Panel-proof' their projects. Staff and management both now agree that the Panel has contributed to better Bank compliance because they are aware of the potential for investigation (Bradlow 2005: 463). The Panel process also fed directly into the Bank's conversion of its environmental rules in the late 1990s and 2000s, as the Bank realised it had to clarify what rules it was able to implement in practice (Treakle, Fox and Clark 2003: 271–2).

Of course the establishment and activities of the Inspection Panel over the last decade does not mean that there are no longer issues of compliance with environmental and social rules. Even the Bank's evaluation reports document this. TEANs continue to campaign against environmentally and socially damaging Bank projects as they emerge. Recent problem projects include the Bujugali Hydropower Project in Uganda; the Chad/Cameroon Petroleum Pipeline Project; a Cambodian forestry concession management project; the Democratic Republic of Congo's economic recovery projects; and a Gas Pipeline Project in Nigeria (World Bank 2007c).[56] While the latter of these projects are still being investigated, most demonstrate that the Bank did not effectively meet its own environmental and social safeguards. The Panel process is therefore a means to rectify projects where environmental rules have not been followed. The argument that the Bank has shifted to become a sustainable development lender is not to state that the Bank has ceased all activities that may degrade the environment. In international development that remains a possibility and evidence exists that it still occurs. Yet it is also important to point to the institutionalisation of the Inspection Panel as a corrective action in cases where the environmental rules and monitoring and evaluation practices have not been systematically implemented. Clearly internalising sustainable development norms is a continuous but uneven process within the Bank. Ongoing TEAN engagement reinforces the importance of finding environmentally sustainable ways to do development.

In this regard, the Panel's existence has led to greater World Bank/TEAN dialogue. Woods states that since 'the World Bank created its independent Inspection Panel in 1993, the organisation has engaged more and more intensively with NGOs both in Washington DC and "on the ground" in countries in which it works' (2000: 835). The mutual constitution between the Bank and advocacy networks is apparent. Moreover, there has been an increased internal TEAN dialogue as Washington NGOs, such as the Center for International Environmental Law (CIEL) and BIC, assist claimants in how to appeal to the new Panel, although Fox notes that this has lessened over time (2002: 132; Treakle, Fox and Clark 2003: 251–3). As such, the role of TEANs has strengthened as a result of the Panel, as have increased links to the Bank through the very mechanisms that TEANs helped establish. TEANs socialised the Bank to establish an institutional accountability mechanism, demonstrating how advocacy networks diffuse norms within IOs. TEAN and Panel activities continue to reinforce the Bank's environmental and information disclosure rules. Along with improvements in the majority of Bank projects detailed earlier, can we therefore speak of a new identity of the World Bank?

New norms of development: the World Bank and sustainable development

Thus far the processes of direct and indirect socialisation have been examined to demonstrate how TEANs, as non-materially powerful non-state actors, have influenced the Bank's projects, policies and institutional mechanisms. This section places these ongoing interactions into context, arguing that the World Bank has incorporated *and is reconstituting* norms of sustainable development. Recall that identity is based upon the organisation's mandate and bureaucratic culture, and is both subjective and inter-subjective. Evidence detailed throughout the chapter suggests that the identity of the Bank has changed significantly since the 1970s, based on environmental staffing, funding, its rules, and its ongoing monitoring and accountability activities, although persistent weaknesses in the Bank's sustainable development practices remain. The following section argues that subjective and intersubjective perceptions of the Bank have also changed. Adding subjective and intersubjective insights from the networks and Bank staff broaden understanding as to the depth of the norm consumption process. As noted at the beginning of this chapter, while the Bank was quick to endorse environmental concerns in its agenda for development in the 1970s, the actual rate of change within the Bank, including both policy changes and project changes, was not fluid or continuous. Rather, it was characterised by ongoing responses to the socialising pressure of TEANs from the mid-1980s.

Bank watchers recognise that the World Bank introduced environmental criteria into the mainstream of Bank operations as a result of TEAN and US activities. Moreover,

> [t]he fact that other multilateral development banks made virtually no moves to integrate the considerations until well into the 1990s (with the example of the World Bank to prod them into action) does support the argument that the NGO campaign was crucial. The NGOs paid much less attention to the multilateral banks than the World Bank, not because they thought it worse than the others but because it had a much higher political profile. (Wade 1997: 731)

The Bank responded to socialisation by TEANs with changes to its operations and policies by focusing on areas that could be tangibly shown as proof of its commitment. Examples include environmental divisions; environmental projects and assessments; national environmental action plans and country environmental analysis. As Wade states, 'the Bank went no further since the NGOs were concerned more with stopping the Bank from doing certain things than encouraging it to grapple with the major causes of environmental degradation' (Wade 1997: 731). Indeed, the Bank

> found itself so sharply attacked in the 1980s for its alleged insensitivity to environmental concerns in poor countries that its first reaction was to instead pull back. Instead of working positively ... the Bank responded defensively ... most by withdrawing projects. (Paarlberg 1993: 347–8)

The Bank's initial response to environmental issues was to 'do no harm' as it grappled with how to mitigate the negative consequences of its development projects.

This changed in 1992–93 when the Bank began to focus on what it could actually achieve within a sustainable development framework. The Bank then moved towards a more integrated approach to the environment. In 1991, Shihata argued that the Bank's role 'in the protection and improvement of the environment' had not been adequately known or appreciated. The Bank, he argued, 'has gone a long way to reconcile this developmental objective with conservation and preservation concerns' (1991: 179). As a result of the anti-Narmada campaign and the increasing strength of the international norm of sustainable development 'around 1992 and 1993 the more comprehensive ideas of the "environmental management" paradigm began to take hold at senior management and operational levels' of the Bank (Wade 1997: 709–10). The Bank's World Development Report for 1992, entitled *Development and the Environment*, signalled a decisive shift towards the full incorporation of sustainable development norms. By 1996, environmental issues had become central to the Bank's overall strategy for its borrowers (Haas and Haas 1995; Wade 1997: 612). Meanwhile, the Bank began to instigate partnerships with environment NGOs demonstrating the depth of the Bank's engagement with environmentalists.

Norms of sustainable development widened the Bank's considerations beyond the project level to link environmental criteria into macro-economic country policies. In the early 1990s this took place through National Environmental Action Plans (NEAPs); work which is now conducted through Country Environmental Strategy Papers (CESPs) (World Bank 2008a: 20). The Bank institutionalised these efforts into its 2001 Environment Strategy and established a Vice Presidential level ESSD network to implement sustainable development. On the basis of environmental staff and project funding levels Nielson and Tierney (2003) locate the Bank's shift in the 1990s, as does the Bank's IEG, the latter on the basis of the Bank's overall activities and environmental performance at the time (World Bank 2008a). These changes signify how the Bank's own perception had changed towards internalising sustainable development, making it part of its identity.

As a result of direct and indirect socialisation the World Bank implemented wide-ranging policy changes that reflect environmental awareness. The suite of environmental rules has drastically improved in breadth and depth since the mid-1980s. As a result, the bank is now a global standard setter in sustainable development (Civic 1997–8; Hunter 2008). In addition, the Bank's monitoring measures have become more extensive, targeted and ongoing. While difficulties remain in ensuring compliance with environmental rules, improvements across the different regional departments in interpreting and applying the safeguards demonstrate measurable achievements in deepening sustainable development norms.[57] World Bank staff argue that it has changed substantially as a result of interaction with TEANs.[58] While activists remain sceptical that the World Bank has internalised sustainable development, this norm has made the Bank very different from what it once was. Indeed, TEANs are highly cognisant of the impact they have had on the World Bank.[59] Even the staunchest of Bank critics such as Bruce Rich, acknowledge that 'substantial change has occurred in the organisation' (cited in Nielson and Tierney 2003: 266). This indicates that while TEANs continue to pressure the World Bank, they are aware of the profound changes that the Bank has undergone, such that intersubjective beliefs about the Bank's shift are demonstrable.

The identity of the Bank has changed in terms of sustainable development being institutionalised through its policies and structures, and habitualised within Bank practices through its procedures. This implies a shift in property effects or beliefs (Risse, Ropp and Sikkink 1999). Further, the Bank remains at the forefront of finding methods to integrate sustainable development into international development lending. Currently it is engaging with new tools such as country, sector and regional environmental analyses in order to go beyond the constraints of the traditional EA tools. Yet there are internal differences and the Bank's internalisation of sustainable development is not unproblematic or linear. The World Bank's increasingly complex mission complicates its development efforts (Einhorn 2001: 22); this was attributed to Wolfensohn's 1996 restructure (Fidler 2001: 41). This is central to current debates over whether the Bank is in fact 'green'. While there has been a substantial shift within the World Bank, TEANs continue to oppose projects that are not environmentally sustainable.[60] Motivated by ongoing accounts of Bank non-compliance, scholars question whether or not the Bank has in fact incorporated the environment into its overall identity (Rich 2002).

While direct socialisation from TEANs and indirect socialisation through the US and other principals have fundamentally reshaped the Bank, this does not mean that norms of sustainable development are prioritised within Bank practices. This does not negate the fact that the Bank is internalising sustainable development. It must be kept in mind that the Bank's identity is not 'fixed' or stable, especially in light of the mutual constitution of agents and structures. The taken for granted nature of sustainable practices in Bank operations – through the habitualisation of integrated safeguard data sheets, through the use of the safeguards, through institutionalising the Inspection Panel investigations and ongoing monitoring through QAG and post-project OED evaluations, does not mean that non-compliance does not exist. Sanctioning procedures to enforce the norm of sustainable development are in place but they are not directly linked to staff actions. Indeed, Vice Presidents, Country Directors and management often do not promote sustainable development norms and may even undermine them. The Bank's approval system means that few are able to focus on innovative approaches to incorporating sustainable development into their project designs, although they are evident.[61] Management has the power to further internalise sustainable development but sustainable leadership is lacking.

Some scholars surmise that the Bank is therefore unable to internalise sustainable development, arguing that routinised operations based on hierarchy and efficiency undermine the incorporation of environmental concerns into the Bank's economic models (Le Prestre 1989; Rich, 1994). A decade ago scholars, such as Wade (1997), concluded that the institutional difficulties meant that complete environmental understanding has not been realised. Activists such as Rich (1994) and journalist Caufield (1996) agreed that the Bank has been 'green-washed' and that environmental criteria have not been implemented properly, and thus the Bank cannot be considered sustainable. More recently Gutner has argued that as a result of 'antinomic delegation', the Bank has 'conflicting or complex tasks that are difficult to institutionalize and implement' (2005a: 11, 21). In addition, Weaver argues that the Bank displays 'organised hypocrisy' as a result of its inability to implement donor-driven agendas including sustainability (2008).

Yet the sum of Bank practices over the past two decades, more so than any other development institution, is evidence that sustainable development norms are being internalised within the Bank, indicating a fundamental identity shift. Compared with other MDBs, Gutner finds that the World Bank is a 'darker shade of green' than either the European Bank for Reconstruction and Development or the European Investment Bank. A greener bank is one 'explicitly addressing environmental issues ... [and it] finances projects with primary environmental goals and attempts to integrate environmental thinking into the broader set of strategic goals it develops' (2002: 26). Gutner further notes that the World Bank moved from initially being a light green organisation to one that is now dark green as a result of pressure from 'major shareholder countries, usually supported or pushed by environmental NGOs' (2002: 47). Other scholars agree that the World Bank has 'undergone a significant transformation in recent years, mostly as a consequence of NGO political activity' (Payne 1997: 470; Nelson 1997).

In 1995 Haas and Haas argued that the Bank had learnt to analyse how environmental concerns fit within its aims by re-evaluating its beliefs about cause and effect, resulting in a change of the organisation's goals. Thus, learning is predicated on understanding the causal linkages between the complex problems that need to be solved and the specific means by which they might be resolved instead of by a trial-and-error approach where the quickest solution is employed. Haas and Haas argued that the World Bank changed its goals to incorporate environmental issues while internalising environmental ideas. They argued that only UNEP and the Bank were capable of integrating environmental considerations into their traditional responsibilities (1995: 266).

Indeed, the World Bank did introduce environmental criteria through a complex re-evaluation of its beliefs, resulting in a change of the organisation's goals to employ environmental components. The Bank in the 1970s superficially adopted environmental concerns as a result of outside ideas and influences. Although it did not initially analyse the underlying complexity of this issue in response to its mandate of economic development at the time, it did attempt to correspond to a broader understanding of development. This brings us back to the degrees of socialisation. First, adaptation or tactical responses to socialisation by TEANs is evident in the Bank's initial responses to halting problem projects and instigating a suite of environmental rules. But the Bank then went much further in responding to and engaging with TEANs over the strengthening of those rules and creating an accountability mechanism, before reconfiguring its operational procedures to monitor and evaluate them.

The Bank institutionalised its commitment to sustainable development with its borrowers, but it has also committed itself to addressing global environmental issues through partnerships with environmentalists including the WWF partnership in 1997 on forest conservation and sustainable development, and with Conservation International to protect biodiversity hotspots in 2000 (World Bank 2008a, 2006a). As previously stated, the Bank is now the largest multilateral development lender for the environment.

In a longer-term analysis, the practices demonstrate that the Bank is consuming sustainable development norms. Normative changes tend to be incremental, showing an unfolding understanding of the complexities inherent in internalising new norms, and how this can be reconciled with the organisation's identity as an economic development lender. Assuming that IOs undertake new operations to keep themselves relevant within the international arena, the World Bank demonstrated throughout the 1990s that it had internalised sustainable development rather than merely affecting the trappings of it. The World Bank now perceives its identity to be based on sustainable development through including the environment into its mission statement, increasing its environmental staff, increasing its environmental lending, continuing and broadening its commitment to environmental monitoring and evaluation systems, and administering environmental facilities and funds. Furthermore, the Bank now engages in dialogue with TEANs as well as partnerships with moderate conservation NGOs. Indeed, NGOs and TEANs recognise the significant shift by the Bank. The project, policy, and institutional changes outlined throughout this chapter, as well as subjective and intersubjective beliefs regarding the Bank's change, demonstrate that the World Bank has become a sustainable development lender.

The extent to which the World Bank identity continues to change depends on the future interactions between TEANs, the Bank and its borrowers. The Bank has been influenced by direct and indirect socialisation as witnessed by project, policy and institutional changes from the 1990s and early 2000s. Although more collaborative interaction with the networks has occurred since then, both direct socialisation through dialogue between networks and the Bank, and indirect socialisation through the Tuesday Group remain (Nelson 1997: 468). The Tuesday Group continues to provide a long-standing institutional basis for the sharing of information and policies between advocacy networks and the US in order to reach consensus on World Bank policies, projects and institutions.[62] TEANs do not constrain World Bank activities; rather they help create shared norms of development between IOs, states and TEANs. Payne argues that the World Bank's implementation of sustainable development and information disclosure practices exemplify constructive cooperation between IOs, NGOs and states (1996: 133).

Recent changes also point to Bank efforts to *reconstitute* the norm of sustainable development from rule-based to market-oriented. Under the leadership of Paul Wolfowitz (2006–7) there was a continuation of Wolfensohn's agenda on the Bank's safeguard policy conversion and the country systems approach, the latter of which has been continued under President Zoellick.[63] Wolfowitz's only major decision on environmental issues was the merger of the ESSD Vice Presidency with Infrastructure to create the Vice Presidency for the Sustainable Development Network (SDN) in August 2006. Wolfowitz stated that the 'purpose of consolidating these two networks is to mainstream environmental issues ... [and] ensure that we strengthen our focus on sustainability as we increase our investment in infrastructure'. The new vice presidency controls approximately forty per cent of the Bank's lending portfolio.[64] TEANs see the move as an indication of 'the gradual erosion of consensus on the appropriate role of the Bank in promoting sustainability' (Seymour 2006), while the Bank clearly views this as a means of reconstituting sustainable development as market-based rather than the rules-based understanding of sustainable development that it seeks to establish with its borrowers.

While identifying how the World Bank has shifted towards an environmental identity (and may be moving towards a market-based sustainability), this chapter provided evidence for two important arguments. First, that the World Bank's environmental shift resulted from engagement with TEANs in a process of socialisation. It has taken on an environmental identity although the norm came from outside the institution and continues to be reconstituted through practice. As a result, the Bank demonstrates that IOs may diffuse norms that do not emerge from within, contra current IO studies (for example, Chwieroth 2008; Finnemore 1996a; Leiteritz 2005).

That international norms may influence IO behaviour and identity, and specifically shaped the Bank's environmental shift, also challenges dominant rationalist explanations, despite a recognition of the role of environmentalists in casting the Bank's orthodox economic development as unsustainable (Gutner 2005a, 2002; Nielson and Tierney 2005, 2003; Nielson, Tierney and Weaver 2006). Some rationalists such as Nielson, Tierney and Weaver (2006) accept limitations to their approach. In examining the efficacy of the World Bank's strategic compact reforms under President Wolfensohn they argue, for example, that an organisation's culture could dilute the extent of organisational change expected from a change in material incentives instigated by either member states or management (2006: 121). Organisational culture therefore becomes an intervening variable in weakening the power of material incentives enacted by states or management, or conversely, by providing an explanation for how seemingly non-important ideas like sustainability are discussed within the World Bank despite disincentives for staff to do so.

Nielson, Tierney and Weaver (2006) therefore incorporate

normative concerns to explain World Bank change, yet they do so by carving out rationalist versus normative spaces for action by either the Bank or its member states. For example, they examine President Wolfensohn's strategic compact by arbitrarily dividing the relationship between the World Bank and its member states. Member states operate in a normative free zone where principals strategically negotiate their interests. This is compared to a sticky internal environment within the Bank where staff follow pre-determined incentive structures that have solidified over time into a World Bank culture (in this regard, both staff material interests and the organisation's culture are the same). Viewing the World Bank in this way leads the authors to argue that constructivists cannot explain change in the World Bank (and by extrapolation any other IO) because they are wedded to organisational cultures as explanations of IO behaviour, which reinforce stasis not change. This therefore gives no room for new norms to take hold, unless they are 'adjacent' to norms already held by the organisation.

In casting constructivism in this form, the authors overlook the central thrust of constructivism: not that material interests are not important, but that norms and social structures shape how these are understood – both inside IOs but also in terms of the actions of those outside the organisation. In some ways Nielson, Tierney and Weaver's approach to action inside the World Bank, where staff material incentives and the Bank's organisational culture are synonymous, could fit within a constructivist framework; after all norms enable strategic action by determining what action is possible. Yet Nielson, Tierney and Weaver do not analyse where environmental norms come from – seemingly emerging from the interests of powerful member states and management rather than the influence of non-materially powerful non-state actors such as TEANs both independently and through states.[65]

The upshot is that while the broader normative environment is not examined to explain where sustainable development came from, Nielson, Tierney and Weaver conclude that the Bank staff have 'partially internalised these new [environmental] norms and new thinking about the nature of development' and that 'behavioral patterns have shifted less dramatically than a pure incentive-based model might predict, yet still more than a stand-alone cultural model would expect' (2006: 123). In other words, both strategic material incentives and organisational culture are important. This is precisely the argument made here but without the need to split rational action from normative understandings of behaviour, or the need to build a bridge between rationalism and constructivism (a bridge that nonetheless maintains the rationalist–constructivist dichotomy, and even creates a new one with ideas inside IOs but not outside them). To reiterate, the argument made here is that the World Bank has undergone an identity shift as a result of the socialisation of TEANs but the Bank's identity determines how it responds to, and reconstitutes, international norms.

This bring me to the second main argument of this book: the chapter demonstrates that IOs may internalise norms that do not resonate with its identity although this runs contrary to much of the recent IO literature (Grigorescu 2002; Momani 2005; Nielson, Tierney and Weaver 2006; Weaver and Leiteritz 2005). Indeed the Bank initially ignored and then rejected, before engaging and responding to, TEAN claims. The Bank's internalisation of sustainable development norms points not only to the importance of international norms in shaping IOs, but that organisations (and states: see Epstein 2008; Risse, Ropp and Sikkink 1999) may take up norms considered to be antithetical to their identity at any given point in time. This accords with nascent research that demonstrates that external normative influences may influence IOs with the effect of revising their practices and reconstituting their identity, which may lead to a reversal of their policy prescriptions over time (Vetterlein 2007).

Conclusion

This chapter analysed how sustainable development norms were diffused within the Bank by assessing its projects, policies and institutions. TEANs emerged to socialise this IO directly and indirectly through influencing member states such as the US via Congress and Treasury. Yet the Bank's identity determined how it was socialised, or how it reproduced and transformed sustainable development in practice. Repeated interaction with TEANs furthered the Bank's environmental commitment. This was evident with the restrictions placed on disbursements for Polonoroeste, and ceasing involvement in Narmada, Arun III, and the GWCPR Project. Direct socialisation challenged the Bank's understanding of development, forcing it to respond to the environmental impacts of its projects. Further, direct and indirect socialisation led the Bank to strengthen its suite of environmental and information disclosure rules, and implement detailed and ongoing environmental monitoring and evaluation procedures. Institutional changes included the dramatic increase in staff and environmental funding, raising the profile of the environment within the Bank's organisational structure and the establishment of the Inspection Panel. The Bank also established partnerships and dialogue with NGOs.

The Bank has changed to incorporate environmental norms – and continues to reconstitute them in light of continued socialisation by the networks and the changing nature of development. The extent of World Bank change over the past thirty years is not only significant, it is an identity shift. The chapter therefore traced how TEANs pushed for the Bank to adopt and internalise sustainable development norms where both material and ideational influences occur simultaneously. Without unpacking where ideas come from, rationalist accounts only explain part of the picture in determining how decisions are made within the international system. Tracking how ideas inform how material incentives are understood and how actors respond, informs our analysis of the socialisation of IOs.

Recent debates about how to operationalise sustainable development continue in relation to the Bank's safeguard policy conversion, the shift towards country systems and the creation of the Sustainable Development Network. These demonstrate that the Bank's identity is not fixed, and that socialisation is a continuous interactive process between IOs, states and TEANs. The recent changes indicate that the Bank is attempting to reconstitute sustainable development norms towards a market-based rather than rules-based understanding of sustainable development. In comparison, IFC and MIGA have not been under the same degree of scrutiny as the Bank, perhaps as a result of less transparent linkages between investment, finance, and ecological destruction. The different operations and identities of the affiliates of the WBG are analysed in light of similar processes of direct and indirect socialisation from TEANs, beginning with the IFC.

Notes

1 A World Bank environment review argues the OEA was created 'in reaction to externally voiced concerns about the potential unplanned effects of Bank-supported projects' (Liebenthal 2002: 3).
2 Similarly the market-driven approach by IFC is determined by the function the market is given in interactions between TEANs, IFC, project sponsors and member states.
3 As 95.6 per cent of environmental lending from 1990 to 2007 came from the IBRD and IDA; the GEF, Multilateral Fund, and the Carbon Finance Unit are not explored here (World Bank 2008a: 141). For more on the extra-curricula 'green' activities of the Bank see Park 2007.
4 The environment became a strategic pillar of the Bank's work in 2000 and was followed by its 2001 Environment Strategy (World Bank 2001c, 2008a: il).
5 Discussion of the Bank's environmental identity is resumed in the conclusion of this chapter.
6 Interview with Lori Udall of International Rivers Network, 7 September 2001.
7 The impact of direct and indirect socialisation on the boomerang pattern is examined in the book's conclusion.
8 The US is highlighted here because it is the largest shareholder within the Bank, because the US political system allows lobbying, and many vociferous environmental NGOs are US based.
9 A second power sector loan for energy to Brazil was cancelled on the basis that the first power sector loan could not meet its environmental and social conditions: personal correspondence with former World Bank ecologist Robert Goodland, 31 October 2008.
10 Personal correspondence with author, 4 July 2008.
11 Local people earn a livelihood from the sustainable extraction or 'tapping' of latex from rubber plants and harvesting fruit; indigenous people sustainably collect Brazil nuts (Revkin 1990).
12 Northern NGOs defend their legitimacy through network links to people adversely affected by Bank projects, as both states and the Bank questioned their role and power in campaigns.
13 Lutzenburger became the Collor regime's Environment Minister in 1990 after Brazil's military dictatorship ended, signifying the nascent environmental movement there.
14 The Narmada protests were against both the Bank and the Indian government although the Indian government remained committed to the project long after the Bank disengaged (Khagram 2004).
15 The Morse commission like the later Hair inquiry detailed in chapter 4 is seen as part of the World Bank and IFC respectively as they were

established on behalf of the IO and were directed in their investigations, although Morse's report was made public and Hair's was not disclosed until after major protest from TEANs.

16 Indeed, 'Morse himself had to get out of his hospital bed to refute [President] Preston': personal correspondence with former World Bank ecologist Robert Goodland, 4 July 2008.

17 The *Financial Times*, 'The World Bank Must Withdraw Immediately from Sardar Sarovar', 21 September 1992: 6; The *New York Times*, 'Why Thousands of People Will Drown Before Accepting the Sardar Sarovar Dam', 21 September 1992: B10.

18 The 2006 *Environmental Matters* publication provides a breakdown of environmental funding. This includes: thirty-five per cent for pollution management and environmental health, twenty-six per cent water resources management, thirteen per cent on land management and ten per cent each on climate change and environmental policy and institutions (World Bank 2006b: 5). It is unclear whether this is for increasing energy efficiency or conservation. See Gutner 2005a and Nielson and Tierney 2005 for more on the coding for environmental lending. Overall spending figures include technical and advisory assistance and policy lending. If assessed on volume of loans for environmental and natural resource management *projects* alone, then this declined from sixteen per cent of overall Bank lending in FY2001 to twelve per cent in FY2006 (World Bank 2007b: 14). In other words the biggest lending spike has been for environmental policy lending. Also it does not take into account the cost of cleaning up traditional infrastructure and energy lending.

19 The numerous projects arousing controversy are well documented (Bramble and Porter 1992: 327; Caufield 1996; Fox and Brown 1998; George and Sabelli 1994; Le Prestre 1989: 174–81; Rich 1994; Wade 1997: 637–57; Wirth 1991: 2650).

20 This section unless otherwise stated is from Fox and Brown (1998: ch 13).

21 Wolfensohn was advised by Maurice Strong, former UNEP Executive Director and Secretary General of the UN Conference on the Human Environment in 1972 and the Earth Summit in 1992, to cancel the project as it was 'a battle he didn't need politically in his first month on the job': personal correspondence with former World Bank ecologist Robert Goodland, 4 July 2008.

22 International Campaign for Tibet, 'Inspection Panel Request', dated 18 June 1999.

23 This umbrella NGO was supported by the broader TEAN including the Bank Information Center and Friends of the Earth.

24 John Fitzgerald, US AID, 'Addendum to July Tuesday Group Notes',

Memo to the Tuesday Group and MDB Watchers, dated 28 July 2000.

25 Robert Wade (2009) rejects this characterisation of the Inspection Panel's results. He argues that TEANs had less and inaccurate information from the project site compared to Polonoroeste and Narmada and that technically the Bank need not have classified the project as a Category A. Without going into details of the Panel's deliberations, Wade opines that the Panel caved in to TEAN social influence and US pressure. While further investigation of the alleged 'bias' of the Inspection Panel is warranted, Wade's argument dovetails with the view here that the power of social influence by TEANs shaped the Bank's actions.

26 The Bank's first ecologist, Robert Goodland, stated that most environmental reforms within the Bank were 'minimalist or tokenistic until [President] Conable arrived'. He further stated that '[E]ven then progress was modest and didn't last long enough to be permanently mainstreamed': personal correspondence with author, 4 July 2008.

27 1987 is seen by the Bank as an environmental watershed (Green and Raphael 2002). Nielson and Tierney argue that the 1987 changes were not as significant as the early 1990s (2003: 243). As detailed below, the environment started to become routinised from the early 1990s.

28 The Brundtland Commission is the World Commission on Environment and Development.

29 Personal correspondence with author, 4 July 2008.

30 In 1999 the Bank introduced a Financial Intermediary category to ensure financial lenders using Bank loans meet its safeguards.

31 Approximately twenty-five per cent of World Bank lending is development policy lending (DPL), formerly structural adjustment lending (World Bank 2005d). There has not been 'a concerted effort to incorporate environmental concerns into these types of operations' (Liebenthal 2002: 11). Under the 2004 OP8.60 Development Policy Lending policy, the Bank determines whether or not the environment is affected by DPLs and how it will be addressed (World Bank 2004).

32 There are numerous environmental and social groups working to improve individual safeguards such as EA (detailed in Hunter 2008); indigenous peoples (in Gray 1998); forestry (in Kolk 1996); dams and involuntary resettlement (in Khagram 2004 and McCully 2001); and pest management (on the Pesticide Action Network website: www.panna.org/resources/ifi). These all feed into the broader network for World Bank sustainability. Hunter (2008) distinguishes

policy or 'horizontal' networks from project-specific 'vertical' networks although this division is not clear cut.

33 This is not to downplay the importance of internal advocates for the safeguards (Bebbington *et al.* 2006; Davis 2004; Hall 2007). Bank ecologist Robert Goodland for example wrote most of the environmental policies and engaged with NGOs comprising TEANs to get the Bank to implement the safeguards such as the Indigenous Peoples policy (Rich 1994). External normative pressure remains a key factor explaining the Bank's shift.

34 A backlash against anti-globalisation protestors occurred after 11 September 2001, which arguably influenced general perceptions of TEANs (for a critical view of environmentalists in relation to the World Bank see Mallaby 2004 and Wade 2009).

35 Confidential interview with Senior Environmental Specialist, 23 February 2007; letter from the Forest Peoples Programme to Steven Pickford, World Bank Executive Director on behalf of 70 environmental organisations from 32 states: 'Concerns about the Weakening of the World Bank Safeguard Policies', dated 2 March 2001. Cited at www.forestpeoples.org/ (accessed September 2008).

36 An MIC is any country eligible for IBRD loans (World Bank 2005b).

37 A later report claims borrower 'ambivalence' while highlighting how successful sustainable development can be with borrower engagement (Liebenthal 2002: 16, 24).

38 This argument does not have much weight as projects must meet the highest standards amongst the donors involved.

39 Letter to the Board of Executive Directors: 'World Bank's Proposed Middle Income Country Strategy Threatens to Weaken Social and Environmental Standards', signed by 186 environmental organisations, dated 7 June 2004. Cited at www.bicusa.org (accessed July 2006).

40 In January 2007 US Congresswomen Nancy Pelosi became Speaker of the House of Representatives.

41 For a detailed list of documents now available from the World Bank Group see the Global Transparency Initiative 2006.

42 Transparency has since become a norm in itself, underpinning calls by critics for greater IO accountability, legitimacy, effectiveness, efficiency, governance and even democracy. For the World Bank, transparency is central to its Governance and Anticorruption strategy (Weaver 2008), and was the basis for the establishment in 2001, and later recommended reform of, the Bank's internal Department of Institutional Integrity (Volcker *et al.* 2007).

43 Only 236 environmental specialists worked for the Bank in FY2004 although this does not include technical specialists in other areas

such as water and sanitation (109 specialists), health and human development (207) and social development (167). Again, the extent to which area staff incorporate environmental practices in undertaking their work is unclear (World Bank 2005e: 14).

44 Another separate network, Operations Policy and Country Services, was later added (World Bank 2005e: 18).

45 Confidential interview with Senior Environmental Advisor, Environmentally and Socially Sustainable Development Network, the World Bank, dated 19 September 2001.

46 OED or IEG is used depending on the unit's name at the time.

47 Confidential interview with Senior Technical Advisor, Quality Assurance and Compliance Unit, Environmentally and Socially Sustainable Development Network, the World Bank, dated 20 September 2001.

48 Confidential interview with Senior Environmental Advisor, The Environment and Socially Sustainable Development Network, the World Bank, dated 19 September 2001.

49 Both the CAS and PRSPs determine the Bank's development assistance for its borrowers.

50 Confidential interview with Senior Technical Advisor, Quality Assurance and Compliance Unit, Environmentally and Socially Sustainable Development Network, the World Bank, dated 20 September 2001. Under President Wolfowitz QACU was moved to the Operations Policy and Country Services network to become the Operational Policy and Country Compliance Unit or OPCQC in 2006.

51 Confidential interview with Senior Environmental Advisor, Environmentally and Socially Sustainable Development Network, the World Bank, dated 19 September 2001.

52 Not all ESSD loans are environmental. ENRM on the other hand includes: industrial pollution; urban environmental management; land, watershed, forest and natural resource management; integrated water basins, fisheries, marine and coastal management; environmental governance; biodiversity; and global ecosystem management – problematically, because ENRM projects cut across so many industries that even ENRM-coded projects may not be mapped to the environment sector to assess their development (rather than environmental) outcomes (World Bank 2008a: 21, 97). On the list of themes versus networks, see World Bank 2007b: 15, 2001c.

53 QAG assessments vary slightly over time as they revise their analytical framework and tools.

54 The Bank instituted an early warning risk system during project

implementation to prevent failure; the system gives 'flags' to projects at risk to facilitate corrective action (Weaver 2008: 272–7).

55 Confidential interview with Sector Manager, Environmentally and Socially Sustainable Department, Latin America and the Caribbean Region, the World Bank, dated 15 October 2001.

56 The World Bank cancelled its loan to Chad for the pipeline on 9 September 2008 after the Chadian government reneged on its commitment to use the project's revenue for poverty reduction. In 2006 President Wolfowitz froze a Chadian account for the same reason.

57 Confidential interview with a Senior Compliance Officer, Environmentally and Socially Sustainable Development Network, the World Bank, dated 19 September 2001.

58 Confidential interview, Former Senior Technical Advisor, Quality Assurance and Compliance Unit, Environmentally and Socially Sustainable Network, World Bank, dated 20 September 2001.

59 Confidential interview with a former Natural Resources Defense Council activist, dated 18 October 2001.

60 Controversy over projects such as the Chad–Cameroon Oil Pipeline project has revolved around the Bank attempting to instigate innovative social and environmental solutions to a traditional high-risk development project with private sector, government and development partners.

61 Confidential interview with a Sector Manager, Environmentally and Socially Sustainable Development Network, the World Bank, dated 15 October 2001; confidential interview with a Senior Policy Analyst of the World Resources Institute, dated 8 October 2001

62 Confidential interview with a Senior Project Manager at the Bank Information Center, dated 21 September 2001.

63 In 2007 President Zoellick identified six strategic aims for the Bank to focus on: IDA and African states; post-conflict lending; lending to middle income countries; fostering global and regional public goods; development in the Arab world; and knowledge and learning. See www.worldbank.org (accessed October 2008). The natural environment is included as a global public good.

64 World Bank, 'World Bank President Assigns Responsibilities to Managing Directors and Announces Organisational Integration', Press Release No: 2006/501/WB, 27 June 2006; www.worldbank.org/ (accessed 31 October 2006).

65 Although they do recognise that norms may originate from elsewhere (2006: 133–4, n 10).

4
IFC and norms of sustainable finance

Introduction

While socialisation of the World Bank began in the 1980s, IFC became the focus of TEANs for investing in environmentally destructive development in the 1990s. This chapter documents how direct and indirect socialisation by TEANs led to an identity shift in IFC through its projects, policies and institutions. Although different from the Bank, these components again demonstrate how IFC consumed sustainable development norms as a result of TEAN interactions. First IFC's finance identity is established and indications that IFC has internalised sustainable development are provided. Then the micro-processes of TEAN socialisation of IFC are traced: TEANs used problem project campaigns previously established by networks against the Bank again using persuasion, social influence and coercion. The first major problem project campaign is outlined, the Pangue dam in Chile, as this had a profound and lasting impact on the organisation. While IFC had already established a token environment department with only one environmental advisor, it was not until the socialisation process began that IFC shifted to institutionalise sustainable development. This occurred through establishment of IFC's comprehensive safeguard and information disclosure policies in 1998, which again occurred in response to direct and indirect socialisation. TEAN socialisation then contributed to the establishment of a Compliance Advisor/Ombudsman (CAO) as an accountability mechanism for IFC. IFC then began internalising its environmental identity with its 2001 Sustainability Initiative. The chapter concludes by arguing that IFC perceives itself as, and is perceived to be, a market-based sustainable development financier.

IFC's identity

IFC has a longer history than the recent opposition by TEANs suggests. Although ideas on the need for an IO as a private sector facilitator had been discussed at Bretton Woods in 1944, it was not formally proposed until 1949 and did not emerge until 1956 (Matecki 1957: 49). Disagreements between states over its purpose persisted, such that it did not operate as it was originally envisaged until 1970 (Mason and Asher 1973: 345). IFC's establishment created the World Bank *Group* for private sector solutions to development; later joined by ICSID in 1966 and MIGA in 1988. IFC's mandate is to supplement the activities of the World Bank by partially financing and facilitating finance for private enterprise in developing countries. It invests in private sector development projects where access to capital is not available. However, as a public institution the project must have some 'prospect of productivity' (Mason and Asher 1973: 351).

As a financial organisation IFC is primarily made up of investment bankers. Although it shares its President and Boards of Governors and Directors with the World Bank, IFC has its own identity based on its own mandate, culture, and operations. IFC is run by the Executive Vice President (EVP), currently Lars Thunell. It has its own Articles of Agreement and its own funding, provided by and for its members, who must be members of the Bank. IFC now has 180 members, and the voting and influence of each is determined by the amount of share capital 'paid in' (currently totaling $2.4 billion). Much like the World Bank, the United States provides the dominant share of IFC funds at twenty-four per cent, followed by Japan at six, and France, Germany and Britain at five per cent each (IFC 2008: 25).

IFC raises capital through international markets and has a triple-A credit rating. IFC began with a smaller loan window and smaller funds to loan per project than the Bank, but the organisation trebled its financing in the 1990s and continued to expand rapidly in the 2000s as a result of the dramatic increase in direct foreign investment (FDI) flowing to developing countries (Lee 2001: 475; UNCTAD 2007). Thus far IFC has invested in 1,490 companies in 122 states (IFC 2008: 37). IFC loans and equity investments are increasingly comparable in size to the IBRD's annual lending budget of approximately $15–20 billion because IFC mobilises additional financing for the projects in which it invests. Owing to its mandate, IFC is restricted to investing less than thirty-five per cent of the total capital of a project so as not to crowd out private financiers; it usually invests between five and twenty per cent. IFC's new investments for financial year 2008 reached $11.4 billion with an additional $4.8 billion mobilised through loan syndications, securities and sales. The combined total project costs for these new investments and loan syndications amounts to $43 billion; which is in addition to IFC's current commitments of $32.4 billion. IFC is now 'the largest multilateral source of loan and equity financing for private sector projects in the developing world' (IFC 2008: 34, 37).

IFC's product mix at time of writing includes: fifty per cent loans, twenty-two per cent in loan syndications, fifteen per cent equity investments, twelve per cent guarantees and one per cent in risk management products (IFC 2008: 27). IFC thus undertakes three types of operations. First, it finances private sector projects in developing countries through equity and quasi-equity investment, and loans and venture capital for private projects. Second, it assists private sector companies to attract international investors, which are known as syndications. Lastly, it provides technical assistance by providing information to the private sector in order to promote investment in developing states, and helps states establish financial markets through technical assistance. As a result, both private sector corporations (project sponsors) and developing country governments are its clients. There is less focus here on the technical and advisory services provided to states as TEANs have not attempted to socialise this aspect of IFC. Although sustainable development norms are spreading throughout the organisation, its technical financial instruments really only began to address sustainability in earnest from the mid-2000s, reflecting its identity shift to a sustainable finance corporation.[1]

Up to the 1990s sustainable development was not an integral aspect of IFC operations.[2] Even in 1998 when environmental aspects of private sector financing came to the fore with the implementation of IFC's own environmental policies, sustainability was not integrated into IFC's mission (IFC 1998a: 8). A consolidation of IFC's environmental shift took place in 2001 when IFC instituted a Sustainability Initiative to centre its approach to sustainable development lending and investment. The initiative introduced environmental sustainability as one of five core strategic aims of the institution with the intention of enhancing IFC's leadership position in sustainable private sector investment (IFC 2001c: 14, 2006a). The Sustainability Initiative was moved from the Environment and Social Department (CES) into IFC's central Operational Strategy Group (COS), thereby legitimising and internalising the environment as central to IFC's operations. The shift exemplifies IFC's push to reorient the organisation's values to include sustainability (Wright 2006a: 73). Since 2001, IFC states that its aim is to 'promote sustainable private sector investment in developing countries, helping to reduce poverty and improve people's lives' (IFC 2005a).[3] While this does not indicate a sustainable development approach, IFC has changed its *understanding* of its mission: sustainable development norms are now incorporated in its triple bottom line assessment of its financial, environmental and social return on capital investments (IFC 2002a, 2001b).

The Sustainability Initiative states that IFC is looking to go 'beyond compliance'. This indicates IFC's shift from a rules-based sustainable development as evident in the World Bank, to a market-based understanding of sustainability that internalises environmental ideas into private sector instruments, investments and thinking. The Sustainability Initiative moves away from the 'preventing harm' Bank model to maximise financial, environmental and social returns on capital investments. For IFC this means 'a more opportunistic, added-value, market incentive-oriented approach', where financially successful projects are not derived from environmental 'distortions' (IFC 2001a: 51). The new approach envisions IFC disseminating and implementing recognised environmental and social best practices, such as eco-efficiency and corporate governance.[4] Current work is therefore attempting to identify environmental, social and governance factors in all IFC investments.

IFC's identity is that of a finance corporation operating within the international project finance industry. Yet throughout the 1990s and early 2000s, a substantial change towards internalising sustainable development norms occurred through incorporating sustainability into its understanding of its mission and into its strategic aims, as noted. Other significant organisational changes involved increasing environmental and social staff from one consultant in 1989, to ninety-nine Environment Department staff in 2004, to 200 in the Sustainability Knowledge Network in 2008 (of 3,325 staff; IFC 2008: 118); decentralising over sixty per cent of environmental and social specialists to investment departments and regional offices in order to be involved at an earlier stage of IFC's project cycle; increasing environmental and social development spending from two million in 1994 to $12.5 million in 2004 (IFC 2005c: 40, 53); its introduction of, and leadership in, the creation of the finance industry's environmental and social standards; and the creation of institutions to monitor, mediate and redress environmental and social damage from IFC-invested projects. In the last year IFC rolled out an Environment and Social Sustainability Business Line of advisory products covering six themes: sustainable investing; sustainable energy and water; cleaner technologies; social responsibility; gender entrepreneurship and biodiversity (World Bank 2008a: xl). Other 'beyond compliance' changes demonstrating IFC's commitment to sustainable development norms include IFC's annual reporting on its greenhouse gas emissions for private sector projects, assessing its own organisational environmental impact, and support for the GEF and carbon financing instruments (IFC 2002a: 57; World Bank 2008a: 45).

These changes are significant in demonstrating not only a change in IFC interests but a shift in its identity; from having no social and environmental conscience, to a position of 'do no harm' to the present 'do good' (IFC 2002b: 2). The Sustainability Initiative places sustainable development norms at the centre of IFC's operations. IFC now markets itself to project sponsors on the positive financial, social and environmental benefits of sustainable development. IFC argues that it is at the forefront of sustainable finance. This was borne out within the industry in June 2003 with the introduction of the Equator Principles by private investment banks, those with whom IFC establishes syndications. The Equator Principles are voluntary environmental and social guidelines that emulate IFC's environmental safeguards.[5]

The Equator Principles are a move towards sustainable development across the project finance industry and were initiated by IFC and ABN AMRO in October 2002 when they co-convened a meeting for nine other investment banks on environmental and social issues (Wright 2006b). These 'Equator Banks' adopted IFC's safeguards, demonstrating how IFC has internalised sustainable development norms into its corporate finance identity and begun to diffuse them throughout the international system.[6] As of October 2008, sixty-one banks are now signatories covering over eighty-five per cent of the project finance industry (IFC 2007b: 22). The Equator Banks have committed 'not to provide financing to projects where the borrower will not, or is unable to comply with our environmental and social policies and processes', making environmental and social safeguards one determinant of investment agreements (Stevastopulo 2003). The Equator Principles indicate that IFC has moved towards normalising sustainable development investing.

Even more importantly in terms of IFC's leadership role in sustainable finance was its 2006 shift from World Bank-adapted environmental rules to more flexible performance standards. These were subsequently adopted by the 'Equator Banks' even though IFC's safeguard policies had already been modified and agreed upon for private sector use. From mid-2007 thirty-two export credit agencies from the Organisation for Economic Cooperation and Development (OECD) states also began benchmarking their activities against IFC's performance standards (World Bank 2008a: 59). According to IFC, the performance standards have 'catalyzed the swift convergence of cross-border project finance and this has leveled the playing field' in financial markets worldwide (IFC 2007b: iv). The aim of the rest of this chapter is to analyse the process whereby IFC moved from a pure financier of private sector projects, to a sustainable development financier.

IFC's 'problem project' campaigns

Having sketched IFC's sustainable development identity, this section analyses how direct and indirect socialisation by TEANs first influenced this IO through problem project campaigns in the 1990s. As IFC monitored the events unfolding between the Bank and TEANs, they themselves came under the scrutiny of advocacy networks soon after. There is a core advocacy network of northern and southern NGOs engaged in continuous dialogue and pressure to incorporate the environmental into WBG identities. Connections between a number of northern, environmental NGOs including BIC, CIEL, Conservation International, Environmental Defense, Friends of the Earth, NRDC, and the Sierra Club, have garnered social influence through public opposition against the WBG (Friends of the Earth 2001; IFC 2002b: 32). These NGOs are engaged in a worldwide network, from Europe to Latin America and Southeast Asia, disseminating information and forming the hub of advocacy opposition to the WBG which is joined to project-specific activists and NGOs.

That TEANs aimed to shape IFC is significant because it is less well known and it is more difficult to garner social influence compared to direct socialisation in relation to the World Bank. IFC's minimal equity percentage in funding private sector projects meant that TEAN influence may have been limited. It was never assured that opposing IFC projects would prevent environmentally degrading practices. However, as will be demonstrated below, TEANs undertook similar campaigns against IFC to that of the Bank. Advocacy networks questioned the role of IFC within the WBG, exposing IFC's harmful environmental practices and seeking to clarify the link between IFC and the Bank's environmental rules. As such, TEANs were able to further the inroads they had made in reforming the Bank through indirect socialisation. IFC came under pressure from TEANs in the early 1990s via the first problem project campaign that had far-reaching consequences for IFC's identity. The focus of the campaign was the Pangue dam and associated dams along the Bio Bio River in Chile. This demonstrates how direct and indirect socialisation (again through principals such as the US) began to reconstitute the organisation first through its projects and later through its policies and institutions.[7] Pangue remains controversial in IFC history because it was the first large project IFC ever undertook and its environmental and social repercussions would further shape IFC projects, policies and institutions (IFC 2005b: 1; Bowles *et al.* 1999: 125, n 137).[8] As the Pangue campaign influenced the establishment and strengthening of IFC policies and institutions, it is imperative to first outline how the Pangue dam became the first IFC 'problem project' campaign.

Pangue dam, Chile

This section outlines the rudiments of the Pangue project, before examining the processes of direct and indirect socialisation. Empresa Nacional de Electricidad SA (Endesa) was privatised in 1989 and is now a Spanish-owned multinational corporation (Nash 1992: 8).[9] Endesa planned to construct six hydroelectric dams along the Bio Bio, one of Chile's largest rivers, which flows 380 kilometres from the Andes to the Pacific Ocean, in order to meet Chile's increasing electricity demands. Over one million people use the Bio Bio for drinking, irrigation, fishing and recreation. The first dam, Pangue, was designed to be the most efficient in the world 'generating 450 megawatts of power while flooding 1, 250 acres, a much smaller amount than other large dams' and purportedly only requiring the resettlement of fifty-three non-indigenous individuals (IFC 1992; Nash 1992: 8).[10] IFC canvassed the project in 1989 when approached by Endesa after Chilean government approval. IFC appraised the project from 1990 to 1992, classifying the project as Category A for its expected environmental and social impacts (IFC 1997c; Hair 1997). The projected costs were estimated at $465 million although the completed project came in under budget. In April 1992, IFC authorised $170 million in loans and approved an equity investment of $4.9 million in Pangue SA, the Endesa subsidiary undertaking the project (IFC 1992). IFC facilitated the project loans, leading to several European banks investing.

TEANs opposed the dam prior to IFC Board approval. TEANs challenging IFC comprised: the Grupo de Accion por el Bibio (GABB); 400 Chilean citizens including indigenous Pehuenche people, and some Chilean Congress members; International Rivers Network (IRN); the American Anthropological Association (AAA); BIC, CIEL, NRDC; Red Bancos – a Latin American and Caribbean NGO network on MDBs; and another forty-seven NGOs from all over the world including Friends of the Earth.[11] They engaged IFC through both direct and indirect socialisation. Indirect socialisation was evident as early as 1991 in relation to IFC Board approval. For instance, IRN was engaged in persuading the US Executive Director (US-ED). TEANs questioned the US-ED's position on the dam, and offered information to persuade the US-ED on the project's perceived environmental, social, economic and political ramifications.[12] Moreover, in

March 1992, a communiqué between the US Chairman of the Foreign Appropriations Committee to the US Secretary of the Treasury requested to know their position on IFC's support of the Pangue project and more specifically 'what actions the US Executive Director has taken in the IFC to comply with US laws regarding alternatives to the proposed project and analyses of its *environmental and social impacts*'.[13] TEANs were therefore persuading the US to invoke its material power to oppose the project.

Significantly, indirect socialisation continued with correspondence between the US EPA and BIC revealing that the US Treasury's 'Working Group on Multilateral Aid' (or Tuesday Group) was aware of the environmental questions 'that have been raised by local and United States non-governmental organisations about the Pangue Dam project'.[14] US Treasury purportedly met with IFC regarding the environmental and social impacts of the proposed dam in January 1992. Pangue SA sent a copy of the EA to the US-ED, and in May the US-ED was one of a number of Directors involved in meetings with TEANs.[15] *The US-ED then abstained from voting on the Pangue project in December 1992.* The Alternate US-ED argued that the dam demonstrated 'what we [the US] see as a general failure of recent World Bank hydroelectric projects to assess adequately, and in a timely manner, the likely impacts of proposed projects to fisheries and aquatic biodiversity'.[16] Thus, indirect socialisation had already begun to affect IFC decision-making based on the indirect socialisation of the Bank. Although the US was increasingly concerned about the negative impact of World Bank dam projects, there can be little doubt that TEANs brought Pangue and IFC to US attention.

Further action by the Alternate US-ED details that the US-ED has been socialised by TEANs. Even more revealing than abstaining from voting on the project, the Alternate US-ED then requested environmental information from Pangue SA on behalf of the network, and listed the specific reports the network would find useful.[17] The implications of these events are clear: while the US had abstained from voting on the project, the US, through Treasury and through its representatives in IFC, were advocating on behalf of TEANs. While indirect socialisation in this project campaign was successful in terms of shaping the US-ED's position on Pangue, it was not able to mitigate the environmental effects of the project, nor its cessation. Pangue, constructed between 1993 and 1996, began operating in 1997.

Direct socialisation was also used in this campaign. Environmental and indigenous groups opposed the project via social influence from 1990.[18] Prior to the loan approval in 1992, petitions were sent to IFC by the consolidating TEAN including Chilean environmental and social groups, North and South American NGOs and NGOs worldwide requesting that IFC reject the project.[19] TEANs argued that the Pangue dam was authorised without any proper baseline environmental studies; that the environmental impact study was completed after the decision to implement the project; that the EIA for Pangue did not adequately assess downstream impacts; that the dam's reduced flow and contaminated water threatened the health of people below the dam and one of Chile's most important fisheries; that an adequate flow management regime had not been developed, as required by the loan agreement between Endesa and IFC; and that the dam endangered wildlands and biodiversity and threatened the cultural property of the Peheunche people (GABB 1995: 16–23). Further, they claimed that the energy was superfluous to Chile's projected future energy requirements (Johnston and Turner 1998: 7).

The Pangue campaign intensified in 1998 over the construction of the second and largest of the dams, Ralco. Although Ralco was not funded by IFC, TEANs argued that the EIA of Pangue did not take into account downstream impacts of the Pangue dam even though it was widely known to be part of an intended six dam construction by Pangue SA, *of which IFC has equity shares*. According to TEANs, Ralco displaced something in the region of 600–1,000 people. Of these people, 400 are Chile's traditional indigenous people, the Peheunches, the most traditional of the Mapuche Indians, Chile's largest indigenous group. The dam endangered their livelihood and traditional culture, and threatened to flood over seventy kilometres of the river valley (IRN 1998b).

TEANs argued that IFC broke its own policies on indigenous people and resettlement. IFC repeatedly claimed that Pangue was an isolated endeavour, even though the more damaging Ralco dam was designed in conjunction with Pangue and four additional dams. TEANs declared that Pangue's environment studies should have analysed the entire impact along the Bio Bio as was normal practice for the impact of assessing dams. IFC stipulations also required Endesa to provide money for a Pehuen Foundation to mitigate the effects of Pangue resettlement on the Pehuenche people. This money was also used to resettle people in the Ralco area and constituted a misuse of IFC funds, thus violating IFC's lending agreement.

In a turnaround of events, in February 1997 IFC threatened to declare the Chilean company Endesa in default for its failure to meet environmental and social conditions for Pangue and its connection to Ralco. Then President, James Wolfensohn, wrote to the Chilean Finance Minister, Mr Eduardo Aninat, urging the Chilean government to mediate between IFC and Endesa. Wolfensohn states that Endesa 'appears to have taken a less than constructive approach to its environmental and social obligations', and that Endesa is therefore 'in a situation of immanent default under the IFC financing agreements'.[20] In doing so, Wolfensohn refers to two independent reviews undertaken to assess Pangue that were especially critical of the role of IFC's 'handling of the environmental appraisal and supervision of the Pangue project and the compliance of Pangue SA and Endesa with their obligations under the IFC agreement'. According to the *Financial Times* these reports had been prepared by the urging of 'green lobbies' on the Pangue and Ralco projects (1997: 3). One of those reports was an independent investigation contracted by IFC undertaken in May 1995, by American anthropologist Dr Theodore Downing, a member of the American Anthropological Association (AAA). Wolfensohn stated that both reports would be made public should Pangue SA not comply.

The Downing report identified extensive deforestation, severe limitation of Pehuenche land rights, and the general failure on the part of the Pehuen Foundation to meet its objectives. The projects along the Bio Bio led to unchecked immigration to a previously isolated area, land speculation, and deforestation inflicted by timber contractors estimated at between $3 and $18 million through unregulated and underpriced logging (Downing 1996: 5). The report stated that the Pehuenche people were asked to sign resettlement agreements, exchanging ancestral land rights for land high in mountains, several hours from their homes, and without an understanding of the effects of Pangue or the ramifications of the proposed Ralco development. TEANs endorsed Downing's statement to IFC that these actions did not constitute an adequate response by IFC to the environmental and social conditions of the area.

The AAA's Committee for Human Rights further accused IFC of a range of human rights abuses linked with its funding of Pangue (Johnston and Turner 1998). The Downing report stated that IFC and Endesa violated the human rights of the Pehuenche by negotiating the future of the ethnic group without their knowledge or participation, or that of the Chilean government authority responsible for indigenous affairs (CONADI). The AAA also claimed that the programme of resettlement failed to compensate adequately those affected. In addition, the AAA argued that the suppression of the Downing report constituted racial discrimination as the report was only shown to non-indigenous representatives on the Pehuen Foundation Board (Johnston and Turner 1998: 2). TEANs also challenged IFC to release the report, which it did a year and a half later.

Direct socialisation came to a head on 17 November 1995 when the local environmental and social umbrella network GABB and close to 400 Chileans, including members of the Pehuenche community and members of the Chilean Congress, filed a complaint with the World Bank Inspection Panel.[21] *This claim was rejected on the basis that the Inspection Panel does not have the power to inspect IFC projects.* This occurred even though, as GABB argued in its claim, IFC must meet the appropriate World Bank environmental guidelines and policies.[22] Additionally, they argued that because IFC has the same President and Boards of Governors and Directors, it should be recognised as being under the mandate of the Inspection Panel (GABB 1995: 4–5).

The claim argued that IFC had violated the following procedures and safeguards: Procedure for Environmental Review of IFC projects (1990); Environmental Analysis and Review of IFC Projects (1993); and the World Bank Operational Directives related to Dam and Reservoir Projects, Indigenous Peoples, Wildlands, Cultural Property, Involuntary Resettlement, and Project Supervision (GABB 1995: 6–7). The incident provided impetus for President Wolfensohn to commission an autonomous internal review of Pangue's environmental and social impacts. In 1996, Dr Jay Hair, the former head of the National Wildlife

Federation and the World Conservation Union (IUCN), was appointed to undertake the evaluation.[23] The Hair report, much like the Morse report in the Narmada campaign against the Bank referred to in chapter 3, outlined IFC's belated and tactical response to TEANs.

The Hair report, completed in April 1997, concluded that IFC was unable to enforce its own environmental and social guidelines.[24] It states that 'IFC did not follow fundamental World Bank Group requirements in any consistent or comprehensible manner throughout the development and implementation of the Pangue Project' (Hair 1997: 35). The report also argues that there 'was no evidence in the record that comprehensive and systematic monitoring of requirements to determine compliance with relevant World Bank Group requirements were either a) identified within IFC or to the project sponsor or b) subsequently monitored' (1997: 38). The report noted that although IFC had complied with 'some aspects of the four step environmental review process that was in effect from March 1990 to December 1992 ... that insufficient attention was paid to downstream environmental impacts, induced impacts on indigenous peoples, cultural properties management, and wildlands protection issues during the early phases of project development' (1997: 41). In sum, the report identified that IFC did not comply with overall project supervision and the following World Bank operational directives: Environmental Policy for Dam and Reservoir Projects; Wildlands; and Management of Cultural Property. Although IFC was in compliance with resettlement of immediate non-indigenous families, the indirect impact of the project on indigenous peoples had not been taken into account and as a result IFC was not compliant in this regard (1997: 60–97). It further endorsed the Downing report on the operation and recommendations for the Pehuen Foundation and recommended the report's public release (1997: 5).

The Hair report revealed fundamental flaws within IFC regarding the implementation of sustainable development. The subsequent findings of the report demonstrated a lack of environmental appraisal and supervision of the Pangue project and non-compliance of Pangue SA–Endesa with their obligation to IFC stipulations (CIEL 1997). TEANs suspected a cover-up, arguing that IFC suppressed both reports, reflecting a fundamental lack of transparency reminiscent of previous World Bank practices. Fuel was added to the controversy with an article in *The Nation* titled 'Wolfensohn, Indian Killer' claiming not only the suppression of the Hair report but also potential ethnocide (Cockburn 1997).

The Hair investigation coincided with public debate in Chile over Ralco's environmental safety. Meanwhile, AAA argued that the Downing report was released only after public discussion over Ralco concluded, thus directly suppressing information for vital decision-making on the impacts of the second dam (Johnston and Turner 1998: 13). TEANs supported 'Downing's evaluation [which] presented evidence that Endesa used IFC loan funds earmarked for Pangue to support Ralco development' (IRN 1998a). Chile's indigenous people opposed Ralco before construction began in April 1998. After protracted legal battles and sustained Penhuenche resistance the dam was completed in 2002 (Alywin 2002: 18).

TEANs repeatedly requested the Hair report's public release, through, amongst other things, letters from GABB, CIEL, IRN, Red Bancos, and NRDC to IFC.[25] The Hair report was released publicly three months after its submission to IFC in April 1997. However, one third of the Hair report was censored when it was made public for 'commercial confidentiality'. According to Dr Hair in a letter to President Wolfensohn dated 25 July 1997, 'there ... [were] numerous deletions that appear to have been made for no other reason than to avoid embarrassing the individuals who made certain decisions regarding the Pangue Project or how it was supervised by IFC' (IRN 1997b).

President Wolfensohn replied to Friends of the Earth claiming that the Hair report contained 'numerous statements of fact and opinion about the actions of Pangue SA, the Chilean company responsible for the Pangue project and its parent company, Endesa, and that other statements in the report disclose information which, in the view of Pangue management, IFC is legally bound to keep confidential'.[26] A fresh investigation into Pangue by IFC's accountability mechanism the Compliance Advisor/Ombudsman (CAO) recommended its complete public release (CAO 2003b: 4).

This demonstrates three significant factors. First, through the Hair report IFC began to discover that environmental transparency was itself controversial, in a similar fashion to the Morse report as detailed in chapter 3. Secondly, President Wolfensohn's comments to GABB exemplify the fundamental shift in thinking about TEANs for IFC. With the report's release Wolfensohn sent a copy to GABB and commented in the letter that the Hair report 'results from your long and continual efforts to raise our awareness of environmental and social issues arising in the Pangue project. Thank you for your efforts.'[27] Wolfensohn encouraged TEAN efforts to socialise IFC on environmental and social issues.[28] Taking its cue from its president, IFC would increasingly recognise the constraining influence of TEANs as legitimate. Thirdly, it demonstrates how IFC retained a position of non-disclosure of its environmental and social practices for commercial confidentiality. This would be challenged by TEANs, as discussed below.

On the Hair report's release, IFC acknowledged the positive statements on how IFC handled the Pangue project, while stating that it had learnt from the report. IFC recognised that it should take a more systematic approach to social and environmental analyses; that it should have waited for more complete information and analysis of the dam's downstream impacts; that it should have handled indigenous issues more thoroughly; and that IFC should have ensured that the project complied with policies on cultural issues, indigenous people, and dams and reservoirs. However IFC challenged the report's methodology, refuting that IFC was not compliant with a number of World Bank requirements and the idea that IFC's Board was not fully informed (IFC 1997c).

IFC did attempt to incorporate environmental and social practices into Pangue by stipulating that Endesa–Pangue SA organise a Foundation to mitigate the effect of the development on the Pehuenche people and to set up an environmental monitoring station to measure the effects of the dam. The failure to regulate the Foundation or to achieve the designated results was a serious error on the part of IFC. Importantly, when IFC was mobilised by repeated TEAN protest, Endesa quashed the issue by repaying IFC's loan. Endesa avoided default by borrowing money from Dresdner Bank to repay IFC. In March 1997, Pangue SA 'unilaterally exercised its prerogative to prepay $150 million in loans outstanding to IFC and participant banks' (IFC 1997a), a situation GABB had foreshadowed in November 1995.[29]

A press release from Endesa and Pangue SA stated that they maintained their 'objective to demonstrate to the IFC with full transparency, its total compliance with environmental issues and policies' (Endesa 1997). As IFC retained a 2.5 per cent equity stake in Pangue, deliberations between both parties continued over 'outstanding environmental and social issues' (IFC 1997a; IRN 1997a). On 30 April 1997, IFC and Pangue SA signed an agreement detailing the steps to be undertaken by the company to meet its environmental and social obligations (IFC 1997b).

According the IFC's CAO, its first complaint was filed over Pangue in 2000 and was resolved after more than a year of mediation (CAO 2003b: 9). In August 2001, IFC and Endesa again agreed on the measures required to meet the original loan agreement's environmental and social stipulations. Local indigenous women then filed another complaint with the CAO on 2 July 2002 on the basis that many of the issues listed in the original 1995 Panel claim, that had been upheld by the 1997 Hair report, remained. Ten days later, IFC 'exited' the project, *of which the CAO was unaware*. The CAO was only informed of IFC's decision on 10 September 2002. Importantly, the CAO viewed the 2001 agreement as binding irrespective of IFC's exit.

The CAO therefore continued its investigation. In October 2002 IFC claimed that it was no longer responsible for the Pangue project. In contradistinction to its statements, IFC then undertook a supervision visit of the project in December, just days after a CAO visit. The CAO assessment called for a renewed commitment by IFC to ensure the 2001 conditions were fulfilled and for the publishing of the Downing and Hair reports in full. IFC's position on Pangue remains defensive, and the CAO remarks that '[t]he cloak of secrecy that covers all things related to Pangue is at odds with evolving attitudes and practices within Endesa, Chile and IFC' (CAO 2003b: 4). The CAO has since closed the investigation but continued to provide funds for community development until December 2008 (CAO 2006a).

In sum, IFC did attempt to alleviate some of the negative social implications of the dam with the Foundation for the affected population. This was a *post hoc* approach to mitigating social aspects of the development, although according to one of the original consultants it 'failed miserably' (Robinson 1998). The lack of structural incentives to adhere to the original plans for the Foundation indicates IFC had not internalised sustainable development norms and is again reminiscent of the earlier attempt by the World Bank with the Polonoroeste project in Brazil to attempt innovative social and environmental practices without having the localised knowledge and supervisory capacity to do so. Moreover, the environmental problems of the dam were not addressed systematically and have since been accepted by IFC as a major flaw. IFC was further implicated in the destructive development of the Ralco area because it was cognisant of the planned dam, although it did not finance the project itself. Thus, the Pangue project demonstrated flaws in IFC practices that did not address environmental and social sustainability.

One aspect of the loan was to initiate the Pehuen Foundation to mitigate the social costs of development. Yet it was discovered that IFC had been unable to ensure these requirements were met. IFC responded by suppressing all information and then ignoring the project's adverse effects. The Pangue project was a 'wake-up call' to IFC over its use of World Bank safeguard policies and revealed inherent weaknesses in adopting but not internalising environmental and social norms into its identity as a financier of private sector development. The flaws in the underlying rationale behind grafting environmental safeguards onto private sector projects was exacerbated when companies such as Endesa did not (and perhaps could not) fulfil such requirements. As a result, IFC's superficial approach to sustainable development was exposed.

To reiterate, TEANs influenced the US, which then abstained from approving the Pangue project. They further shaped the Alternate US-ED's actions; he undertook lobbying on their behalf. In addition, direct socialisation by TEANs aimed to shape IFC through persuasion including letters and meetings with IFC staff as well as social influence via petitions, protests and marches.[30] TEANs attempted to ensure that IFC incorporated sustainable development practices by advocating further information on the project's social and environmental impacts, leading to two independent reports. The network then filed a claim with the World Bank's Inspection Panel which contributed to the establishment of the CAO (below), which complainants would then use. By filing a claim the TEAN highlighted that IFC could no longer escape their attempts to constrain the actions of this IO and to socialise its identity through constant interaction. After Pangue, TEANs aimed to influence IFC to improve its environmental and information disclosure policies, again via direct and indirect socialisation.

IFC's environmental safeguard and information disclosure policies

Until recently, IFC escaped public scrutiny because of its relative anonymity as a multilateral development lender and investor. This changed when IFC was exposed for its inability to meet World Bank environmental rules in relation to the Pangue project (Lee 2001: 475, n 20). This section details how TEANs used direct and indirect socialisation to influence IFC to establish its own environmental and transparency rules via persuasion, social influence and coercion. This led to broader organisational changes including the expansion of its environment department. IFC already had an Environment Division with *one* environmental advisor in 1989. The division introduced environmental classifications for its projects, mimicking the Category A, B and C projects of the World Bank.[31] Yet in 1990, only seven of 160 projects reviewed were deemed to have potentially significant environmental impacts. Now even IFC agrees that the volume of projects to review was beyond the capacity of one permanent staff member (IFC 2002b: 30).

TEANs were able to continue the socialisation process of the WBG because they engaged in persuasion, social influence and coercion to convince IFC to adopt the World Bank's recently strengthened environmental and social safeguard and transparency policies. The lessons so harshly learnt by the World Bank thus served as an example and a template. Prior to Pangue there was a vague assumption that IFC would adhere to World Bank environmental and social standards, and while there had been no official adoption of policies, IFC used Bank staff to assess its projects.[32] During 1993, at the height of the Pangue campaign, IFC began to revise its use of World Bank environmental safeguards. IFC began to realise that more specific private sector policies were needed rather than the *ad hoc* use of World Bank policies that had been tentatively in place since 1988 (IFC 2002b: 31). The 1993 environmental policy and 1994 information disclosure policy signalled the introduction of environmental rules purely for IFC.

Direct socialisation was used to shame IFC to strengthen its safeguards. It was the social influence of the TEAN Pangue campaign that convinced IFC of the need for a complete review of its approach to environmental and social issues (Crawford 1997; Morgera 2007: 155). TEAN's Inspection Panel claim over the Pangue project in 1995 was an attempt by TEANs to apply strict interpretations of all of the World Bank's environmental rules to IFC projects, which required a more detailed policy application than IFC had given in relation to Pangue. Carol Lee, an IFC staff member, states that environmentalists were right to question IFC because the 1993 policy did not expound precisely which of the Bank's safeguards applied (2001: 477). This was compounded by the 1997 Hair report recommendations on improving IFC's environmental policies, which came in response to the rejected Panel claim. Both informed the wide-scale review and comprehensive upgrading of IFC's environmental and social safeguard policies in 1998 (IFC 2002b: 31). Direct socialisation as a result of the Pangue campaign and Inspection Panel claim therefore influenced IFC's decision to take up environmental safeguards. Indeed, IFC 'clearly considered NGO comments when formulating its policies' (Bowles *et al.* 1999: 128). Indirect socialisation was evident with TEAN-backed US support on the Board of Executive Directors in voting to establish a suite of environmental rules for IFC.

In 1998, IFC introduced more comprehensive and strengthened environmental and social safeguard policies, as shown in Box 4.1.

Concurrent with the mass campaign against Pangue and Ralco, IFC introduced a new public disclosure policy (discussed next) and drafted a 'Best Practice Manual' for clients. IFC then began to improve the standard of its procedural environmental criteria and established guidelines for specific industries as well as the *Pollution Prevention and Abatement Handbook*; *Occupational Health and Safety Guidelines*; the *Safe Disposal of Hazardous Wastes*; *Techniques for Assessing Industrial Hazards*; and the *Environmental Consideration for Port and Harbor Development* (IFC 2000).

By the late 1990s, IFC's Environment Division comprised the Environment Projects Unit (EPU) for specific environmental projects, the Environment and Social Review Unit (ESRU) to

Box 4.1 *IFC's 1998 environmental and social safeguard policies adapted from the World Bank's safeguards.*

OP4.01 Environmental Assessment (1998)

OP4.04 Natural Habitats (1998)

OP4.36 Forestry (1998)

OP4.09 Pest Management (1998)

OP7.50 International Waterways (1998)

OD4.30 Involuntary Resettlement (1990)

OD4.20 Indigenous People (1991)

OP4.37 Safety on Dams (1996)

OPN11.03 Cultural Property (1986)

Policy Statement on Child Labour and Forced Labour (1998) – unique to IFC

determine project compliance, and the Capital Markets Environment Services Team (CMEST) to oversee financial sector projects. The EPU was created in 1996 as an incubator for projects with specific environmental benefits; it prepared potential projects for funding by IFC's investment departments (World Bank 2001a: 184). Both ERSU and CMEST were to ensure 'that IFC investments are environmentally and socially sound and meet IFC and World Bank Group policies and guidelines' (IFC 1998a: 98).

In 2000 the Environment Division was upgraded to become the Environment and Social Development Department (CES) (World Bank 2008a: 6). CES reports directly to the EVP rather than line operational management to maintain its independence (World Bank 2001a: 182). The department continues to provide environmental and social review services for all IFC investments, to catalyse projects with specific environmental benefits, and to provide training services for environmental staff and clients (IFC 2001b). Environmental and social specialists are located in the central CES that serve the six regional, nine industry, and eight thematic departments, and in investment project teams. By 2000 IFC had increased the number of its environmental specialists to fifty; thirty-nine of which were located in CES reviewing project compliance (IFC 2002b: 29; World Bank 2001a: 182). Within the regional, industry or thematic departments there may be units with environmental expertise. For example, the Renewable Energy and Efficiency Team was located in the Power Sector of the Infrastructure Department (World Bank 2001a: 184). In 2002 IFC initiated three additional environmental and social development facilities: the Corporate Citizenship Facility, established to 'mainstream' environment related work in projects; the Sustainable Financial Markets Facility, designed to build capacity in financial markets; and the Environmental Opportunities Facility, created to develop new environmental projects and environmental components of projects (IFC 2002a: 60). In 2006 these units were incorporated into IFC's environmental advisory centre, which controls IFC's Sustainable Business Innovator programme.

Like the World Bank, IFC consolidated its environmental approach between 1998 and the early 2000s from 'do no harm' to 'do good'. The comprehensive suite of environmental rules adopted by IFC in 1998 would be compounded by the increase in environmental staff to ninety-nine and its increase in environmental funding from $2 million in 1994 to $12.5 million in 2004 (IFC 2005c: 40, 53). Furthermore, it would also substantially devise and improve its monitoring and evaluation procedures, as detailed below. As a result, IFC was internalising sustainable development norms through the institutionalisation of environmental rules and mainstreaming their integration into IFC investment operations. As part of this process IFC management asked the CAO to undertake a review of the safeguards since their establishment. The CAO was established in 1999 with assistance from TEANs (see below) at the same time that IFC appointed its first liaison to the NGO community. The CAO completed the review in 2003, circulating a draft version for public comment in 2002. The draft states that it is intended for IFC and NGOs and communities,

> *who in the past have played a critical role in the development of the SPs [safeguard policies] their concept and detail*, and who look toward the policies, sometimes in the absence of other information and measures to seek reassurances that the projects undertaken will do no harm and will enhance the development of their communities and regions. (CAO 2002a: 10; emphasis added)

The CAO found a 'steady progression and evolution of practice' in IFC's activities (CAO 2002a: 23). It noted a marked improvement in project public consultation, which it found influenced the effectiveness of the safeguards and project outcomes. The CAO reported that the safeguards do contribute to positive environmental and social impacts (CAO 2002a: 23–42). The final report signalled that the safeguards often go beyond the 'do no harm' approach and provide a demonstration effect on other stakeholders (CAO 2003a: 6).

However, the report stated that IFC was not capitalising on the 'excellence displayed by many of the environmental and social specialists' (CAO 2003a: 7). Overall it argued that IFC had a 'weak system supporting the safeguard policies, including lack of specific objectives, weak project monitoring and supervision, and poor integration of SPs [safeguard policies] into IFC's core business' (CAO 2003a: 7). The review also found need for greater transparency in decision-making; that the EA umbrella policy for all other safeguard policies required tighter quality control; and that a more comprehensive approach to social safeguards was needed.

CAO recommended that IFC better assess borrower capacity for environmental and social governance; that IFC strengthen its system for environmental and social project preparation; that IFC integrate safeguard policies into early project design; that IFC management be held accountable for environmental and social goals at the project and portfolio level; that environmental and social decisions be transparent and peer-reviewed; that interpretations of the safeguards be made available to sponsors and affected communities; that the environment and social development department become a more central part of investment decision-making throughout IFC; and that a number of safeguard policies be updated and have a 'regular, if not continuous, monitoring and update system' (CAO 2002a: 45–8). This, it was argued, was necessary for IFC to 'remain an industry standard leader' (CAO 2003a: 7).

Both the CAO Review and the concurrent Extractive Industries Review fed into IFC's decision to update its safeguards in October 2003. By now TEANs were considered legitimate influences on IFC practices and were extensively consulted along with industry, states and specialists. The consultation period was IFC's largest ever with stakeholder workshops in four regions of the world

(IFC 2006b: 8). Consultations lasted from 2004 to 2005, with an additional sixty-day window for comments in late 2005. A majority of submissions (fifty-nine per cent) were from civil society including TEANs (IFC 2006b: 8). Although the establishment of the safeguards was influenced by TEAN direct and indirect socialisation, IFC's decision to update its safeguards did not lead to the outcomes TEANs expected from their previous experiences.

TEANs became disaffected by the consultation process: they argued that more time was needed for engagement with IFC than the time allocated for input. Only four months were allocated for consultation on *all* of the policies compared to years of consultation with the World Bank on a *single* policy (Lawrence 2005b: 13). They further claimed that the workshops were not open, that many documents were only in English, and the integrity of the process was undermined.[33] Significantly, the guidance notes meant to supplement the new standards were belatedly provided for comment and TEANs argued that they had to fight for the release of the standards second draft.[34] Perhaps even more important was the lack of clarification on how the consultations were included, leaving many in the network feeling as though the entire process was compromised.[35] A number of NGOs boycotted in protest (Lawrence 2005b: 13).[36]

The process converted the safeguards into what IFC would call performance standards. This process demonstrates how IFC began to internalise and reconstitute sustainable development as market-based sustainability for a private sector financier. As discussed below, IFC's shift from the 'do no harm' perception of sustainability to the 'do good' increasingly meant viewing sustainability through the lens of its investment finance identity rather than through the World Bank's rule-based sustainability. On 21 February 2006 the Board of Executive Directors adopted the new performance standards to replace the safeguards. IFC's EVP Lars Thunell argued that the standards are 'stronger, better and more comprehensive' than the safeguard policies (IFC 2006b: 3). They include the standards listed in Box 4.2. These were supplemented by 'companion' Guidance Notes for project sponsors, and Environment, Health and Safety Guidelines to replace the Pollution Prevention and Abatement Handbook for staff and project sponsors (IFC 2006b: 21).

TEANs actively opposed the performance standards which

Box 4.2 *IFC's policy and performance standards on environmental and social sustainability effective 30 April 2006*

Performance standard 1: Social and Environmental Assessment Management System
Performance standard 2: Labour and Working Conditions
Performance standard 3: Pollution Prevention and Abatement
Performance standard 4: Community Health, Safety and Security
Performance standard 5: Land Acquisition and Involuntary Resettlement
Performance standard 6: Biodiversity Conservation and Sustainable Natural Resource Management
Performance standard 7: Indigenous People
Performance standard 8: Cultural Heritage

Source: IFC 2006c: 1.

they saw as weakening the stringent, credible safeguard policies. TEANs claimed that IFC was 'lowering the bar' of international lenders because they allow environmental and social assessments to be undertaken by the client rather than by independent experts, and that these standards are weaker than those of the World Bank (Lawrence 2005a). TEANs argue that IFC's new policies make IFC less accountable because of their 'flexible, discretionary nature' such that the standards 'remove unambiguous benchmarks' (Lawrence 2005a; Halifax Initiative 2006: 1).[37] TEANs highlighted that the standards include 'aspirational statements' and allow 'a lot of discretion' in their implementation.[38] Finally, they state that the performance standards are 'permissive', and contain 'broad caveats allowing exceptions'.[39]

The CAO also commented on the draft standards in late 2005 and again in January 2006. While many of the CAO's comments were integrated into the new performance standards they still did not incorporate a commitment to measuring impacts at the project level. Further, key commitments outlined in the Extractive Industries Review were omitted along with a statement as to how current problems in applying the safeguard policies would be addressed.[40] Finally, the CAO argued that assurances that the new performance standards would not weaken the existing institutional commitments to sustainability remained absent (CAO 2006b: 1). These points are echoed by TEANs (Halifax Initiative 2006).

In shifting from the safeguards to the standards IFC updated its Environmental and Social Review Procedure (ESRP). While the ESRP remains consistent in monitoring project sponsor compliance, the distinction between the safeguards and the performance standards is illuminating. Specifically, IFC now distinguishes between IFC policies and policies for IFC clients. IFC must adhere to its overall Sustainability Policy, its ESRP and its Disclosure Policy. Its clients are required to meet the Performance Standards, the Guidance Notes and the Environmental, Health and Safety Guidelines (IFC 2006f). The safeguards had made no such distinction.

Specifically, the umbrella safeguard, Operational Policy 4.01, required an EA for Category A and Environmental Reviews for Category B projects. The categorisation, EA criteria and the monitoring for compliance were undertaken by IFC although the project sponsor undertook the project. In comparison, Performance Standard 1 (PS1) requires IFC to assess whether the project sponsor has a management system in place to address likely environmental impacts (thereby overriding the project category A, B, C as the primary determinant of environmental and social assessment requirements, although the categories remain in place).

On paper the performance standards are a mix in terms of whether they have weakened or strengthened IFC's sustainability. The performance standards are much clearer in identifying IFC's expectations of client compliance and staff interpretations of the standards in a number of safeguard areas and specific sectors such as the extractive industries (CAO 2005a: Annex II; Halifax Initiative 2006: 6). The performance standards further state that the project sponsor must meet national and host country obligations under international law as well as the standards which are subject to IFC loan conditions.

There are some improvements that TEANs recognise, such as the expansion of the EA procedure in PS1 from the safeguards.[41] PS1 now specifically refers to the project's 'area of influence' rather than merely the project site and refers to broader supply chain management by project sponsors (IFC 2006c: 5; Morgera 2007: 160). Second, the performance standards now recognise labour, working conditions and human security (PS2 and PS4), which establishes human rights as a concern for international financial institutions and was the result of engagement with trade unions and human rights groups. IFC is further ahead than the Bank and MIGA in terms of its rights-based development agenda which incorporates eight of the International Labour Organisation's conventions (IFC 2006c: 7), although TEANs argue that the standard does not go far enough (Herz *et al.* 2008). PS3 on pollution prevention and abatement now includes greenhouse gas accounting on carbon emissions (IFC 2006c: 13), which 'seems to respond to' recommendations made by TEANs and the CAO (Morgera 2007: 168). More generally the performance standards do reference important multilateral environmental agreements (see Morgera 2007: 183), and although there is room for improvement IFC has broken new ground for a multilateral financial institution.

On the other hand, TEANs argue that IFC's performance standards on involuntary resettlement and indigenous peoples do not meet the Bank's safeguard policies, which raise serious questions about whether IFC will face more problem projects in the future (Halifax Initiative 2005: 17; Lawrence 2005a: 13). Other standards are not so clear cut: PS6 on the conservation of biodiversity and natural resources is seen as mixed, such that it 'maybe a bit of a gain but not really backwards'. IFC has devised a more inclusive definition of 'critical natural habitats' including language on alien species, and it has 'more explicit conditions pertaining to legally protected areas' as well as incorporating analyses of ecosystem impacts (Morgera 2007: 171).[42]

Yet the new standard does not include the previous provision (under Natural Habitats Policy OPN4.04) that projects should be 'sited on land that has already been converted or degraded where feasible' (CAO 2006b: 4, 2005a: 37; IFC 2006c: 24–5). Nor does it include a specific 'no-go' provision TEANs advocated in order to ensure protected sites would remain so. Morgera argues that PS6 retains an economistic understanding of natural resource use (2007: 174–6). TEANs argue that some private banks such as ABN AMRO and Bank of America have stronger environmental policies in sector specific areas such as biodiversity conservation and forest protection, raising questions about IFC's leadership in project finance.[43] Yet IFC argues that it continues to have higher standards overall and remains a sustainable finance leader.[44]

Although it is too early to tell what the impact of the performance standards on IFC projects will be, the CAO continues to advocate for IFC to assess specific environmental impacts at the project level as it recommended in 2003, rather than merely present aggregate data on its environmental performance. The CAO notes that IFC's shift from procedurally based environmental requirements (from Category A, B, C and FI designations, with the latter for loans to financial intermediaries not requiring environmental assessments) to an 'outcomes based framework ... gives IFC and its clients greater flexibility' for determining how to balance desired project outcomes from their risk (2007a: 2). Thus, determining a project as Category B no longer signals the extent of public consultation or its environmental and social risk, which was the case for IFC under the safeguards and remains the case for the World Bank.

Yet the CAO also notes that IFC is now applying formerly Category A only concerns to Category B projects, such as environmental and social impact assessments and engaging external experts to verify monitoring (2007a: 3, 5). This flexibility means that project specific environmental and social conditions are viewed through an ongoing environmental management system by the project sponsor, although the extent to which IFC can ensure their commitment remains to be seen. IFC will release a three-year implementation report on the performance standards in 2009 with the intent of updating them in 2010 (IFC 2007b: 5).

Arguably, the shift from the safeguards to performance standards demonstrates a process of internalising and reconstituting sustainable development norms for a sustainable financier. To explain, Wright argues that the move by IFC is one away from a TEAN- and civil society-centred compliance approach toward industry understandings of sustainability (2006a). This shift must be seen in the context of operationalising sustainable development norms. IFC has attempted to mainstream environmental ideas throughout its operations and the life of the projects its finances (see PS1, IFC 2006c: i; Morgera 2007: 160). IFC's shift therefore exemplifies a market-based approach to development that emphasises the life cycle of the project rather than a rules-based approach, or from ‘avoiding harm to value added activities’ (CAO 2005a; Wright and Rwabizambuga 2006). It has reconstituted sustainable development norms as part of internalising them for a private sector financier and investor. As a result, the implementation of the performance standards is crucial to IFC’s sustainable finance identity.

The change has raised warning flags with TEANs and the CAO over the potential downgrading of absolute environmental and social commitments. To date only half of projects approved under the performance standards have disbursed some funds (IFC 2007b: 17). The IEG reports in its review that IFC has played a positive role in helping clients develop management systems on environment and social issues which directly correlates into high environmental and social effectiveness outcomes (World Bank 2008a: 56). To ensure that environmental commitments have not been downgraded by the introduction of the performance standards requires ongoing interaction between TEANs, the CAO, IFC, project sponsors and states.

Beyond the rules versus flexible sustainability approach there is further evidence that mainstreaming of sustainable development norms is occurring within the organisation. In terms of its ‘do good’ sustainability initiative, IFC is now becoming a more selective investor with an exclusion list prohibiting investment in a range of practices (IFC 2006b: 13). Furthermore, to undertake its sustainable development work, the number of environmental and social specialists at IFC increased to ninety-nine in 2004, up from fifty in 2000 (IFC 2005c: 53, 2002b: 29). In addition, sixty-three per cent of environmental and social staff are located in regional or industry departments where investment deals are made (IFC 2006a: iii). Environment staff are now integrated into the initial investment contract negotiations thus incorporating environmental concerns at the beginning of a project cycle (IFC 2005a: 18, 22). From 2006, sustainability began to be integrated into IFC’s core internal training programmes to further mainstream sustainable development norms. IFC has also substantially changed its position on disclosing information on its environmental practices – again a result of direct and indirect socialisation by TEANs. Information disclosure is integral to IFC’s sustainable development shift, for reasons discussed below.

Environmental transparency

IFC continued to consume norms of sustainable development from TEANs by establishing its own information disclosure policies. Information disclosure became an issue for TEANs as a means of accessing information to monitor IFC's environmental impacts. IFC operates within the realm of private sector lending for development, a process that is subject to business confidentiality and secrecy, which is not transparent to the wider community. TEAN opposition to the degree of IFC confidentiality again took two distinct forms of direct and indirect socialisation, effectively repeating the same processes that established the World Bank's disclosure policy. Direct socialisation entailed persuasive practices including writing letters, emails and faxes on behalf of a growing number of concerned groups all over the world, as well as informal meetings and telephone calls with IFC staff related to information disclosure issues. The indirect process was based on influencing the US, again through the US-ED. This was done by persuading US Congress to ensure that IFC adhered to the 1989 Pelosi amendment on the timely release of information by MDBs.

In 1991 Nancy Pelosi, the US Congressional member who had enacted the amendment, personally questioned IFC's adherence to the amendment in a letter to President Conable. The amendment requires the release of Category A project environmental assessments at least 120 days prior to the meeting of the Board with the time limit for Category B projects being sixty days.[45] President Conable sought to reassure Congress member Pelosi that IFC was meeting its information disclosure requirements on environmental aspects of projects as far as it possibly could within the legal constraints surrounding private sector lending agreements.[46]

IFC adopted its own policy on disclosure of information in July 1994 (Chamberlain 1997: 8). However, this was not before continued pressure from TEANs to ensure that IFC complied with the US Pelosi amendment, which they argued the new policy did not. Persuasion via letters from the National Wildlife Federation and the Sierra Club to the US Secretary of the Treasury outlined arguments that the 1994 policy would not meet information disclosure requirements.[47] Coercive pressure was evident when congressional member Pelosi sent a letter to the US Secretary of the Treasury, advocating that the US-ED oppose the adoption of the Disclosure of Information Policy.[48] The letter pointed to the lack of sufficient documents being released by IFC on environmental and social issues for projects; their reliance on sponsor agreement to release such documents; and the limited time of their release before Board approval of such projects. Irrespective, IFC approved the Disclosure of Information Policy in 1994.

IFC's 1994 policy was adapted from the World Bank's new disclosure policy, but it allowed a greater restriction of information on the basis of business confidentiality. IFC's policy allowed the release of general publications regarding specific sectors such as mining, the 'Summary of Project Information' (SPI) documenting which projects were being considered for approval, the EIA for Category A projects and the Environmental Review Summary (ERS) for Category B projects. Significantly, the 1994 disclosure policy came under review soon after, as mass opposition by TEANs continued unabated, calling for greater access to project documents, specifically those assessing the environmental and social issues. As such, the information disclosure policy of 1994 was already subject to review in 1995, with substantial TEANs input via public consultation by IFC on the internet, and continued until a new revised policy was established in 1998, coinciding with IFC's updated safeguards.

In September 1998, IFC completed its revised policy on disclosure of information as a result of direct and indirection socialisation from TEANs (Bowles *et al.* 1999: 128). IFC had attempted to

> broaden the scope and information about its activities that it makes publicly available and to broaden the methods of dissemination of project-specific information, including that pertaining to environmental and social impacts, to locally affected people and other interested parties. (IFC 1998b)

In reality the 1998 policy added little to the previous policy. IFC would release the SPI while the project was under consideration. EIAs for Category A projects and ERSs for Category B projects were to be disclosed to the public at, respectively, sixty days and thirty days prior to Board deliberation.

TEANs insisted that these periods were neither sufficient for the public to ascertain the effect of the project, nor enough to mobilise efforts to counteract or halt its harmful environmental aspects. In addition, they claimed SPIs were too vague and limited in terms of specific environmental concerns. The network argued that only releasing SPIs was futile because they were only early information releases for projects while later more detailed documents remained inaccessible. While IFC proclaimed that it followed its environmental and social policies, TEANs vehemently denied this. The inability of IFC to satisfactorily implement its own policy guidelines as documented in the Pangue case (and elsewhere, see Bowles *et al.* 1999) highlighted this deficiency. The 1998 disclosure policy stated that any legal documentation was confidential, including the actual agreement between IFC and the borrower (minus specific social and environmental mitigation measures). What was publicly available included the 'typical' standard list of environmental and social covenants that IFC borrowers were required to comply with. Non-disclosed documents included the monthly operations report (MOR), any project specific Board papers, any documents or related information on negotiations between IFC and the client, or any IFC communication with member governments. Further, IFC allowed itself a waiver over all information if it so desired (IFC 1998b), which it retained from the 1994 policy (Hair 1997: 20–1).

The core difference between the World Bank and IFC's 1998 policies was the amount of information and the timeframe within the project cycle in which such information was made available (Chamberlain 1997: 8). While IFC argued that its position was based on a presumption of disclosure, statements protecting private clients qualified this. Nominally available documents including the SPI and the EIA for Category A projects are released to the public at thirty days prior to the Executive Director's Board meeting for project approval, and the ERS for Category B projects is released at sixty days. This is in contradistinction to the release of Category A and B assessments by the World Bank which occur at the project appraisal stage in the project cycle – that is at the beginning of the project design stage, rather than at the end. Moreover, the release of the SPI by IFC was predicated on 'market conditions or timing requirements [which] may prevent observance of the 30 days period'. Further, releasing Category A EIAs, and Category B ERSs were conditional on the consent of the project sponsor and IFC management (Chamberlain 1997: 10).

However, the 1998 policy did make a number of documents available to the WBG information shop (infoshop) in Washington, DC, its regional or country offices, and through the internet. Available documents included: EIAs for Category A and ERSs for Category B projects, environmental data sheets, national environmental action plans, indigenous people development plans, and resettlement plans. Releasing these documents highlighted the importance of making information available to affected communities, but also demonstrated the increase of IFC policies covering communities and their environments. This was supplemented by the publication of a *Guide to Public Consultation and Disclosure* for IFC sponsors, and followed up in 1999 with the establishment of the CAO (examined next). As such, while TEANs continued their efforts to socialise IFC with regard to further information disclosure, it is recognised by TEANs, sponsors, and IFC themselves that information disclosure and public consultation have improved. Furthermore, IFC staff recognise that information disclosure has improved drastically, and has improved the development effectiveness of IFC projects (CAO 2001a).

IFC initially established its policy on information disclosure in 1994: it was opposed by the networks and the US. IFC then strengthened its information disclosure policy in 1998 but retained its qualified position in favour of 'disclosure where disclosure would not materially harm the business and competitive interest of clients' (IFC 1998b). Yet continued pressure and criticism of the revised 1998 policy, through direct and indirect socialisation, has meant that advocacy networks have kept information disclosure on IFC's agenda. Advocacy networks continued to argue for the release of more information such as the Monthly Operations Report, which provides project summaries before the appraisal stage of the project cycle; the removal of management's right to waiver the SPI; and the establishment of an appeals mechanism similar to that of the Inspection Panel for peoples adversely affected by IFC projects to ensure IFC follows its own safeguard policies. This led to the revision of IFC's information disclosure policy from 2001, which included extensive public consultation throughout 2003 and 2004.

On 21 February 2006, an updated disclosure policy was

adopted by IFC's Board, which came into effect with the performance standards. The new policy states that after IFC undertakes its Environmental and Social Review Summary (ESRS) will be released to the public along with an EIA and SPI (renamed the Summary of *Proposed* Investment) for Category A projects sixty days prior to the Board meeting – along with an ERS and SPI for Category B projects at thirty days prior – retaining the timeframes established under previous policies (IFC 2006d: 4). The new policy is explicit that any revisions to the ESRS will be made public (through the infoshop, online and by request), addressing TEAN concerns that up-to-date information is provided on the environmental and social components of a project as it progresses.

IFC's performance standards further outline the disclosure obligations of the project sponsor via management systems and action plans. Morgera argues that these information disclosure changes 'set the bar for the private sector's primary responsibility of disclosing information regarding IFC-funded activities to the public' (2007: 164). Both the performance standards and the disclosure policy require the client to 'engage with affected communities, including through the disclosure of information', although TEANs argue that this does not go far enough. The performance standards state that consultation will be based on 'free, prior and informed consultation' rather than ensuring the 'free, prior, and informed *consent*' of project affected communities as is increasingly codified in international law (Morgera 2007: 166) and was recommended in the 2003 Extractive Industries Review (Halifax Initiative 2006: 8–9; IFC 2006c: 5, 29–30). It also does not specify timelines for community consultation (Lawrence 2005b). Once the project sponsor has established a management system, devised an action plan and undertaken community consultation, IFC will disclose project information (IFC 2006d: 4).

In relation to IFC's performance, the disclosure policy states that it will release information on its own developmental effectiveness 'at least annually' (IFC 2006d: 8). TEANs argue that IFC's evaluation mechanism restructure in 2005 (which consolidated all the evaluation mechanisms of the WBG) 'caused confusion as to what they produce and publicly disclose' (Global Transparency Initiative 2006: 3). The Independent Evaluation

Group for IFC (IEG-IFC) has recently implemented its own disclosure policy stating that it will release half of its reports tracking IFC operations, which is unprecedented (IFC 2006g: Annex I). Additionally, since 2006 all IEG-IFC reports sent to the IFC's Board of Executive Directors have been disclosed. Significantly, in 2005 both the World Bank and IFC began to disclose Executive Director Board meeting minutes, signalling a distinct shift in stance in favour of transparency, although these are incomplete (IFC 2006b: 14, 2006d: 7). Finally, IFC has established an administrative appeals process for requesters that are unfairly denied access to information, which TEANs argue is 'an important and positive first step' that the rest of the WBG should follow (Global Transparency Initiative 2006: 4–5; IFC 2006d). They also note that IFC has improved its position on information excluded from disclosure, and applaud IFC's decision to monitor the disclosure policy and update it within five years (Global Transparency Initiative 2006: 7, 14).

According to the transparency scorecard devised by TEANs to assess international financial institutions, IFC has progressed in a number of areas but they call for IFC to further disclose how staff are evaluated; to provide more project and programme information, especially on evaluation and monitoring; and for IFC to provide full disclosure of its Board meetings (Global Transparency Initiative 2006: 7). TEANs continue therefore to push for maximum disclosure.[49] In response IFC has now created a 'Disclosure Portal' on its website for tracking project information, although the organisation retains the position of not providing project level development effectiveness information (IFC 2007b: 4, 12).

In sum, TEANs have influenced IFC towards a more comprehensive understanding of information disclosure and IFC has substantially improved its environmental transparency since the early 1990s when no disclosure was needed, although TEANs continue to push for maximum transparency and engagement with affected communities. Such changes contribute to IFC's overall identity shift, emphasising the role of TEANs in diffusing norms within this IO. These changes are evidence of a progression towards fuller disclosure. They indicate an internalisation of environmental transparency and an internalisation of sustainable development norms. Yet sustainable development is also about the outcome of IFC practices. IFC has increasingly turned its attention to tracking and evaluating its projects, and this is examined next.

IFC's institutional mechanisms

Significant changes have taken place within IFC as a result of direct and indirect socialisation. IFC adopted and adapted the World Bank's suite of environmental and transparency rules for its private sector development projects before internalising and reconstituting them as performance and disclosure standards. TEANs were central to that process by using direct socialisation through persuasion and social influence on the need for a private sector financier but public institution to have minimum environmental rules. Direct socialisation continued from the Pangue project, but both direct and indirect socialisation were crucial in establishing greater environmental transparency. After making substantial changes to its policy framework, this section shows how IFC then began to incorporate sustainable development norms throughout its operations by detailing its efforts to institutionalise and habitualise environmental and social monitoring and evaluation procedures. It then traces how TEANs successfully engaged IFC through direct and indirect socialisation to create an accountability mechanism, the Compliance Advisor/Ombudsman (CAO).

Environmental evaluation and monitoring in IFC

In 1995 IFC created the post-project evaluation body, the independent Operations Evaluation Group (OEG, which became the IEG-IFC in 2005), the same year that the Pangue Inspection Panel claim was filed and rejected.[50] Much like the World Bank's OED/IEG, the OEG/IEG-IFC undertakes project 'post-mortems'. From 1996, half of all projects completed were subject to a detailed OEG audit. The OEG developed a project-level environmental and social effects (ESE) indicator to evaluate and rate the development outcomes of its investments (World Bank 2008a: 14). It designates four ratings: unsatisfactory, partly unsatisfactory, satisfactory and excellent. From 1999 the OEG/IEG-IFC examinations would be based on a random selection of Expanded Project Supervision Reports (XPSRs), which are completed by the IFC investment officers undertaking the project.

From 2006, all of the lessons derived from the XPSRs are fed back into IFC through its new Lessons Retrieval Network, an intra-network database for IFC staff.[51] After 1998, the OEG began providing *Good Practice* publications on integrating environmental and social concerns into operations and *Lessons of Experience* papers on past projects in order to improve operations (including on Pangue, Chad/Cameroon and the Baku–Tbilisi–Ceyhan Pipelines: see IFC 2005b, 2006e, 2006f). The OEG itself states that its findings and recommendations 'with respect to environmental and social safeguard policies, guidelines, and procedures' are being implemented by IFC, including guidelines on hazardous material and on offshore oil and gas. The OEG further argues that the 'body of policies, documents and procedures that codifies IFC's environmental and social operating procedures is adapting constantly' and that IFC staff often go beyond the 'minimum standards of the guidelines' (Liebenthal *et al.* 2005: 114).[52]

In 2001, the OEG evaluated 171 randomly selected recently matured investment operations approved between 1993 and 1995. The OEG concluded that two-thirds of the projects were deemed satisfactory or excellent for their environmental, social, and health and safety (ESHS) requirements. A small percentage of projects were deemed unsatisfactory, which IFC argues were the result of being located in highly risky unregulated states (IFC 2002c: 2–4). Between 2001 and 2004, OEG results hovered between sixty-two and sixty-six per cent of projects meeting ESHS requirements, spiking to sixty-nine per cent in 2005 (Park 2007a: 548). In 2004 the IEG-IFC then began to 'benchmark projects in meeting performance criteria established at appraisal, and in 2006 it developed an evaluation framework using the new performance standards'. IEG-IFC currently identifies most investments evaluated through this system (157 investments to date) as meeting the standards detailed in the appraisal stage, although there is a high degree of variation amongst the different industries IFC invests in (World Bank 2008a: 53, 55).

Overall, the IEG undertook an evaluation of IFC's environmental impact by examining 604 randomly selected matured investments evaluated between 1996 and 2006. It found that sixty-seven per cent of the organisation's investments were satisfactory in meeting their environmental and social policies and demonstrated positive development impacts (World Bank 2008a: 49). Those deemed partly unsatisfactory (thirty-three per cent of projects evaluated) had not met IFC's environmental and social safeguards but were being addressed through ongoing action plans and were not considered to be contributing to permanent environmental damage. The unsatisfactory seven per cent of projects evaluated had 'mitigation prospects [that] were uncertain or unlikely' (World Bank 2008a: 49). Project success rates fluctuated over the decade between sixty and seventy-seven per cent which IEG argues is a result of tightening standards, increased complexity and a broadening of assessable issues. Over IFC's entire portfolio, Category A projects performed better, at seventy per cent on average (World Bank 2008a: 49–50).

IFC has instituted a range of monitoring mechanisms in line with its implementation of the 1998 safeguard policies which have been carried over to the 2006 performance standards. Within CES the Investment Support Group (CESIG) was created to ensure the shift from the safeguards to the standards. CESIG includes forty-five specialists and two managers for project review and supervision (IFC 2007b: 7). Environmental monitoring of projects is done through the ESRP, created in 1998 to guide staff in applying environmental and social analysis to all investments (World Bank 2001a: 182). This includes requiring assessments for all projects at the project appraisal stage, and reviewing project compliance by IFC's environment and social specialists (from 2000 by CES). In 2001 the CAO stated that the 'centralized system of compliance provided by the environment and social team in IFC has helped establish a strong culture of compliance' (CAO 2001a: 2). ESRP was updated in 2006 and again in mid-2007 after the shift to the performance standards. The 2007 update provides more specific IFC requirements for FI investments to meet ESHS requirements after revealing their weakness in meeting the performance standards (World Bank 2008a: 47).

Further evaluation procedures have been instituted to ensure compliance and monitoring throughout the project cycle. In 2000 IFC responded to its increasing size and expanding portfolio by establishing a Quality Portfolio Management (QPM) system to ensure consistency in project processing. QPM provided environment and social specialists with a reference manual and a 'work flow' to direct staff on when to complete reviews in the project cycle. Under QPM project managers were audited and the system was regularly reviewed (World Bank 2001a: 183). Once the performance standards were introduced in 2006, IFC created a new Quality Assurance (QA) system within CES to manage the project cycle from pre-appraisal through to supervision.

Concurrent with its attempts to improve its monitoring and clearing systems, IFC introduced an Environment and Social Risk Rating (ESRR) system in 2001 to identify projects in high-risk sectors and projects that are not complying with IFC safeguards and standards (CAO 2002a: 19). The ESRR system evaluates investments on a four-point scale of risk. This adds to IFC's seven-point scale of risk for its credit and investment rating systems. In measuring the risk of investments according to their financial, environmental and social likelihood of success, IFC identified a correlation between poor environmental and social ratings, and risky financial performance (IFC 2003: 4; Park 2007a). In many ways this confirmed the 'business case for sustainability' by indicating that financially high-risk projects are also more likely to be environmentally and socially damaging. In line with IFC's development commitment to promoting the private sector investment in often fragile developing states this became known as its 'high-risk, high-reward' strategy where IFC knowingly invests in high-risk sectors to improve their development outcome (IFC 2007b: 7). This instrument demonstrates how IFC internalised sustainable ideas into its financier identity by assessing and monitoring high-risk environmental, social and financial investments.

In undertaking these assessments, IFC began to identify a substantial environmental safeguard compliance gap between better performing investments in 'real' projects compared to IFC's equity investments. In 2003 the OEG stated that IFC had difficulty negotiating environmental and social clauses into equity agreements because it had 'little legal leverage' and 'no legal right to obtain Annual Monitoring Reports' as a minority shareholder in private companies. Indeed, IFC's environmental rules and procedures did not distinguish between investment instruments (Liebenthal *et al.* 2005: 129). Since 2006 there has been a dramatic increase in the number of FI projects IFC undertakes, outstripping the capacity of environmental and social supervision (World Bank 2008a: 55–6, 161, n 25). As of 2007 IFC has quadrupled the number of environmental and social specialists assessing FI project compliance, and the first FI projects to apply the performance standards are now being supervised (IFC 2007b: 8). Moreover, the updated 2007 ESRP now incorporates detailed guidance on how to address environmental and social issues when investing in financial intermediaries on the basis of their risk assessment (IFC 2007b: 8).

Both the process of detailing projects' environmental and social impacts through the ESRP and the rating of investments' environmental and social risks through the ESRR are integral to IFC's overall monitoring and evaluation process. The ESRP details IFC's 'ongoing project processing requirements' (IFC 2007b: 3) and indicates project compliance while the ESRR draws attention and resources to high-risk projects requiring detailed attention. IFC states that all projects triggering IFC's performance standards will now be reviewed annually by a CES specialist (in addition to normal monitoring and auditing procedures) and the ESRR will be used to determine the frequency of site reviews of a project's environmental and social compliance (IFC 2007b: 10).

Indicators from both the ESRP and the ESRR feed into IFC's Development Outcome Tracking System (DOTS) which IFC established in 2005 to evaluate the ongoing ability of IFC investments to meet their financial, economic, environmental and social, and private sector development aims throughout every stage of the project cycle. Beginning in 2007 'real time' DOTS results are published in IFC's annual report. In 2008 it posted results that seventy-one per cent of its currently operational projects had high development ratings; overall sixty-five per cent of IFC's portfolio had high environmental and social outcomes compared to sixty-four per cent of projects with high financial performance ratings. Development results for IFC's advisory services remain lower although these are much newer than the rest of its advisory functions (IFC 2008: 42–5).

Through DOTS IFC states that it is 'the first multilateral development bank to report on its current development results for its entire portfolio'. Moreover its reporting is now externally verified, increasing the legitimacy of its reporting (IFC 2008: 41). The

IEG's recent review of the World Bank, IFC and MIGA stated that IFC's monitoring of environmental impacts is more systematic than the World Bank, and IFC continues to break new ground including trialling a carbon dioxide tracking system (World Bank 2008a: 13, 56). Yet the IEG argues that IFC could improve its 'baseline and performance indicators for later monitoring and evaluation'. It further recommends IFC extend its analysis to 'measure more fully the aggregate and supply chain impact – beyond individual project performance – of projects with large environmental dimensions', which fits within the parameters of the new performance standards (World Bank 2008a: xxiii). However, weaknesses in IFC's environmental performance do continue to exist. These are demonstrable in specific industries such as agriculture, food and beverage, forestry, textiles, and tourism, and regionally in areas such as Sub-Saharan Africa (World Bank 2008a: 52–3). These are discussed in relation to IFC's environmental accountability.

The rapid changes demonstrated here, from the detailed evaluations undertaken by the OEG/IEG-IFC to the variety of monitoring and evaluation instruments devised by IFC (including the ESRP, ESRR and DOTS) indicate that sustainability is institutionalised and habitualised within this organisation. The extensive manner in which environmental policies and feedback mechanisms are increasingly incorporated throughout IFC's operations demonstrate that IFC has internalised sustainable development norms. Processes of direct and indirect socialisation by the network, as demonstrated throughout, led to a reformulation of IFC's identity through the establishment and internalisation of environmental policies which were reconstituted in the process to fit IFC's identity as a financier. The next section analyses how advocacy networks influenced the establishment of an accountability mechanism for the private sector lender and investor of the WBG.

Environmental accountability in IFC: the CAO

TEAN processes of direct and indirect socialisation were again evident in instituting a new accountability mechanism for IFC. After the rejection of the Pangue claim, advocacy networks tried to further sustainable development norms by persuading IFC to increase its environmental and social accountability. CIEL,

Friends of the Earth, and BIC were all engaged in direct socialisation through meetings and interaction with IFC (and MIGA) staff as well as providing comments to the WBG's Committee on Development Effectiveness (CODE) on the proposals for an accountability mechanism's operating guidelines and functions in 1996.[53] Early on, the structure and function of such a mechanism was being compared to the World Bank's Inspection Panel. CIEL favoured establishing a similar Inspection Panel, although it was later determined that a private sector accountability mechanism for both IFC and MIGA should be more flexible than the quasi-judicial proceedings of a panel.[54] However, TEANs were both informed of and responded positively to the creation of a Compliance Officer/Ombudsman.[55]

In terms of indirect socialisation, the accountability mechanism had long been supported by the US Executive Director (US-ED) Jan Piercy, where the US Executive Director had already been socialised by TEANs on an accountability mechanism for all MDBs and their affiliates. In 1997, at a CODE meeting regarding the establishment of an accountability mechanism, Piercy stated that:

> The IFC/MIGA process for developing a proposal can proceed now ... The CIEL/Friends of the Earth proposal received by CODE members yesterday provides a launching point. We understand that the NGO proposal has been reviewed by the private sector and incorporates many of their concerns. *This proposal can provide the basis for reconciling differences and to help focus the discussion and negotiations.*

Piercy therefore favoured the input from TEANs, while identifying the 'lack of progress since the last CODE meeting' as the result of 'time spent dealing with the Pangue review'. Piercy reaffirmed the US's commitment to such an accountability mechanism because the Pangue project 'illustrates the need for having an inspection mechanism in place to avoid ad hoc approaches'.[56] The US-ED's support for making an accountability mechanism part of both IFC's and MIGA's identities has remained consistent throughout.

Direct socialisation has also been consistently applied in all stages of the establishment of an accountability mechanism: TEANs used persuasion and the social influence from problem projects to push for such a body, and they were engaged in its creation and its initial operations. CIEL was part of the search committee established to find a suitable candidate for the job of the CAO.[57] CIEL, BIC, the Berne Declaration (a Swiss-based environmental NGO), and Friends of the Earth were original members of the CAO's Reference Group, assisting in the establishment, operation, and procedures of the CAO through roundtable workshops in 1999, 2000 and 2001. The Reference Group is 'an independent body of stakeholders from the private sector, the NGO community, academia and other institutions' which has 'guided the development of operational guidelines for the CAO and participated in the safeguard review process' (CAO 2002c: 4). Furthermore, TEANs have consistently monitored the CAO's operations since its inception in 1999, directly engaging with the CAO to ensure that it operates transparently.[58] The CAO has enabled the input of both TEANs and industry. The CAO has gained the trust of TEANs with regard to its intentions to provide an accountability mechanism for IFC (and MIGA) projects, although some NGOs remain critical of its efforts (Friends of the Earth International *et al.* 2006). The next section describes the CAO's role and how it furthers sustainability within IFC to support the argument that IFC has consumed norms of sustainable development.

President Wolfensohn set up the CAO in 1999. The CAO has vice presidential status within IFC and reports directly to the WBG President. There was strong participation from TEANs from the CAO's inception. Wolfensohn was committed to a multi-stakeholder approach to appoint a CAO agreeable to both the private sector and TEANs. The committee was made up of IFC and MIGA staff, international and local NGOs, business groups and sector experts, who selected Meg Taylor. Further, the CAO 'Reference Group' is comprised of experts in social, environmental and private sector issues (especially in IFC and MIGA operations) that serve as a body of knowledge for the CAO for its investigations. In addition to the environmentalists previously mentioned, the Reference Group initially included: Conservation International, the World Conservation Union (the Netherlands), Survive (Paraguay), Pro-Natura (Brazil), and the World Wildlife Fund (Pakistan). The broad dialogue with TEANs continued with open forum discussions on the CAO's operational guidelines.

Drafts were available to TEANs for comment and roundtable meetings were held in September 1999 and early 2001 in four regions (Africa, Latin America, Asia and the United States). A third roundtable meeting was held in May 2001 to review the CAO's first year of operations.

The CAO assists IFC and MIGA to 'enhance the social and environmental outcomes of the projects in which they play a role' (IFC 1999: Appendix). As the title may suggest, the CAO has three functions: compliance auditor, advisor and ombudsman. The first entails the evaluation of IFC's and MIGA's compliance with their environmental policies through either an informal analysis or a full-blown compliance audit. Compliance audits may be triggered by the WBG president, IFC or MIGA management, the CAO, or from the ombudsman function (see below). The second role is as an advisor to IFC and MIGA staff, management, and president on environmental and social issues, either informally or formally through regular reporting to the president and periodic reporting to the Boards. The final role is the ombudsman role, which was established to respond to and mediate problems regarding people adversely affected by IFC- or MIGA-related projects.

The ombudsman is significantly different from the quasi-judicial Inspection Panel process established by the Bank although both were established to address environmental and social issues as a result of direct and indirect TEAN socialisation. The CAO acts as an independent mediator compared to the World Bank's Inspection Panel, which determines whether people were adversely affected as a result of Bank non-compliance with its own safeguards. Like the Inspection Panel, the CAO becomes involved when it receives a complaint from peoples adversely or potentially affected. Like the Panel, the CAO validates the claim. From there, the Panel and the CAO diverge.

While the Panel investigates Bank compliance, the CAO directly mediates between the affected community, IFC or MIGA, the project sponsor and the host government. However, the ombudsman can only persuade parties to reconcile through conflict resolution and problem solving. Consequently, the only leverage the CAO has is the cooperation of IFC or MIGA in investing in or guaranteeing the project. This depends on the percentage IFC has invested or at what time the complaint occurs and how much IFC has invested or recouped. Thus, the CAO has less power than the Inspection Panel, which may require a change in Bank behaviour if it has breached its own safeguards. Unlike the Panel however, the CAO directly attempts to influence IFC or MIGA project sponsors where they have breached IFC or MIGA policies, something which the Inspection Panel only does indirectly through investigating the cause of non-compliance.

Of the three functions, the ombudsman is the most crucial in terms of its immediacy for environmental accountability. The ombudsman recommends 'practical remedial action' while addressing 'systemic issues that have contributed to the problems' (IFC 1999: Appendix). Between 1999 and mid-2007 the CAO received sixty-four complaints on approximately twenty-four projects in its ombudsman role; the overwhelming majority are IFC claims. Of those eligible for assessment, the CAO has closed mediation for seventy-three per cent of claims while fourteen per cent were ongoing at time of writing. Approximately twelve per cent of closed mediations have since been referred to the compliance function of the CAO on the basis that IFC or MIGA may not have ensured that the project sponsor met IFC or MIGA's environmental and social policies (CAO 2007b).

The process of mediation, dialogue, and conciliation concludes with a report to the president, notification to the parties and, hopefully, a settlement agreement. The complaint is then closed, subject to continued monitoring and follow-up. Possible outcomes include: the successful settlement between the parties; an unsuccessful settlement of the parties with a report to the president outlining recommendations for investigation; or unsuccessful efforts to reach settlement with a report to the president outlining that no CAO action could resolve the problem. Under the 2007 revised operational guidelines for the CAO, the second outcome now automatically triggers the CAO's compliance function (CAO 2007b, 2006c: 6). A compliance audit may ascertain whether IFC and MIGA policies or lack of monitoring failed to prevent adverse effects. The CAO therefore incorporates environmental and social feedback for IFC and MIGA.

In April 2002, the CAO commissioned an independent investigation of its own operations. The 2003 report stated that the CAO is committed and successful in its ombudsman role but it found that the office was overextended and that its compliance audit function was underdeveloped. Overall it stated that the CAO had contributed to the increased knowledge and improvement of IFC and MIGA functions, while recommending further environmental and social integration within both organisations (Dysart, Murphy and Chayes 2003: 1–14).

In 2006 the IFC and MIGA Boards commissioned a review of trends in complaints to assess common triggers for CAO mediation. The review discovered that the CAO is involved in one per cent of IFC and MIGA projects, and is receiving an increasing number of complaints. This is likely to be from increasing knowledge of its existence and from IFC investing in the world's largest cross-border infrastructure construction project, the BTC pipeline running through Azerbaijan, Georgia and Turkey (the project generated twenty-six claims up to the end of 2007), rather than from an increase in the number of problem projects. However, the 2006 review identified that fifty-two per cent of the complaints were on extractive industry projects such as oil, gas and mining, followed by manufacturing (thirty-two per cent) and infrastructure (sixteen per cent), even though extractive projects only make up eight per cent of IFC's project portfolio (CAO 2006c: 9–10).

In terms of environmental accountability, environmental and social issues, consultation and disclosure practices dominate both the claims and the audits. Environmental claims are often based on 'water quality, emissions, noise, conservation, spills, siting and cumulative impacts' (CAO 2006c: 13–14). Environmental problems were raised in fourteen of the nineteen projects reviewed and were the second most frequent complaint after social issues, while consultation and disclosure issues ranked third, and implementation of EAs ranked fourth (CAO 2006c: 14). CAO recommendations to IFC and MIGA in relation to both ombudsman complaints and compliance triggers have also been dominated by environmental and social mitigation and capacity (CAO 2006c: 27).

Since the review the CAO's compliance function has been increasingly utilised: to date it has undertaken four compliance audits from eight cases, the majority of which are triggered by the ombudman process (CAO 2007b: 12, 2006c: 7, 13). However one audit was generated by IFC's EVP Peter Woicke in 2004 to assess IFC's project categorisation (B) as a result of TEAN social influence. The CAO determined that the project, the Amaggi soybean plantation in Brazil, could not be justifiably identified as Category B until IFC could ensure that the project sponsor's environmental management system was satisfactorily implemented.[59] In 2007, the IEG concluded that the project sponsor's corrective action plan had not been supervised and that pollution levels exceeded IFC limits (World Bank 2008a: 52). IFC management argues that this does not recognise the efforts of IFC in this project and more broadly to further responsible best practice in the soy sector (World Bank 2008a: 159).

Regarding its advisory role, the CAO has undertaken a review of IFC's environmental and social safeguards, reported on IFC's role in the Extractive Industries Review and provided feedback on the implementation of IFC's performance standards and new environmental and social safety guidelines. As a result of the trends report, the CAO reviewed its operational guidelines during 2006 including a period for public comment (CAO 2007b). Changed CAO practices include complete neutrality in the ombudsman process, engaging in monitoring during the ombudsman and compliance processes to ensure that parties meet agreed upon practices from the mediation or compliance audit, and opening a window post-compliance audit for IFC, MIGA and project sponsors to demonstrate compliance (CAO 2007b: 3, 8).

The CAO argues that the 'positive impact of CAO's work on social and environmental performance has been incremental and cumulative' (2006c: 30). It has improved IFC and MIGA environmental and social capacity in fifty-six per cent of the complaints that it has been involved in (CAO 2006c: 23). TEANs have also tested the efficacy of the CAO. This is evidenced by NGOs querying CAO decisions regarding the Pangue dam in Chile, the Jordan Gateway project and more recently on its conflict resolution process in the Antamina mine in Peru (Friends of the Earth International *et al.* 2006). While the networks question specific decisions made by the CAO, it is clear that the CAO does have the overall support of TEANs (CIEL 2000).

There is also evidence that the CAO, with its aim of assisting local communities in resolving issues with IFC- (or MIGA-) backed projects, and its open stance on information disclosure, continues to advocate for broader information disclosure and environmental accountability at the project level for IFC (CAO 2006c). The work of the CAO has become an important part of the identity of IFC, contributing to furthering sustainable development within IFC. As argued in relation to the World Bank, that problem projects continue to come to light does not mean that IFC is not internalising sustainable development. This is pertinent considering IFC's decision to engage in high-risk, high-reward projects to improve their development outcome, including in agribusiness such as soybean plantations and palm oil production.[60] Yet the IO has put in place systems to ensure that environmental and social issues are incorporated into its investment and lending decisions. The role of the CAO is to ensure that project sponsors, IFC and MIGA, and TEANs are able to resolve issues where these standards are not being met. The very existence of the CAO, like the Inspection Panel, has contributed to increasing IFC's compliance and the CAO provides another legitimate voice in ensuring that IFC continues to improve its environmental practices.

IFC's identity shift

IFC has changed significantly since the early 1990s. This is more than just superficial change in response to states' material power. It is an identity shift. This section reflects on the subjective and intersubjective understandings of IFC's environmental metamorphosis. IFC first employed an environment advisor in 1989 in relation to the Pangue project yet it was not until direct and indirect socialisation by TEANs culminated in the Pangue Inspection Panel claim in 1995 that IFC began to realise the importance of preventing negative environmental and social impacts. As one staff member stated, Pangue really affected IFC's outlook.[61] This view is supported by TEANs who argue that IFC became much more responsive after the Bio Bio claim, by adopting, and then institutionalising, World Bank safeguard policies.[62]

TEANs reconstituted IFC's identity by pressing for the adoption of IFC's own environmental rules. The full establishment of comprehensive environmental, social and transparency policies in 1998 resulted from continued socialisation in the form of persuasion via calls, meetings and consultations and through indirect socialisation via the US-ED and US Congress. This was followed the establishment of the CAO, again as a result of direct and indirect TEAN socialisation. IFC and the CAO recognise the influence TEANs had in establishing such an accountability mechanism (CAO 2002a: 10).[63] The CAO provides an invaluable feedback mechanism, along with the IEG-IFC on how to improve its environmental impact, furthering its environmental accountability to peoples, regions and ecosystems affected by IFC-invested projects.

Indirect socialisation has influenced the US, who began to support a sustainable IFC. A recent annual report to US Congress on the *Environment and the Multilateral Development Banks* outlines how the Treasury Department and the US-EDs of MDBs 'continue to use their voice and vote to improve policies, procedures and specific projects' while advocating for further integration of environmental issues and social policies into project development processes, effective independent Inspection Panels, better management and protection of natural resources, and clear project performance indicators (United States Treasury 2001: 2, 4, 16–17). The US has consistently and actively advocated for a sustainable IFC. The US has shared concerns with TEANs over IFC's activities and the US-ED has abstained or voted against projects deemed too risky. Furthermore, the US was the only principal to provide comments publicly on drafts of IFC's performance standards.[64]

This demonstrates the US's adherence to sustainable development norms through its advocacy and leadership in IFC. As argued throughout, the US has been shaped by the persistent persuasion of TEANs in diffusing norms within IOs: from the initial acceptance by US public agencies of sustainable development norms advocated by TEANs outlined in the previous chapter, towards a committed US government policy reflecting TEAN concerns. This has shaped interactions with IFC, not only on individual US-ED voting decisions, but also in furthering IFC's environmental policies and supporting environmental accountability.

The perception of a shift in IFC is supported by TEANs. They argued that IFC's environment department is both useful and growing, and that IFC seems genuinely concerned with environmental improvement and global issues.[65] While there remain concerns about the implementation of performance standards, and 'problem projects' currently being mediated by the CAO, IFC has become a leader in integrating environmental and social considerations into its operations and lending requirements. As one CAO officer notes, IFC is attempting to integrate environmental and social considerations through the entire organisation, and this is being promoted by a progressive IFC management.[66]

IFC internalised sustainable development norms through its Sustainability Initiative, which it shifted from the CES into IFC's central Operational Strategy Group (COS), thereby legitimising and internalising the environment as both business throughout the organisation and a strategic priority (Wright 2006a: 73). In the early 2000s TEANs perceived IFC to be 'better than the Bank' in terms of interacting with the networks. IFC was seen to be less bureaucratic and more efficient in responding to environmental problems and incorporating environmental issues into its work.[67] In 2004 IFC appointed Rachel Kyte, a former activist (for the World Conservation Union) and CAO officer to head their Environment and Social Sustainability Department indicating the incorporation of TEAN ideas into IFC.

Yet IFC's identity as an investor and financier informs how it reproduces and transforms sustainable development through its operations. The relationship between TEANs and IFC soon became strained when IFC articulated the replacement of its safeguard policies with new performance standards. TEANs were opposed to the rushed consultation and saw little reason for the change. In IFC's haste to create standards that are more easily operable for private sector financiers it has lost the support of many groups within TEANs. In an attempt to be a leader in sustainable development, IFC may have become 'cocky'.[68] IFC's performance in implementing the new standards will determine how they affect its operations, and TEAN support.

IFC's internalisation of sustainable development norms led to their reconstitution as sustainable development norms for private sector financiers. This is evident in the flexible performance standards and the revised Equator Principles, which have now become global norms for private sector investors in project finance. As established at the beginning of the chapter, IFC's understandings of its mandate incorporated sustainability from 2001. IFC has introduced environmental and social policies, widespread training and sophisticated and more transparent monitoring systems. Yet an identity shift also includes subjective and intersubjective beliefs about IFC's concerns for sustainable development. IFC became committed to incorporating social and environmental concerns into its operations as a strategic aim of the organisation.[69] IFC now argues that 'it has a solid track record of investments and leadership in sustainability' (2006a: i). The organisation's culture has changed also, with a substantial increase in environmental and social staff and ongoing commitment to sustainability from IFC management even after a change in leadership in 2006.[70] This demonstrates that IFC has shifted its identity to become a sustainable financier. Clients agree. Recent client surveys undertaken by IFC demonstrate that project sponsors choose IFC as a financier based on its environmental, social and governance expertise – and that they are more likely to stay with IFC as a result of their experience (IFC 2006a: 5, 2006b: 9). This provides further impetus for IFC to maintain its sustainable finance practices.

The distinct identity of IFC from the Bank has meant that norms of sustainable development have been internalised differently. Like the Bank, IFC has dramatically increased its professional social and environmental specialists; instigated far-reaching environmental and social policies; moved towards increased transparency through its information disclosure; and established an accountability mechanism to address peoples and ecosystems adversely affected by IFC-funded projects. Yet there remain noticeable differences such as the shift to the performance standards as a result of the private sector investor identity of the corporation. This is further reinforced by the establishment of a mediation accountability mechanism compared with the quasi-judicial Inspection Panel established by the Bank. However, as has been amply demonstrated throughout, IFC has internalised sustainable development norms into its identity as a sustainable lender and investor.

Conclusion

IFC has made substantive changes to its project operations, environmental policies and institutions which comprehensively demonstrate the institutionalisation, habitualisation and internalisation of sustainable development norms. Yet IFC's identity determined how it was socialised and how it reproduced and reconstituted sustainable development through its operations. This chapter detailed how TEANs socialised IFC through direct and indirect processes to become a sustainable development lender and investor. This was first demonstrated through continued TEANs processes begun against the Bank: through socialising the US-ED not to vote for IFC investment and funding of the Pangue dam in Chile in 1992. While the US-ED abstained from voting, the Alternate US-ED continued to advocate for sustainable development norms within this project, even acting on behalf of TEANs, demonstrating the socialisation of key components of the US government. From there the network continued to constrain the actions of IFC in this problem project campaign by directly influencing IFC through protests, letters, petitions, draft proposals and meetings to the point where independent reports were commissioned to verify the environmental and social damage resulting from Pangue.

While TEANs were unable to halt or effectively mitigate the negative environmental and social impacts of Pangue, they were able to continue socialising IFC at the policy level. The networks aimed to establish a comprehensive suite of IFC's own safeguards, which until that point had been vaguely based on using Bank policies and advice. Without network influence there may have been little reason to clarify IFC's use of Bank policies. This is especially pertinent as MIGA, the third affiliate to be analysed within this book, had only just begun to harmonise its safeguard policies – again just as TEANs attempted to socialise sustainable development norms into its identity.

Further, TEANs were effective in instigating the need for an IFC information disclosure policy through indirect socialisation through the US via US Congress and the Pelosi amendment, but also through direct socialisation from discussions and meetings with IFC staff ultimately leading to a more environmentally transparent IO. More importantly, IFC staff all agree that these measures not only are important, but that they improve the development effectiveness of IFC projects (CAO 2002b: 10–12). The drastic improvement of information disclosure, while not enough to satisfy TEANs, is significant compared to the early 1990s when there was no perceived need to release information.

Lastly, TEANs socialised IFC on the need for an accountability mechanism for the private sector affiliates of the WBG, making this an important aspect of the development lender and investor identity of IFC. While IFC's implementation of new performance standards in February 2006 led to TEAN disaffection, it demonstrates that IFC has internalised and reinterpreted sustainability for private sector investors. This has damaged relations with TEANs but it also shows how far IFC has progressed in terms of making sustainable development central to its operations. While the development lender and investor identity of IFC now has a strong grounding in sustainable development norms, the extent to which TEANs have shaped the political risk insurance identity of MIGA requires analysis, and is examined next.

Notes

1 Between 1990 and 2007 twenty-four per cent of IFC's advisory services were on environmental and social sustainability; these had some positive outcomes but were not documented enough to assess comprehensively. IFC has now established sustainability indexes in Brazil and India, indicating the mainstreaming of sustainability into financial markets. As of 2006 all advisory services are assessed for their environmental and social impact (World Bank 2008a: xvii, 58).

2 See IFC's Annual Reports during the 1990s at www.ifc.org Accessed: October 2008.

3 Again, see IFC's Annual Reports at www.ifc.org (accessed October 2008).

4 IFC, 'A Sustainable Development Roadmap for IFC': internal IFC PowerPoint presentation, n.d.

5 Prepared Statement by Peter Woike, Executive Vice President of the IFC, Equator Principles Press Conference, 4 July, 2003. See www.ifc.org (accessed November 2003).

6 For the full list of Equator Banks see www.equator-principles.com/ (accessed October 2008).

7 Since Pangue, other campaigns have included: the Jordan Gateway Project; the Bujagali hydropower project in Uganda; the controversial Chad/Cameroon Petroleum Development and Pipeline Project, a joint World Bank/IFC-funded venture; the Amaggi soy bean plantation in Brazil; the Orion Pulp Mill in Uruguay; IFC's investment in a forestry company in the Democratic Republic of Congo; and the Baku–Tbilisi–Ceyhan Pipeline. These would all be subject to CAO mediation except the Chad/Cameroon pipeline which would come under the Inspection Panel. See the CAO website at www.cao-ombudsman.org.

8 Like Polonoroeste in Brazil, the Pangue-Ralco campaign would

become a defining moment in Chile's environmental movement and would stimulate Chile's environmental regulatory framework (Alywin 2002; Lee 2001: 474, n 16).

9 See www.endesa.es (accessed October 2008). Prior to privatisation the project was to be supplemented by World Bank funding and the Bank warned IFC of the significant environmental and social impacts of the project. Personal correspondence with former Bank ecologist Robert Goodland, 2 November 2008.

10 Disagreements exist over the number of people directly and indirectly affected by the dam but indigenous people were displaced (Johnston and Turner 1998).

11 Open letter by GABB to the Executive Directors of IFC and to the Inspection Panel (dated 10 December 1995); forty-seven NGOs from all over the world protested the Pangue dam project not being investigated by the Inspection Panel (Hair 1997: 1).

12 Letter from Owen Lammers of IRN to the US Executive Director Patrick Coady, dated 17 April 1991.

13 Letter from Patrick Leahy, Chairman of the Foreign Appropriations Committee to The Honorable Nicholas Brady, Secretary of the Treasury, dated 10 March 1992; emphasis added.

14 Letter from Timothy Atkeson, Assistant Administrator of the United States Environmental Protection Agency to Mr Chad Dobson of BIC, dated 31 March 1992; original spelling.

15 GABB's claim 'does not list numerous other letters, FAX or phone contacts, or meetings with Pangue, *US Treasury, US Directors Office*, NGO groups, the press and the public' (GABB 1995: attachment 1; emphasis added).

16 Statement by Mark M. Collins Jr, US Alternative Executive Director to the Board of Directors, dated 17 December, 1992, 'IFC Proposed Investment in Empress Electrica Pangue SA – Chile', IFC Board of Directors.

17 Letter from Mark Collins Jr, US Alternate Executive Director to Mr Christian Maturana of Erupresa Electrecan Pangue SA, dated 3 April 1992; original spelling.

18 Letter from Frances Hamilton, IFC Divisional Manager of Public Relations to Brent Blackwelder of Friends of the Earth, dated 18 September 1990; letter from Jack Garrity, IFC Manager of Corporate Relations to Mr Orrego of GABB, dated 2 March 1992. In 1997 President of GABB Juan Pablo Orrego won the Goldman Environmental Prize for his work to protect the Bio Bio.

19 Letter from GABB representing 13 Chilean environmental and social groups to President Preston, dated 4 February 1992; letter from NRDC representing twenty-five environmental and social NGOs to

President Preston, dated 20 April 1992; letter from Friends of the Earth International on behalf of twenty-five NGOs to IFC, dated 4 March 1992; letter from Jack Garrity, IFC Manager of Corporate Relations to Elka Morgan of Friends of the Earth International, dated 30 March 1992.

20 Letter from James D. Wolfensohn to Eduardo Aninat, Minister of Finance, Chile, dated 6 February 1997. See also the *Financial Times*, 'World Bank Arm Warns Endesa', 21 February 1997: 3.

21 Letter from GABB to the President and Executive Directors of IFC, and the Inspection Panel, dated 10 December 1995.

22 Although it was never specified within Endesa's investment agreement which policies applied. For example, IFC staff member Carol Lee argues that 'some IFC staff maintained that the World Bank's policy on dams and reservoirs did not apply to IFC' (2001: 477).

23 Letter from President Wolfensohn to GABB, dated 6 December 1995.

24 The following section is from the Hair Report (1997).

25 Letter from David Hunter of CIEL to President Wolfensohn, dated 15 November 1996; letter from Glen Switkes of IRN to President Wolfensohn, dated 22 November 1996; letter from Maria A. Espinoza of Red Bancos to President Wolfensohn, dated 6 December 1996; letter from Barbara Bramble of NDRC to President Wolfensohn, dated 30 January 1997; letter from Mark Constantine, IFC Manager of Corporate Relations to David Hunter of CIEL, dated 9 December 1996.

26 Letter from President Wolfensohn to Andrea Durbin of Friends of the Earth, dated 2 June 1997.

27 Letter from President Wolfensohn to Mr Orrego and Mr Opaso of GABB, dated 15 July 1997; emphasis added.

28 Comments from Wolfensohn could be attributed to his position as WBG president rather than IFC. However, IFC Executive Vice President Peter Woicke was a strong supporter for promoting and internalising sustainable development within IFC.

29 Letter from GABB to President Wolfensohn, dated 17 November 1995. For another example see Bowles *et al.* 1999.

30 Monti Aguirre, 'Mapuches to make 220 kilometre march', *Chip News*, email from Bio Bio campaign mailing list, 27 February 2001.

31 A Financial Intermediary loan (FI) category was added in 1993 requiring IFC to ensure that a loan to a financial intermediary in a developing country meets IFC's environmental stipulations. The Bank later adopted this category.

32 The lack of supervision over Pangue came from the fact that many of the social initiatives were from Bank staff but were not followed up by IFC (Hair 1997).

33 Interview BIC activist (1), 10 September 2005; interview Environmental Defense Activist, 8 September 2005.
34 Interview BIC activist (2), 15 February 2006.
35 Letter from Yuki Tanabe and Kazuko Suzuki from the Japan Centre for a Sustainable Environment and Society to IFC EVP Peter Woicke, dated 24 August 2004.
36 Interview with WRI activist, 9 September 2005.
37 The Global Rights Rules and Responsibility Coalition, comprising thirty-five NGOs, documented their engagement with IFC at www.grrr-now.org (accessed November 2006).
38 Interview with WRI activist, 9 September 2005.
39 Letter from BIC, Bretton Woods Project, BanglaPraxis, Campagne per la Riforma Della Banca Mondialle, CIEL, Earthrights International and Peregrine Environmental Consulting to Rachel Kyte, Environmental and Social Sustainability Department Director IFC, dated 23 October 2006.
40 A key omission in IFC's standards in response to the Extractive Industries Review is the lack of analysis of poverty reduction. TEANs also argued for more explicit commitments and recognition of community engagement, disclosure, international environmental standards and human rights law (Lawrence 2005c).
41 Interview with BIC activist (2), 15 February 2006.
42 Interview with BIC activist (2), 15 February 2006.
43 Interview with FOEI activist, 14 February 2006. Many of the Equator Banks agreed with TEANs that the safeguards did not need to be changed: interview with BIC activist, 15 February 2006. Yet they adopted IFC's performance standards as the Revised Equator Principles on 1 July 2006.
44 Interview with IFC Environment and Social Department Director, September 2005.
45 Letter from Nancy Pelosi, Member of US Congress to IFC President Conable, dated 28 June 1991. This was also circulated to US Treasury and the House Subcommittee on International Development, Trade, Finance and Monetary Policy.
46 Letter from IFC President Conable to US Congress member Pelosi, dated 29 July 1991.
47 Letter from Lyn Greenwalt of the National Wildlife Federation to the US Secretary of the Treasury Lloyd Bentson, dated 12 July 1994; letter from Larry Williams of the Sierra Club to the US Secretary of the Treasury Lloyd Bentson, dated 12 July 1994.
48 Letter from Nancy Pelosi, Member of US Congress to US Secretary of the Treasury Lloyd Bentson, dated 12 July 1994.
49 BIC, 2005, 'Comments on IFC's Disclosure Framework', 31 March.

Cited at www.bicusa.org/ (accessed November 2006); Japan Center for Sustainable and Environmental Society, 'Recommendations for the Review of IFC's Policy on Disclosure of Information', 12 March 2004, on file with author.

50 IEG-IFC denotes the specific reports undertaken by the IEG-IFC unit; IEG denotes the World Bank's body or reports undertaken jointly by the IEG, IEG-IFC and IEG-MIGA.

51 Interview with IFC Officer, 16 February 2006.

52 This report was completed and originally published in 2003 but currently available copies have the same version dated as 2005.

53 Dana Clark and David Hunter of CIEL, 'Extension of the Inspection Panel to IFC/MIGA Operations', report to CODE, the World Bank, IFC and MIGA, 3 July 1996; Friends of the Earth, 'Friends of the Earth's Comments on the Draft Operational Guidelines for the Office of the Compliance Advisor/Ombudsman at IFC/MIGA', manuscript, n.d.; letter from Kay Treakle from BIC, Claudia Saladin of CIEL and Doug Norlen from the Pacific Environment and Resources Center, to Meg Taylor, the CAO, on the Draft Operational Guidelines for the Office of the Compliance Advisor Ombudsman, dated 2 March 2000.

54 Owing to their size it was determined that the new mechanism cover both IFC and MIGA. Nonetheless the CAO has different effects on these organisations because of their distinct identities as detailed throughout.

55 Report from the Secretary, CODE, 'Options to Enhance Environmental and Social Compliance and Accountability in IFC and MIGA', World Bank, IFC and MIGA, 4 March 1998: 7.

56 Statement by Jan Piercy, 'Consultations with Private Sector on IFC/MIGA Inspection Function', CODE meeting, 8 October 1997; emphasis added.

57 Other members included the World Wide Fund for Nature, and the International Institute for Environment and Development. See IFC 1999.

58 Letter from David Hunter and Claudia Saladin of CIEL, to Meg Taylor, the CAO Officer, 9 February 2001.

59 See the CAO website at www.cao-ombudsman.org/ (accessed October 2008).

60 This points to a broader debate in environmental politics as to whether organisations should attempt to green essentially degrading industries. On the one hand reducing the environmental impact of palm oil and soy production (not to mention oil, gas and mining) further justifies their continuation; on the other, it does reduce some of their most egregious impacts while demand for products from

these practices continues.

61 Confidential interview with NGO Liaison Officer, IFC, dated 19 September 2001.

62 Confidential interview with a Bank Information Center activist, dated 21 September 2001. Notably, IFC has many sector specific guidelines for particular industries as well as a policy on Slavery and Child Labour that the Bank does not.

63 Confidential interview with NGO Liaison Officer, the IFC, dated 19 September 2001.

64 Interview Environmental Defense activist, 14 February 2006.

65 Confidential interview with a Bank Information Center activist, dated 21 September 2001.

66 Confidential interview with an Officer from the Compliance Advisor Ombudsman Office, the IFC, dated 14 September 2001.

67 Confidential interview with Conservation International activist, dated 18 October 2001; confidential interview with Friends of the Earth activist, dated 26 September 2001.

68 Interview with a CAO Officer, 9 February 2006.

69 Confidential interview with NGO Liaison Officer, the International Finance Corporation, dated 19 September 2001.

70 Thunell, like Woicke, is concerned with environmental issues although his leadership had little to do with the establishment of the performance standards set in motion under Woicke.

5
MIGA and green political risk?

Introduction

Following the increased intensity of TEAN interactions with IFC, MIGA also began to attract TEAN attention for providing political risk insurance to investors funding projects with severe environmental impacts. Attempts to socialise MIGA roughly followed the same pattern established in the previous two cases. This chapter argues that MIGA is only now beginning to follow a market-based sustainable development. Arguably this is a result of its political risk insurer identity: MIGA underwrites projects in developing countries rather than investing in a project sponsor like IFC or lending for a development project like the Bank.[1] MIGA's once removed position in the development process makes it less responsive to TEAN socialisation and until recently pointed to limited change rather than the more pervasive understandings of sustainable development that took hold within the World Bank's lending and IFC's corporate financing.

MIGA's early reactive and reluctant stance is evidence of its resistance to norms of sustainable development, unlike the identity shifts now apparent within the Bank and IFC. However, improvements to MIGA policies are increasingly apparent: MIGA's safeguard and information disclosure policies were permanently adopted in 2002 and MIGA subsequently adopted IFC's performance standards in October 2007. MIGA has also gone further than IFC by announcing in 2007 that it will disclose information on the development impact of the highly sensitive projects it covers (MIGA 2007c). These changes are indicative of a move toward institutionalising sustainable development norms.

The process of socialising MIGA again began with problem project campaigns similar to those outlined in previous chapters. First, an early campaign is detailed, a mining project in the mid-1990s in West Papua, Indonesia. Indirect socialisation again was based on the networks socialising parts of the US although this was based on influencing the US's publicly funded Overseas Private Insurance Corporation (OPIC) rather than parts of the US government (although this means of indirect socialisation also took place in terms of creating sustainable development institutions for MIGA). Throughout this period TEANs continued to pressure MIGA to institutionalise sustainable development through persuasion, social influence and coercion in relation to its environmental, social and information disclosure policies and this is analysed in section two. Section three then assesses the changes undertaken by MIGA in relation to compliance monitoring and the CAO, the accountability mechanism for (IFC and) MIGA guaranteed projects. The final section argues that MIGA resisted TEAN socialisation before belatedly beginning to follow market-based sustainable development through institutionalising IFC's environmental standards. This highlights how an IO's identity shapes how it consumes international norms.

MIGA's identity

Like IFC, ideas for creating MIGA existed well before the organisation did. Drafts for the organisation were circulated in 1948 but negotiations continued through to the 1970s (Meron 1976: 31; Shihata 1988: 31–2). Wavering over the need for a multilateral political risk insurer continued much longer than debates over a multilateral private sector investment facilitator such as IFC (Matecki 1957: 49). Attempts to institute a multilateral risk insurer under the United Nations Conference on Trade and Development (UNCTAD) failed and the World Bank maintained proposals for an international insurance agency for over thirty-five years, but state support for such an organisation was weak (Shihata 1988: 54). With increased fears of expropriation in the 1970s, the need for a multilateral political risk guarantor was revived to support FDI to developing countries (MIGA 2001a).

Arguably a multilateral insurance agency would fill the gaps between the profit-driven but small private insurance sector and the self-interest of national insurance agencies. After the industry downturn in the 1980s, the private sector viewed international political risk insurance as too unpredictable and the majority of political risk insurance was issued by national credit export agencies (Moran 1998: 139; Stephens 1998: 149). Unlike a national insurer, a multilateral institution would not be constrained by nationality while complementing the work of national agencies and advancing the development objectives of client states (Shihata 1988: 18). By the late 1980s it was assumed that international political risk would be better undertaken by the public sector, leading to MIGA's emergence.

MIGA provides non-commercial financial guarantees to foreign investors for development projects in developing countries (MIGA 2001b). MIGA's mission statement is 'to promote foreign direct investment into emerging economies to improve people's lives and reduce poverty' (MIGA 2007f: 4). The Agency offers two services to its clients: political risk insurance or guarantees to investors and lenders, and technical assistance to aid developing states attract private investment including investment dispute mediation (World Bank 2001d).[2] MIGA covers four types of non-commercial risk to investors in developing countries: currency transfer risk; expropriation; the risk of civil disturbance and war; and the risk of breach of contract by a host government towards an investor. The Agency operates on a case-by-case basis in determining the political risk of each investment, usually insuring seventy to ninety-five per cent of the investment (MIGA 2001b). As such the organisation has a small staff of one hundred political risk analysts who identify acceptable political risk levels to insure or co-insure.[3] Currently MIGA can guarantee $110 million per project, while the maximum coverage per country is $420 million, although reinsurance and co-insurance via syndicates with other insurers supplement this capacity. To date, MIGA has paid only three claims on its insurance (MIGA 2008a).

Although small, MIGA plays a central role in the political risk insurance industry. As part of the WBG, MIGA has 'leverage value' or the ability to reduce exposure for investors and to deter moral hazard on behalf of the investor or host country while aiming to provide amicable settlement of disputes before arbitration (West 1999: 28–30). The renewed growth of private sector insurers in the 1990s further enabled syndicates of co-insurance and reinsurance to be spread across more insurers, thus diversifying risk (Moran 1998: 140).

MIGA grew throughout the 1990s and in 2000 the World Bank gave MIGA $150 million to increase its operations, and approved $850 million to be used from member country subscriptions to reach $2 billion in callable capital (World Bank 2001d). The expansion of the Agency's capital gives it a larger role in providing political risk insurance for a greater number of projects. In 2008 MIGA issued $2.1 billion in guarantees, bringing its overall portfolio to $6.5 billion, its largest ever. To date, the Agency has issued 900 guarantees for $17.4 billion dollars in coverage in ninety-six states. MIGA estimates that it has facilitated over $80 billion in guarantees since its inception (MIGA 2008a: 6, 8).

MIGA was established by agreement of the World Bank's Board of Governors. MIGA has its own Chairman, Council of Governors, Board of Directors, convention (articles of agreement) and budget, although in practice the Executive Directors of MIGA also sit on the Boards of the Bank and IFC. The WBG President was nominated as Chairman of MIGA's Board of Directors, enabling the President to determine the Executive Vice President (EVP), who is usually Japanese. The current EVP, Izumi Kobayashi, was appointed in December 2008 (MIGA 2008b). MIGA membership is based upon subscription to the Agency in the form of ten per cent payable capital, ten per cent promissory notes, and eighty per cent callable capital. All members subscribe to the capital stock of MIGA, which gives the Agency its underwriting capacity. This structure allows MIGA to pay out a claim, or increase its coverage to an amount several times larger than its size if needed. Despite its protracted beginning MIGA now has 173 members. MIGA members include capital-exporting states seeking political risk insurance and capital-importing states primarily seeking technical assistance in increasing foreign investment, although some states like Brazil are both.

Membership shares are determined by the Special Drawing Rights determined by the World Bank and the IMF's Development Committee, and member states' economic strength based on their shares in the World Bank's capital (Shihata 1991: 303). The largest members on the Council of Governors vote for their own representative on the Board of Directors, while the remaining Executive Directors are voted in by the rest of MIGA's members (MIGA 2001b). Like both the World Bank and IFC the US dominates member subscriptions. In MIGA the US has 15.08 per cent, followed by Japan at 4.24 per cent, Germany with 4.22 per cent, and France and Britain with 4.07 per cent each; China now has 2.66 per cent (MIGA 2008a: 102). Voting on the Board is equal, except where a special majority is required for decisions of general application and overall financial exposure (Shihata 1991: 284).

MIGA was designed to insure sound investments with positive development impacts for states with the option of long-term coverage, all of which differentiate it from private political risk insurance agencies (Shihata 1988: 19).[4] In the early 2000s TEANs and MIGA engaged in a heated debate over its role in international development, with TEANs arguing that the organisation does not do enough to support sustainable development and poverty alleviation. In 2000 MIGA reoriented its business model to focus on its development mandate including facilitating south–south investments; covering investments in IDA eligible countries and Africa; guaranteeing small to medium enterprises; and partnering with national insurers and other MDBs (World Bank 2001d). These development objectives serve to direct investors towards investments otherwise not undertaken, but with the added safety of MIGA's guarantees. The Agency provides security to its investors by requiring host country government approval of the issuance of MIGA guarantees and the risks designated for cover (Shihata 1991: 307, 329; World Bank 2001d).

TEANs argued that MIGA was a 'dinosaur' regarding its views on sustainable development (Park 2007b: 174). Heated debates with TEANs demonstrate how MIGA moved from initially rejected TEAN claims, to engaging with them, to then recognising the challenges of grappling with its (sustainable) development mandate and its political risk insurer identity (MIGA 2000). MIGA began to thaw in 2004 when it explicitly announced for the first time that it was 'committed to promoting projects with the greatest development impact that are economically, environmentally, and socially sustainable' (MIGA 2008c: 4, 2007f: 4). MIGA adopted a new business model and strategic directions in

2004 although the Agency's strategic aims for the 2005 to 2008 period did not include environmental sustainability *even though they were devised by MIGA's Policy and Environmental Department* (MIGA 2003a: 7). Yet MIGA claimed that it had a comparative advantage with environmental and social compliance on the basis of a MIGA-commissioned study that concluded that the Agency was 'at the top of its peer group' for political risk insurers in its environmental and social requirements (MIGA 2008c: 4, 9).

From 2004 MIGA established annual meetings with TEANs, although TEANs continued to argue that it was 'not taking environmental and social standards seriously'.[5] Up until 2006, TEANs pointed to a lack of information on MIGA's environmental practices as evidence that it had not changed. However the Agency's 2007 disclosure policy does demonstrate a significant shift for a political risk insurer although it may be too early to tell what impact this will have on its operations. The formal adoption of environmental safeguards in 2002, updated to performance standards in 2007, suggests that internalising sustainable development norms or 'going beyond' compliance may be emerging. The 2007 performance standards are seen as an 'important milestone' in outlining MIGA's 'vision in implementing sustainability' (World Bank 2008a: 64). Arguably then, MIGA, along with thirty-five other OECD export credit agencies, is beginning to follow IFC's market-based sustainable development lead, although the Agency has the opportunity to be a standard setter in the investment insurance industry (MIGA 2007b, 2007c; World Bank 2008a: 59, 54).

As this chapter reveals, political risk insurers, even ones with development mandates like MIGA, have a long way to go towards internalising sustainable development. The Agency does not promote sustainable development in its underwriting. MIGA 'does not have a strategy or business line to actively promote free-standing environmentally beneficial guarantee projects' and has 'only recently begun to move towards environmental stewardship' (World Bank 2008a: 64). For example, in 2006 MIGA provided coverage for its first carbon credit finance project (MIGA 2008c: 14; World Bank 2008a: xl). The next section examines how TEANs attempted to socialise MIGA to internalise sustainable development, again beginning with MIGA's 'problem projects'. The Freeport campaign was the precursor to bigger and more direct campaigns against MIGA, and, as demonstrated below, followed discernible attempts at direct and indirect socialisation.

MIGA's 'problem project' campaigns

TEANs first aimed to socialise MIGA to internalise sustainable development through a 'problem project' in the mid-1990s in order to reconstitute its identity as a political risk insurer of sustainable development. TEANs therefore extended their efforts to diffuse sustainable development norms to all development lenders, investors and insurers. This was based on the recognition that the added security of political risk insurance may determine whether a project eventuates. Political risk insurers could play a pivotal role in international development and could be another means of diffusing sustainable development norms.

Compared to IFC, MIGA is further removed from engaging in environmentally degrading projects. MIGA does not undertake project lending or invest in the project sponsor. As demonstrated below, MIGA as a political risk insurer had less of a reason to respond to TEANs. The properties that constitute MIGA: finance staff, a corporate sector mission and the quick operating speeds necessary to identify acceptable political risk levels to insure or co-insure, mean that sustainable development has been viewed as antithetical to its identity. The small size of MIGA (only one hundred staff, compared to IFC's more than 3,300 and the World Bank's approximately 9,000), and its once removed position from the development process, not as a lender or investor of development projects but as a political risk insurer, meant that in opposing MIGA it could be more difficult to establish the social influence that triggered change within the World Bank and IFC. As with IFC, opposing MIGA projects might not stop or mitigate environmentally degrading projects. Rather, it could lead to a change in insurers by the project's investor. Yet, as with the Bank and IFC, the aim of socialising MIGA is predicated on reconstituting IOs because they diffuse norms. The political risk insurance industry relies on co-insurance and reinsurance for guaranteeing large development projects. Changing the identity of one could affect them all.

Previously, TEANs were able to mitigate or halt World Bank and IFC activities through direct socialisation at the project level through social influence, and indirect socialisation via persuasion and coercion at the policy level. TEANs undertook relatively similar processes with MIGA, questioning MIGA's development role and challenging its adherence to WBG environmental policies. TEANs attempted direct and indirect socialisation of MIGA through its 'problem projects'. MIGA's involvement in the development process was highlighted by TEANs attempting to stop environmentally and socially destructive mines, including the then largest gold mine in the world in West Papua. This campaign had limited success on the project sponsor but it did emphasise the key role that political risk insurers can play in promoting sustainable development. This diverges from problem projects outlined in previous chapters, in that socialising MIGA was not the initial aim for the problem project campaign *per se*. Rather, MIGA was implicated in the campaign for underwriting a project sponsor accused of environmental and social devastation. TEANs drew MIGA into the international campaign against Freeport McMoRan; soon after MIGA introduced environmental safeguard policies.

TEANs here included the Berne Declaration, BIC, Campagna per la Riforma della Banca Mondialle, CIEL, Friends of the Earth (US), International Rivers Network, the Wahana Lingkungan Hidup Indonesia (WALHI or the Indonesian Forum for the Environment), the International NGO Forum on Indonesian Development (INFID), ProjectUnderground and Urgewald. Persuasion and social influence were enacted through TEAN publications and posts on the internet. The campaign was supported online by the Bretton Woods Project, Fifty Years is Enough, Down to Earth, Mineral Policy Institute, Probe International, and the Sierra Club. Online list server Forests.org carried substantial information regarding the West Papuan campaign while articles were printed in major US newspapers as documented below.

Keck and Sikkink argue that '[n]onstate actors gain influence by serving as alternate sources of information. Information flows in advocacy networks provide not only facts but testimony – stories told by people whose lives have been affected. Moreover, activists interpret facts and testimony, usually framing issues simply, in terms of right or wrong, because their purpose is to persuade people and to stimulate them to act' (1998: 19). The initial process of direct socialisation was attempting to constrain MIGA's activities by appealing for them to halt underwriting investments in environmentally and socially disastrous projects. Meanwhile, the process of indirect socialisation emerged in a distinct fashion: by influencing the US's OPIC the TEANs indirectly affected MIGA. OPIC was the primary insurer of the project – change to its coverage necessarily affected MIGA's coverage. The next section establishes the concerns surrounding the project before detailing both the processes of direct and indirect socialisation on MIGA.

Freeport McMoRan mine in West Papua, Indonesia

Freeport McMoRan Copper and Gold (FXC) is a US corporation that is one of the largest and lowest cost producers of gold and copper in the world (Perlez and Bonner 2005). Freeport McMoRan is the majority shareholder of subsidiary PT Freeport Indonesia (PTFI), which is located in Jakarta, Indonesia and operates in the mountains of West Papua (Leith 2003: 68–76).[6] The mine's operations include mineral exploration and the mining and milling of ore containing copper, gold, and silver (Freeport 2003).[7] The Freeport mine is located in the traditional lands of the Amungme and the Kamaro peoples. Freeport became interested in the area in the early 1950s after the discovery of the Gunung Bijih (Ertsberg) copper deposit in West Papua's mountainous interior.

According to Freeport's historical account, in 1966 the company was invited to Jakarta to negotiate a mining contract for the deposit. In April 1967, the contract of work was signed with the Indonesian government, allowing Freeport a thirty-year mining concession from the beginning of its operation, and including all areas within ten square kilometres. This occurred two years before the United Nations sponsored Act of Free Choice in West Papua, which essentially ceded West Papua to Indonesian control.

The Freeport mine opened in 1974. By 1987, the mine was producing 16,000 tons of ore daily, with an estimated 100 million tons of ore reserves. A new deposit, Grasberg, was discovered in 1988, leading to a massive expansion of the mine's operations, with total daily production increasing to 18,600 tons per day with an estimated 200 million tons of ore reserves. In 1991, under the new contract of work for Grasberg, Freeport was permitted to explore another 6.1 million acres in the West Papuan highlands. Improvements in technology and new discoveries led to Freeport McMoRan becoming the world's largest gold producer, milling 300,000 tons of rock per day in 2001. Most of this is dumped as waste or tailings into the rivers.[8] At the time Freeport McMoRan was the largest US investor in Indonesia (*United Press International* 1995).

The mine's environmental impacts are extensive. Prior to Freeport's involvement the land was inhabited by semi-nomadic tribes that used the area for hunting, gathering and spiritual purposes. According to Leith, 'West Papua is believed to be the most diverse and pristine ecosystem in the Pacific and one of the most biologically significant regions on Earth.'[9] Specifically,

> the Freeport mining concession is an area of unique biodiversity, encompassing five clearly defined zones within which fourteen separate and diverse ecosystems or habitats exist. Originally ranging from the pristine equatorial glaciers rising more than 4,500 meters above sea level in the alpine zones, the Freeport concession passes through rain forests and down to coastal mangrove forests and the sea in the space of just over a hundred miles. (Leith 2003: 163)

The mining has affected 'the alpine zone around the mine site; the tailings deposition area in the lowlands, which includes four ecosystems (tidal swamps, peat swamps, meander belt, and alluvial fans), and the coastal region' (Leith 2003: 163).

The original contract for the mining concession contained no environmental clauses, and environmental issues were not considered prior to the discovery of the Grasberg deposit in 1988. With the expansion of the mine came the realisation that Freeport's environmental record could endanger its financing should environmental campaigners succeed in having their criticisms heard. In 1990, Freeport established its first environmental department although this was not given much credence either within or outside the company.[10] Meanwhile, the impacts of the mine continued to grow with increased production.

Freeport's main environmental impact is its tailing waste.

Tailings are the 'residue of finely ground ore from which precious metals have been extracted' (Leith 2003: 166). Freeport's initial operations discharged 7,000 tons per day into the local river system, although by the early 2000s this had increased to approximately 300,000 tons per day, accounting for over 70 million tons per year being dumped. This is substantially more than the 30 million tons dumped into the Fly river system by BHP at the Ok Tedi mine in Papua New Guinea, which was closed down because of extensive environmental damage and environmental opposition. Tailings dumping in West Papua has changed the flow and direction of the Ajkwa river, leading to 'sheeting' of the Ajkwa into the Minajerwi river (Leith 2003: 167). The result was the destruction of 'at least 33 square kilometres of forests where the changing course of the river left behind swamps and destroyed rainforests, hunting grounds and agricultural land' (Leith 2000: 236). In response, Freeport formulated a tailings and river management plan in an effort to contain their impact. However, concerns remain that the high copper content of the tailings may poison the underground water system used by the lowland villages and the town of Timika. Company sponsored environmental audits in 1997 and 1999 did not satisfactorily detail Freeport's adequacy in meeting these environmental concerns (Leith 2003: 169). The tailings are contributing to massive vegetation die-off and may smother aquatic life (Perlez and Bonner 2005).

Further environmental devastation is related to the waste from the mine. This is the excess soil and rock dumped during excavation to reach the ore below. In 2001, Freeport was moving more than 750,000 tons per day, with 230,000 tons becoming tailings and the remainder discarded as overburden. Current and future overburden is to be dumped into the surrounding valleys and lakes of Carstensz Meadow, West Grasberg, and the Wanagon Valley, where an environmentally satisfactorily plan to store the toxic overburden had yet to be devised (Leith 2003: 171). Overburden storage problems have been blamed for landslides in 1998, and twice in 2000, endangering the lives of villagers and taking the lives of three workers (Abrash and Kennedy 2001: 65). Concerns about the thoroughness of Freeport's measures to ameliorate environmental degradation from overburden continue (Leith 2003: 174). Evidence revealed in a *New York Times* article in 2005 suggests that acid leaching from the waste is already flowing into groundwater and has been located in the Lorentz World Heritage Site nearby (Perlez and Bonner 2005).

The social impacts from the mine have been equally devastating. Throughout this period the Amungme and Kamaro people suffered the all too familiar problems associated with mining and the encroachment of modernisation: social upheaval, dependence on tobacco and alcohol, unemployment, illiteracy and malnutrition. An influx of other Papuans and Indonesians to the region has caused internecine rivalry and ethnic tension as people vie for work and related services from the company. Existing tensions have been further exacerbated by the continuing struggle for national independence waged by the West Papua resistance movement (Organisasi Papua Merderka – OPM) counteracted by severe reprisals from the Indonesian military. Freeport has the protection of the Indonesian army and has been strongly criticised for what is seen as its collusion with the former corrupt regime and for providing goods and services to an army that has engaged in gross human rights violations, including killing. In April 1996, tribal leader Tom Beanal of the Amungme people brought the first of two civil lawsuits in the US District Court in New Orleans against Freeport, claiming its activities in West Papua violate international human rights and environmental laws. Both lawsuits were unsuccessful (Yerton 1996: F1).

Direct and indirect socialisation in the Freeport problem project campaign

As with the previous chapters detailing problem project campaigns, the transnational nature of TEANs is strengthened in the linkage of northern NGOs and activists to southern NGOs, activists, and indigenous groups. The connection in the West Papuan case were links between the indigenous leaders of the Amungme people, an Indonesian umbrella NGO WALHI, INFID, and northern NGOs such as IRN and ProjectUnderground, and academics and journalists. The West Papuan project is analysed because it reveals MIGA's role in guaranteeing environmentally harmful projects and how TEANs attempted to enforce environmental and social change.[11]

In 1995 TEANs argued that 'Freeport has been under increasing criticism from Indonesian and international NGOs both for its environmental record and for its close relationship to the Indonesian military, which is responsible for a series of human rights violations in and near Freeport's concession area around the mine' (IRN 1995). Opposition culminated in 1995 when WALHI sued the Indonesian Department of Mines and Energy over its approval of Freeport's environmental management and tailings plan (Chatterjee 1995b). WALHI claimed that Freeport's management plan 'does not offer alternatives to dumping tailings into the local river systems, and fails to adequately address other key environmental issues such as extensive destruction of forests' (IRN 1995).

Indirect socialisation of MIGA, via the US, came into play in November 1995, when the US's OPIC cancelled its $100 million political risk insurance coverage of PTFI operations, its first ever cancellation. OPIC's 'landmark' decision to cancel Freeport's insurance was not only unprecedented but also impacted directly onto MIGA, which was also underwriting Freeport (Perlez and Bonner 2005). It was alleged in the *Times Picayune* of New Orleans, that the cancellation was linked to environmental damage from the mine in West Papua (Yerton 1996). OPIC initially refused to comment on the decision to unilaterally cancel PTFI's coverage. Freeport McMoRan sought immediate arbitration. The *New York Times* reported that the issue seemed to have arisen because of environmental problems at the Grasberg mine and that,

> [e]nvironmental groups in Indonesia and the United States that oppose Freeport's operation in the region say that the company has done little to contain tailings below the mine site and that runoff from the tailings has killed fish in nearby rivers ... Freeport McMoRan officials deny that the mine tailings are toxic. (Bryce 1995: 6)

Other reports claimed that 'the company said OPIC had cancelled the contract for environmental reasons and because it has expanded beyond its original plans' (*United Press International* 1995). Freeport McMoRan claimed that the cancellation was because OPIC had 'expressed concerns about new environmental issues associated with the expansion' but that '[c]ontrary to OPIC's statements, the expanded scope of FCX's mining operations does not violate the insurance policy' because 'the environmental concerns expressed by OPIC have no basis in fact'. Freeport argued that the company meets all Indonesian environmental regulations. The *Mining Journal* further states that Freeport

> is convinced that pressure from some foreign interest groups, who 'wrap themselves in the banner of environmental protection,' and who are 'intent on shutting down economic development projects by US companies in Irian Jaya,' was largely responsible for ... [the] abrupt withdrawal of political risk insurance for Grasberg by the US government agency OPIC. (*Mining Journal* 1995: 483)

The *Mining Journal* continued to state however, that 'the rapid mine expansion and the consequent big increase in waste discharge, was far beyond that originally envisaged, [which] present[s] a real environmental issue and are the main reasons cited by OPIC for its withdrawal' (*Mining Journal* 1995: 483).

The *New York Times* noted that the cancellation came despite lobbying from Freeport's directors including former US Secretary of State Henry Kissinger, and questions raised by Indonesian President Soeharto during his last meeting with US President Clinton (Bryce 1995: 6). The cancellation closely followed more serious concerns raised by two separate reports stating that a number of human rights violations had occurred within the region. According to the report released in April 1995 by the Australian Council for Overseas Aid (ACFOA), twenty-two civilians and fifteen guerillas had been killed or disappeared in or around the mine site, and suspicions were raised about possible involvement by Freeport security personnel. In August 1995 the Roman Catholic Church of Jayapura released a report supporting many of the allegations (ACFOA 1995; Catholic Church, Jayapura 1995). In 2003 the company admitted to paying up to $5.6 million for 'Government provided security' from the Indonesian army (Donnan 2003). Recent clashes with OPM, different ethnic groups and the army have led the Indonesian Human Rights Commission to begin investigating the role of Freeport's security personnel in human rights abuses (New Zealand Press Association 2006).

Freeport McMoRan has denied any involvement of its security personnel in human rights abuses. Indeed it threatened to take legal action against 'three University of Texas professors, two environmentalists and two journalists' for 'false and damaging accusations that it is involved in human rights violations in Indonesia' (Haurwitz 1995: B1). Freeport Senior Vice President Thomas J. Egan sent letters to seven individuals suggesting legal recourse against parties disseminating such accusations in the future. One of the environmental activists, Lori Udall of IRN, stated that 'Freeport was attempting to silence critics with the letters and with an effort to discourage US funding for an Indonesian environmental group' (Haurwitz 1995).

Freeport tried to get US AID to withhold funding for WALHI, arguing that it promoted the nationalisation of Freeport. In response, US AID determined that WALHI 'was serving a proper role in encouraging a transition to a more democratic society in Indonesia and approved a two year grant of $250,000 to the NGO' (Haurwitz 1995).

In an about-face in 1996, OPIC reinstated its coverage of Freeport's insurance in West Papua. At the same time, Freeport announced that it would establish 'a trust fund to pay for environmental remediation programs' which OPIC would monitor throughout the eight-month period of reinstatement (Associated Press 1996). The trust fund was estimated to raise $100 million at the end of the forty-five year productive life of the mine for environmental programmes (*Journal of Commerce* 1996: 5A). Following the reinstatement, the *Times Picayune* uncovered that OPIC had been concerned about the environmental impact of Freeport's mining operation in Indonesia as early as 1989, and confirmed that environmental reasons were behind the cancellation of coverage in 1995. The article also claimed that new documents suggested that personal lawsuit threats were made against OPIC personnel and that evidence released under the US Freedom of Information Act demonstrated that OPIC cancelled the policy 'because of material breaches in the contract which relate to substantial adverse environmental impacts' (Yerton 1996: F1).

According to Freeport's account, it was not until 1996 that the company undertook voluntary social and environmental audits with 'positive results' (Freeport 2003). An environmental audit of Freeport in West Papua in 1996, noted that '[u]ntil recently, PTFI was slow to meet its environmental challenges adopting a reactive rather than a proactive response' (Dames and Moore 1996: 1).

These were the first environmental assessments of the Freeport mine made public (Leith 2003: 163). INFID argued in April 1996 that 'neither the settlement with OPIC nor the environmental audit prepared by Dames and Moore provide a seal of approval of PTFI's environmental performance'. They further stated that the audit 'makes clear that Freeport's commitment to the environment is relatively recent, and that many of the environmental management measures deemed "appropriate" by the audit team are only in the initial stages of implementation, or were only agreed to in the course of the audit itself' (Abrash and Kennedy 2001: 65; INFID 1996). Indeed, WALHI would later submit a lawsuit against Freeport claiming that Freeport had not met Article six of the Indonesian Environment Management Law, in July 2000 (Leith 2000: 246).

In a rapid about-turn, Freeport then cancelled its insurance coverage with OPIC in September 1996 even though the independent environmental consultants had approved Freeport's tailings management programme at the Grasberg mine and negative publicity seemed to be dying down. Freeport argued that it 'had grown beyond [OPIC's] policy' and that 'political risk insurance is no longer the best use of our shareholder dollars' (*Wall Street Journal* 1996: Section B, 10J).

This was then followed by Freeport deciding not to renew its $50 million insurance coverage by MIGA due to expire in January 1997 (*Wall Street Journal* 1996: Section B, 10J). ProjectUnderground argue that MIGA's coverage was cancelled just as MIGA was preparing to send a three-member investigation team to assess recent environmental and human rights abuse claims in West Papua (ProjectUnderground 1996). In the press, MIGA downplayed the connection between the cancellation of the coverage and the environmental investigation (Chatterjee 1996). However, there is evidence to suggest that MIGA had been reviewing its coverage of Freeport based on the actions of OPIC, which had, in turn *been influenced by pressure from WALHI* in relation to the Freeport mine (Leith 2000: 252, 263). According to Leith, the network's pressure and influence with OPIC *was* the reason behind OPIC's cancellation of Freeport's coverage (Leith 2000: 263).

Attempts at direct socialisation took place through repeated letters from TEANs to MIGA calling for it to assess the allegations of Freeport's environmental and human rights abuses, and for MIGA to drop its coverage of Freeport. WALHI had also been advocating for MIGA to cancel its coverage of Freeport as a way of exposing Freeport's environmental and social degradation as early as June 1995 (Chatterjee 1995a) and again in early 1996 .[12] MIGA noted in an internal report that it had 'received a number of letters from NGOs pressing the Agency to cease supporting this project as did OPIC'.[13] Therefore, while MIGA had not been the focus of the campaign in West Papua, as had IFC with Pangue or the World Bank with Narmada and Polonoroeste, TEANs still attempted direct socialisation of MIGA through persuasion and social influence. Persuading MIGA was a very small component of the campaign, but it was effective. Not because MIGA cancelled Freeport's coverage, but because MIGA was roused to investigate the claims made by TEANs. MIGA was aware that TEANs wanted their response to Freeport's actions in West Papua, especially after OPIC's decision to withdraw as a result of the TEAN campaign. Both provided impetus for MIGA's investigation.

However, MIGA's coverage was cancelled prior to its investigation – an act which put the media spotlight on both MIGA and Freeport. Freeport may have been worried about having to meet the environmental and social standards of OPIC and MIGA. Had Freeport remained a client, it is conceivable that the insurers would have strengthened their monitoring efforts on environmental and social safeguards. In 1998 OPIC strengthened its existing policies (OPIC 1999). Also in 1998, MIGA began drafting its own policies as other problem project campaigns were coming to light.

In terms of indirect socialisation the process with MIGA varied from the diffusion pathways established to diffuse norms within the Bank and IFC. To recall, indirect socialisation is the process whereby international norms through TEANs influence states, and states then use material power to shape IO behaviour, thus changing their actions and their identities. In the case of the World Bank, advocacy networks were successful in shaping key parts of the US government (Treasury, members of Congress, and establishing the 'Tuesday Group') regarding problem project campaigns, environmental safeguards, and transparency and accountability mechanism upheld by US legislation. The process of indirect socialisation of IFC took a similar trajectory, again influencing the US to use material power to further diffuse norms of sustainable development, first through attempting to halt environmental degradation at Pangue, then through stipulating the need for IFC safeguards, and finally through furthering environmental transparency and establishing an accountability mechanism.

The process of indirect socialisation regarding MIGA's problem project is significantly different. It is not Congress or Treasury that constrained and influenced MIGA behaviour. Rather, indirect socialisation occurred because the advocacy network opposed the activities of Freeport in West Papua that were insured by both the US's OPIC and MIGA. Influencing the largest underwriter of the project (OPIC) in turn undermined the capacity of the remaining insurer (MIGA) to maintain its coverage. By raising awareness of, and campaigning against, the environmental and social negligence of PTFI in West Papua, TEANs rang alarm bells in OPIC on the nature of their coverage of the mine. The resulting public fiasco led to OPIC's cancellation and then reinstatement of its coverage to PTFI, which was then cancelled by Freeport soon after. As MIGA was also insuring the mine in West Papua, it too wanted assurances that Freeport was complying with environmental and social guidelines, even though MIGA did not at that stage have its own safeguards. This investigation was averted by the cancellation of Freeport's coverage before an investigative team could be sent to West Papua.

Problem project campaigns raise public awareness and heighten social influence through shaming and shunning. The publicity of Freeport's alleged involvement in human rights abuses and massive environmental destruction in relation to the mine's expansion spurred OPIC's decision to halt its coverage even though it had been concerned about the negative impacts of the Freeport mine in West Papua since 1989. MIGA, as another political risk insurer, aimed to investigate the validity of such claims and had its coverage cancelled before such an investigation could be undertaken. The immediacy of such an action on behalf of Freeport is suspicious although it claims that its cancellation of the coverage was based purely on shareholder interests.

While Freeport would go on to have external environmental and social audits of its operations in West Papua in 1996, 1997 and 1999 and attempted to structure a sustainable development plan, a more detailed analysis of MIGA's sustainable development identity was yet to come. The network did not target MIGA or OPIC as vociferously as had been the case with the World Bank and IFC. While local, regional, national, and international groups such as ACFOA, the Catholic Church in Jayapura, INFID, IRN, and ProjectUnderground were concerned with the environmental destruction and human rights abuses in and around the Freeport area, issues that were taken up by the US and international media, the campaign was severely restricted thereafter regarding MIGA's involvement.[14]

The Freeport campaign roughly follows the same trajectory as other problem project campaigns detailed in previous chapters. What is significant here is that rather than mechanisms of US government being influenced, such as Treasury, Congress and the Tuesday Group, the US government's corporation was the focus of direct socialisation. OPIC's role in guaranteeing a major environmental and social disaster as an investment guarantor was enough for it to drop Freeport as a client, and to strengthen its own environmental and social policies. The case exemplifies indirect socialisation whereby international norms through TEANs shape state controlled agencies, which then influence the actions of an IO, which may then reconstitute the IO's identity. Within this process, MIGA had its coverage cancelled by Freeport effective 1997 thus limiting MIGA's operations and its attempts to respond to OPIC's environmental stance. In 1998, MIGA began to draft environmental and social safeguard policies rather than implicitly using IFC's.

This reveals a pattern with regard to WBG affiliates not having their own safeguard policies until TEANs attempt to ensure that minimum requirements for sustainable development are met. However, what this case also shows is that while MIGA was not the sole target of the first 'problem project' campaign it was involved in, it did make MIGA aware that environmental and social problems may affect business as usual. More problem project campaigns implicating MIGA's involvement in environmental and social destruction emerged during and after the Freeport campaign. A 2001 report by Friends of the Earth, Urgewald, and Campagna per la Riforma della Banca Mondialle, claimed that MIGA had guaranteed investments in problem projects in the 1990s including mines in Guyana, the Kyrgyz Republic, Papua New Guinea, Peru and Russia as well as a gas pipeline from Brazil to Bolivia and a soft drinks plant in Bosnia-Herzegovina (Friends of the Earth *et al.* 2001). Many problem projects are mines. The high environmental impact of mining led to mass opposition to financiers and insurers of mining culminating in the Extractive Industries Review by the WBG and major stakeholders akin to the World Commission on Dams (see EIR 2003). Some of these MIGA-backed projects would go to the CAO for mediation and are discussed further in the section on environmental accountability. The importance of Freeport was its scale, the extent of, and secrecy over, the environmental damage and the triggers for change that TEANs used to mitigate it. The following section analyses how MIGA incorporated environmental and social safeguard policies and information disclosure soon after the Freeport campaign, and examines the influence of direct and indirect socialisation.

MIGA's environmental safeguard and information disclosure policies

While the previous section focused on direct and indirect socialisation of MIGA through a high-profile project campaign mounted by TEANs, this section analyses how the networks then attempted to socialise MIGA to create a suite of environmental protection and transparency rules. Interactions between TEANs and MIGA are recounted while detailing the emergence of MIGA's safeguard and transparency policies. This section again demonstrates how ongoing engagement between TEANs and MIGA led to policy changes within the Agency through the same interactive processes of direct and indirect socialisation.

Much like earlier efforts by TEANs to socialise the Bank and IFC, TEANs challenged MIGA's practices, which they characterised as environmentally destructive (Friends of the Earth 2000). TEANs drew international attention to MIGA's traditional political risk insurer identity by asking how it furthered sustainable development. MIGA's activities had not previously been questioned. Insuring development projects in developing countries was automatically assumed to be worthy and claims of its positive development impact were not therefore examined. As with IFC's investment activities, TEANs challenged this conception of development. They argued that MIGA's coverage of development projects in developing countries was not the most effective means to alleviate poverty or to further sustainable development. They highlighted that MIGA had not internalised sustainable development as the Bank and IFC had and wondered why MIGA had weaker environmental and social protection measures than the rest of the WBG (Friends of the Earth *et al.* 2001). TEANs argued that MIGA should be 'applying the bank's environmental and social policies ... applying the bank's stronger information disclosure policy ... and giving the bank's inspection panel jurisdiction to review private sector investments' (Durban 1998).

TEAN characterisations of MIGA activities were vehemently rejected by the organisation. A heated exchange in the early 2000s, detailed below, highlights how both TEANs and MIGA rejected each other's understanding of the Agency's operations. This confrontation may be the first stage of socialisation, where social influence triggers awareness inside the IO that its practices are not universally accepted. Social influence thus challenges the organisation's understandings of its practices, leading to an engagement with dissenters and opening the way for dialogue. Certainly this was the case in the 1980s with the World Bank and in the 1990s with IFC. Indeed MIGA would begin to accept that there are 'challenges' in reconciling its insurer identity with sustainable development goals (MIGA 2000). It would then go on to adopt IFC's safeguards and disclosure policy and then the performance standards as its own. I argue that MIGA got to this stage as a result of TEANs enacting direct and indirect socialisation.

Environmental and social policies

Interactions between TEANs and MIGA over its environmental policies demonstrate resistance by the Agency to internalise sustainable development. As an underwriter, MIGA only becomes involved once a project has been devised by the project sponsor and approved by the host country. Often this means that a project sponsor must provide the Agency with independent EAs of the project and may include some or all of the following: environmental and social impact assessments (ESIAs) for Category A projects, environmental audits, hazard or environmental risk assessments, and an environmental action plan. The ESIA is the 'responsibility of the project sponsor' (MIGA 1999: 6, 10). Procedurally, once MIGA receives a definitive application for insurance from a project sponsor it then undertakes a preliminary environmental screening, which 'identifies additional information that is required for MIGA to provide environmental review and clearance of the project' (MIGA 1999: 13–14).

Although MIGA was established in 1988, it began implicitly using World Bank and IFC safeguard policies in its appraisals from 1991 (MIGA 2003b: 7). Just as IFC had previously adhered to the World Bank's, there was the same assumption that MIGA would adhere to IFC's standards, with MIGA using the experience of IFC staff on a case-by-case basis. In 1996, TEANs began questioning the 'double standards' evident between the World Bank, and IFC and MIGA (Bosshard 1996a). TEANs identified that EA guidelines were less strict and comprehensive for MIGA projects, while MIGA's guarantee process allowed very little time for proper appraisal. By the late 1990s, TEANs were demanding that MIGA institute its own policies.

TEANs argued that MIGA did not have an environmental department of its own, rather subcontracting its environmental project analysis to IFC. At that time IFC had a small department with seven staff and three consultants reviewing between 200 and 250 new IFC and MIGA projects a year while supervising approximately 1,000 ongoing projects. TEANs claimed that up to 1993, only ten of MIGA's 185 projects had been classified as Category A even though MIGA underwrites high environmental impact projects such as mining (Bosshard 1996b). In response, in 1997 the Agency created an in-house environmental unit, MIGA's Policy and Environment Department (MIGPE). By 2001 MIGPE had two environmental specialists (a social specialist was hired in 2004), and employed consultants on a regular basis for project appraisals. According to the WBG's evaluation departments MIGA's environmental and social performance improved after MIGPE's creation (Liebenthal *et al.* 2005: 190–5).

After Freeport cancelled its coverage in 1998, MIGA began to draft its own environmental, social and information disclosure policies (Van Veldhuizen 2000: 54). In doing so, MIGA allowed for a fifty-day comment period open to all stakeholders on the draft policies. The period of consultation demonstrates that MIGA began to follow the practices established by the Bank and IFC before it. In May 1999, MIGA's Board of Directors adopted IFC's environmental safeguard policies for a two-year pilot period after extensive discussions between the Board and management. According to Harvey Van Veldhuizen, MIGA's lead environmental specialist, this 'formalizes an approach' that MIGA has followed 'for many years' (2000: 54). MIGA introduced the project classification system of environmental impacts based on IFC's Categories A, B, C and FI (MIGA 1999: 3–4). This demonstrates MIGA's shift to institutionalise environmental and social rules.

While TEANs agitated over the policy process, MIGA expressed that adopting IFC's safeguards had been 'less than satisfactory' while it awaited the CAO review on IFC's safeguards (2001–3). It adapted four updated IFC safeguards: Natural Habitats, Pest Management, Forestry, and Projects on International Waterways while issuing interim policies based on the World Bank's policies on Involuntary Resettlement, Indigenous Peoples, Cultural Property, and the Safety of Dams (MIGA 2002).[15] In 2001, the CAO undertook a review of MIGA's environmental and social review procedures which are discussed in the section on environmental monitoring and evaluation. The CAO did not address 'adequacy of MIGA's interim safeguard policies; whether MIGA addresses broader sustainability issues not embedded within these policies; or compliance with specific policy provisions' because the safeguards were too recent (CAO 2002e: iii). Yet they did indicate that MIGA was institutionalising environmental rules. The safeguards were permanently adopted in 2002 (see Box 5.1).

During this period, TEANs provoked a reaction from MIGA with a publication entitled *Risky Business*. In it TEANs stated that MIGA had a 'lack of environmental and social accountability for the projects it guarantees and continuously struggle[s] to prove that its operations have demonstrative effects in poverty reduction and development impacts' (Friends of the Earth *et al.* 2001). MIGA quickly challenged the report, questioning its veracity, declaring that it contained factual errors about MIGA's operations. The Agency stated that its market orientation is fully compatible with its development mandate, rebutting claims that it

Box 5.1 *MIGA's 2002 permanently adopted environmental and social safeguard policies*

Natural Habitats (adapted from IFC's 1998 OP4.04)

Forestry (adapted from IFC's 1998 OP4.36)

Pest Management (adapted from IFC's 1998 OP4.09)

Projects on International Waterways (adapted from IFC's 1998 OP7.50)

Safety of Dams (adopted from World Bank's 2001 OP4.37)

Involuntary Resettlement (adopted from World Bank's 2001 OP4.12)

Physical Cultural Resources (originally Safeguarding Cultural Property adopted by IFC from World Bank's 1990 OD4.30)

Indigenous Peoples (adopted by IFC from World Bank's 1991 OD4.20)

Source: MIGA 2002.

does not meet the WBG's environmental and social safeguards. MIGA argued that they have 'turned down and cancelled projects' for not meeting its environmental rules (this would be upheld by a CAO evaluation: see CAO 2002e: 9 n 9).[16]

MIGA then responded more fully and aggressively in September 2001, arguing that it only dealt with corporations which were 'good corporate citizens' and that 'statements made in the report that MIGA's activities are anti-environmental and fail to promote economic growth or alleviate poverty are untrue'. They concluded that 'there is no evidence to support the claims that MIGA's clients have poor environmental and human rights records'.[17] In response, in April 2002 the report's authors rejected MIGA's claims. They argued that the factual errors were in fact radical differences of perception regarding acceptable corporate behaviour. They suggested that MIGA was stuck in an outdated understanding of development and that more needs to be done beyond promoting FDI to further sustainability and poverty alleviation. TEANs argued that MIGA's environmental and social safeguards and disclosure policies are flawed and they refuted MIGA's claims that it only deals with good corporate citizens, arguing that MIGA's clients are not screened for their past social, environmental, labour and human rights records. They concluded that MIGA's response was 'disappointing and unproductive', and on the basis of the exchange argued that the Agency shows 'little interest in recognizing its weaknesses as a development institution. We have found MIGA to be duly resistant to reform and find MIGA's progress in reform efforts to be wholly inadequate.'[18] TEANs simply do not see MIGA as an organisation that can further, or is interested in furthering, sustainable development.

Another letter from MIGA was sent to TEANs in June 2002. It reiterated that MIGA operations are compatible with its development mandate and that the Agency is 'very focused on reputational risk and the record of the project sponsors we support'.[19] Other pertinent issues were raised including environmental evaluation and disclosure, which are discussed further in the chapter. For now it is important to note how MIGA moved from ignoring, to rejecting and engaging with TEANs. Direct socialisation continued with TEANs publishing a similar report in 2003 that reiterated MIGA's weak environmental and social safeguard policies compared with the WBG (Environmental Defense *et al.* 2003: 4).

Regarding indirect socialisation, TEANs are engaged in further strengthening MIGA's policies within the Tuesday Group, particularly in relation to improving its environmental transparency (discussed next). The network also engages in the indirect socialisation of MIGA via the US Congress, where TEANs use persuasion to shape US oversight in reforming MIGA's policies. Friends of the Earth claimed victory in 2001 when the US gave partial lending of $5 million to MIGA rather than the $10 million requested for MIGA's capital increase.[20] Moreover, the US Treasury has made it clear that MIGA's environmental and social policies remain a focus (US Treasury 2006, 2005). Indirect socialisation has contributed to keeping MIGA's policies consonant with IFC. In 2006 MIGA's Board gave the institution twelve months to review IFC's performance standards in order to determine how they could be adapted to its political risk insurance activities. MIGA's new Policy on Social and Environmental Sustainability came into effect on 1 October 2007. MIGA's new performance standards now cover financial sector products, which is important as they constituted sixty-one per cent of MIGA's portfolio in 2008, up from thirty-three per cent between 1990 and 2007 (MIGA 2008a: 4; World Bank 2008a: 61).

Box 5.2 *MIGA's performance standards covered in its Social and Environmental Sustainability Policy, effective 1 October 2007*

Performance standard 1:	Social and Environmental Assessment Management System
Performance standard 2:	Labour and Working Conditions
Performance standard 3:	Pollution Prevention and Abatement
Performance standard 4:	Community Health, Safety and Security
Performance standard 5:	Land Acquisition and Involuntary Resettlement
Performance standard 6:	Biodiversity Conservation and Sustainable Natural Resource Management
Performance standard 7:	Indigenous People
Performance standard 8:	Cultural Heritage

Source: MIGA 2007b.

In addition to the performance standards MIGA has adopted IFC's exclusion list of practices that it will no longer cover. Therefore MIGA is now institutionalising sustainable development. At the same time thirty-two OECD export credit agencies also began to use IFC's standards as benchmarks under the *Revised Council Recommendation on Common Approaches on the Environment and Officially Supported Export Credits* (OECD 2007b; World Bank 2008a: 59). The Common Approaches were drafted as voluntary guidelines by the OECD in 2001 after TEAN pressure led to a statement of intent in 1998 and a draft action plan in 1999. The common approaches were formally adopted by the OECD in 2003, modified in 2005, and revised in 2007. TEANs have continuously pressured the OECD to meet the World Bank's environmental and social safeguards to ensure sustainable development for export credit agencies.[21] MIGA's endorsement of the 2007 converged performance standards and OECD common approaches shows that MIGA is a follower rather than a leader in market-based sustainable development (IFC 2007b: iv; MIGA 2007e).

It is too soon to assess how these policies are understood and disseminated within the organisation. TEANs do note that there is a lack of transparency in export credit financing making it difficult to assess the extent to which export credit agencies meet even minimum environmental assessment compliance (Harmon *et al.* 2005: 12).[22] The extent to which MIGA-backed projects can be monitored for their developmental effectiveness – in terms of their adherence to norms of sustainable development – is also based on the information made available by MIGA to the public. The next section analyses how TEANs attempted to directly and indirectly socialise MIGA to become more transparent.

Environmental transparency

MIGA was established in 1988 at the height of World Bank–TEANs interaction, yet it did not have an information disclosure policy for its first decade of operations. MIGA, like the IFC before it with the World Bank, had vaguely followed the practice of using IFC's information disclosure policy, based as it was on private sector client confidentiality. This section demonstrates how advocacy networks attempted to socialise an IO to consume norms of sustainable development through increased environmental transparency. Direct socialisation was undertaken by TEANs using persuasion and social influence from 1995, to encourage MIGA to disclose more environmental and social information, through letters and reports. TEANs argued that as separate legal entities MIGA and IFC should have their own policies (Chamberlain 1997: 19). TEANs declared that MIGA 'shrouds itself in complete secrecy about its ongoing operations' and that it 'does not even inform [the public] about project approvals by the Board, as long as guarantee contracts have not been finalized with its clients' (Bosshard 1996a).

Indirect socialisation was also taking place. In December 1995 the US-ED was arguing on behalf of TEANs and the Tuesday Group for a separate MIGA information disclosure policy during deliberations over IFC's information disclosure requirements

(Chamberlain 1997: 19). More specifically, Jan Piercy the US-ED at the time is quoted as stating that:

> MIGA is not subject to IFC's policies and standards, and therefore, the strengthened approach to IFC disclosure will not apply to MIGA . . . Now that IFC has had an opportunity to review its experience and refine its practices, there should be no further delay in undertaking an examination of MIGA. (Quoted in Chamberlain 1997: 19)

According to TEANs, MIGA claimed that it would implement a policy on information disclosure in 1996 (Chamberlain 1997: 8). Yet it was not until 1998 that MIGA began to adapt IFC's policies. BIC argued that the 'significant disclosure improvements across the MDBs in recent years have completely left MIGA behind' and that 'MIGA's secretive and uncommunicative nature serves as a reminder of how far other MDBs have progressed'. In its defence, MIGA argued that it was awaiting the outcome of information disclosure policy debates within the rest of the WBG even though the TEANs claimed they had been promised an information policy for public comment by 1998 (Chamberlain 1998).

In 1999 MIGA drafted an information policy with input from business and civil society, enacting a process previously undertaken by both the World Bank and IFC. MIGA maintained that it is one of the most transparent political risk insurance agencies.[23] The policy came into force in 2000. In 2001 the network continued to argue that MIGA's 'environmental and information disclosure policies remain weak' because its disclosure policy 'only requires the agency to make public those documents that will not "harm business and competitive interests of MIGA's applications" and that will not violate confidentiality obligations' (Friends of the Earth *et al.* 2001: 1). They further argued that MIGA's environmental policy allows it to waive community consultation on a project if the local disclosure requirements are deemed adequate.

TEANs further argued that client contracts, including their environmental covenants, were not disclosed. They pointed out that information on project proposals, monitoring and evaluation, and assessment of country risks remained confidential.[24] They voiced dissatisfaction that MIGA's disclosure requirements were only for Category A projects, while these EIA documents are 'difficult to access, especially for affected communities' (Down to Earth 2001). They questioned the discrepancy of listing the ESIAs for Category A projects but not making the actual assessment available, while Category B and C projects did not require any EAs at all. This is, they argued was 'clearly unsatisfactory for a publicly-financed development institution', even though MIGA's standards are equal to national insurers such as OPIC (CAO 2002e: 14).[25] TEANs reiterated that 'MIGA has not given any concrete sign of becoming more transparent or accountable' and that its 'lackluster disclosure and environment policies' are of serious concern (Friends of the Earth *et al.* 2001: 7).

In June 2002 MIGA stated that while it is policy for the ESIA of Category A projects to be released to the public sixty days before the Board meets to consider the project, in practice MIGA manages to release these reports on average 140 days prior to the meeting. MIGA also signalled its intention to review deficiencies in accessing information on environmental and social aspects of MIGA-covered projects.[26] Meanwhile, the CAO urged MIGA to review its non-disclosure of Category B projects in December 2002 (2002e: 8, 17). It also recommended that MIGA 'more systematically evaluate and report on the environmental and social risks associated with projects' because its documents 'rarely reflect the level of effort that MIGA has invested in environmental and social due diligence' (2002e: 16).

Confidentiality is a major concern for an underwriter. MIGA's role as a political risk insurer is based upon assessing the non-commercial political risk of an investment in a project in a developing country. Insurers are required to evaluate the risks of a project quickly to determine whether or not to cover the investor. MIGA has a longer timeframe than private insurers although government insurers like OPIC also have a longer processing period. As a political risk insurer MIGA has a much shorter timeframe than the World Bank, which has the longest design and deliberation time of the WBG regarding lending for proposed projects and IFC, which aims for shorter and quicker evaluations of proposed investments in projects. MIGA does release information much earlier than is required to its Board of Directors.[27] However, TEANs maintained that MIGA had the weakest information disclosure policies of the WBG, such that it would not release information on Category B projects prior to

Board approval (Environmental Defense *et al.* 2003: 4). MIGA responded that it would provide more regular access to information online and that it had a staff member dedicated to information requests.[28]

While MIGA's annual reports from 2003 to 2006 only discuss information dissemination in relation to MIGA's online products, the organisation did improve the environmental information available online.[29] Specifically MIGA's website made clear that it did have environmental, social and information disclosure policies and an accountability mechanism for affected peoples, and made the policies publicly available. In 2004, TEANs argued that MIGA still lacked transparency. They argued that there was an absence of basic information on proposed investments such as project summaries or information on their potential development impact, or what happened to them once they had been approved by the Board, therefore omitting any information on environmental monitoring and evaluation. With so little information MIGA is hard to monitor.[30] TEANs continued to push MIGA to release Category A ESIAs earlier than sixty days before Board approval and to provide even basic project information for Category B projects, but especially requesting that MIGA provide their environmental review summaries.[31]

MIGA's EVP Yukiko Omura responded to these concerns by stating that its decisions in 1999 and 2002 to provide information on Category A project impacts but not Category B meant that it was in line with IFC for the former but in line with industry standards in the latter, and that this was 'not an easy decision'. This highlights the identity conflict within MIGA as a development institution and a political risk insurer. Omura announced that MIGA would be updating its disclosure policy and it did agree to meet specific TEAN requests including linking MIGA's website to the WBG infoshop to make it easier to access ESIA information. Finally, she stated that MIGA would be developing an 'online alert system' that would announce new project information along with providing project descriptions, environmental information and anticipated development impacts.[32] You can now access MIGA's project database through its website. These changes are significant for MIGA.

Continued TEAN criticism did therefore shape MIGA's decision to update its information disclosure policy in 2007, which it did after waiting for IFC to update its own performance standards. MIGA opened the process to stakeholder comments through its online commentary tool. The disclosure policy brings MIGA into line with IFC such that it now makes available the Environmental and Social Review Summary (ESRS) of each proposed guarantee (for projects likely to have an impact and classified as Category A, B or FI). Any environmental assessment documents will now be made available, at sixty days before Board approval for Category A projects and thirty days for B and FI projects, as well as in the guarantee holders' management action plans as determined by the new performance standards (MIGA 2007c: 6).

MIGA's new disclosure policy now releases a Summary of Proposed Guarantee (SPG) that includes a project's details including its environmental classification, any available environmental information and its proposed development impact prior to MIGA Board approval (MIGA 2007c: 5). Even more significant is that MIGA commits to provide information on the 'development impact on the local community of sensitive projects for which it is providing guarantee support' which it will make publicly available per individual project. This goes beyond IFC's disclosure policy but follows OPIC in this regard (IFC 2007b: 12; MIGA 2007c: 7; OPIC 2004: 5).

MIGA has also fallen into line with the Bank and IFC is making its Board minutes available as well as its evaluation reports from its independent evaluation unit, something strongly advocated by TEANs and the US-ED (US Treasury 2005: 12). These changes demonstrate a distinct shift within MIGA in terms of its environmental transparency. While it is too early to determine the impact of these changes, they are significant and in some cases, such as project level development impact information being released for sensitive projects, surprising. Prior to the 2007 policy update there was a significant gap between the demands of TEANs and MIGA's practices, which demonstrated the difference in MIGA's identity to the rest of the WBG. MIGA stated that the new disclosure policy 'aims to enhance transparency . . . with a view to increasing MIGA's development effectiveness and *strengthening public trust in the agency*', (MIGA 2007d; emphasis added). Clearly MIGA is aware of its reputation.

Direct and indirect socialisation attempts by TEANs aimed to internalise sustainable development norms within MIGA. The networks did influence MIGA's adoption of environmental and social safeguards through initial social influence and persuasion and coercion at the policy level. The evidence outlined thus far demonstrates that problem projects like Freeport had little impact at the project level although they did contribute to MIGA realising the need for its own policies. The socialisation attempt continued when TEANs tried to make environment and social policies and transparency part of MIGA's insurance identity. Of course, instituting environmental and disclosure policies alone does not imply an identity shift. The next section reviews how direct and indirect socialisation from TEANs aimed to further improve MIGA environmental and social impact, including its accountability.

MIGA's institutional mechanisms

As with previous efforts by TEANs to socialise the World Bank and IFC, advocacy networks aimed not just to stop problem projects already under way but to ensure that these IOs had environmental standards that applied to their entire portfolios and that they had the means of monitoring and evaluating their environmental practices. This section examines MIGA's monitoring and evaluation procedures before reiterating how the CAO was established as a result of direct and indirect socialisation. The CAO has since undertaken reviews of MIGA's environmental practices and audited MIGA-backed projects contributing to a broader understanding of MIGA's environmental behaviour. While TEANs were engaged in persuasion, social influence and coercion to make environmental monitoring and accountability part of MIGA's identity, the organisation would create an environmental unit, would separate its evaluation function, and would have its environmental practices periodically reviewed.

In the late 1990s TEANs argued that MIGA had done little to monitor the environmental and social impacts of the projects it was underwriting. They argued that MIGA's monitoring capacity was weak because the organisation was 'not equipped' for monitoring so that the projects it covers 'adhere to MIGA's standards and policies' (Down to Earth 2001). From 1996 MIGA would begin to think about how to establish internal evaluation processes and in 1998 MIGA released its first of two periodic internal Development Impact Reviews evaluating twenty-five MIGA-backed projects (West and Tarazona 1998). Also in 1998 MIGA hired its first environmental specialist (World Bank 2008a: 60).

The number of environmental specialists would increase to two full-time environmental staff and one consultant to review projects in MIGPE in 2001 (Down to Earth 2001). However, MIGA did not have a monitoring system in place but would follow up on a project when it 'learns of a potential problem ... or when it receives a complaint from stakeholders' (MIGA 2003a: 10). Another periodic Development Impact Review was undertaken in 2001 evaluating fifty-two projects representing seventy-five per cent of all active projects covered by MIGA between 1990 and 1996. It delineated developmental impacts into direct, indirect, and diffused effects from the projects guaranteed, where direct effects included economic and environmental impacts (West and Tarazona 2001: 25, 40).

Only ten of the fifty-two projects were seen to require environmental monitoring (West and Tarazona 2001: 29). Twenty-two were not measured, none failed, and none were unable to be measured although the reasoning for this was not provided. Environmental impacts were assessed as superior, above average, average, or failed. Four projects were deemed to be superior and 'were expected to significantly reduce or reverse impacts to the environment ... [and] perform well beyond the expected levels of compliance and mitigation'. Sixteen projects were above average and 'avoided a significant contribution to local environmental problems', while ten were average, meaning they 'typically complied with the local environment regulations' and met 'MIGA environmental guidelines on an ongoing basis' (West and Tarazona 2001: 49). The latter included four mining projects, even though they are known for their high environmental impacts.

In the heated exchange described earlier between TEANs and MIGA in 2002 MIGA announced that it had 'established a new and separate Operations Evaluations Unit to carry out independent assessments of the development effectiveness of MIGA's activities'.[33] In July 2002, MIGA separated its review and evaluation functions (previously under MIGPE) in order that its screening and monitoring teams did not evaluate themselves (CAO 2002e: v). The Operations Evaluation Unit (renamed in 2005 the IEG-MIGA) became an independent evaluation institution under the oversight of the World Bank's Operations Evaluation Director General thus bringing the WBG's evaluation departments under one roof. A recent analysis by a working group on private sector evaluation systems recognises a dramatic improvement in evaluating MIGA practices since the OEU/IEG-MIGA was established, although MIGA itself remained 'non-compliant' for meeting self-evaluation standards (MIGA 2007f: 3, 7, 2005: 10). The IEG-MIGA assesses the development outcome and MIGA effectiveness of 'matured' projects, which were initially five years after guarantee approval (later three years after guarantee). A project's development outcome includes its environmental and social impact while MIGA effectiveness includes analysing MIGA's internal procedures, underwriting and value added. From 2003 IEG-MIGA would also begin to pilot tracking projects' quality-at-entry much like the World Bank (MIGA 2005: 11).

While MIGA was separating its monitoring and evaluation functions, the CAO reviewed MIGA's environmental and social compliance on forty-two Category A and B projects between 2000 and 2002. The CAO discovered that MIGA followed its review procedures and that its capacity to review projects was adequate but its compliance monitoring was inadequate and social issues 'often rated as less than satisfactory' (CAO 2002e: iii). This was due to MIGA's 'informal and unsystematic' reliance on the guarantee holder or partner organisations for environmental and social compliance monitoring (CAO 2002e: iv–v, 10). Further reviews demonstrate that MIGA's reliance on its partners for monitoring remains the case, raising questions as to what value MIGA adds to underwriting projects being invested in, or that have loans provided by, other development institutions such as IFC, the World Bank or MDBs (MIGA 2004: 21, 2006: 26).

Soon after, the WBG's evaluation bodies reviewed the WBG's role in the extractive industries. Released in 2003, their report reviewed MIGA's mitigatory measures to prevent adverse impacts for twelve extractive industry projects (mostly mines) guaranteed between 1990 and 2001 including nine Category A projects and three Category B projects (Liebenthal *et al.* 2005: 176, 180). The review stated that MIGA had improved over time and that all projects benefited from MIGA's 'incorporation and/or enforcements of safeguards' (Liebenthal *et al.* 2005: 190–5), although a subsequent review of eighteen projects evaluated in 2006 would demonstrate the opposite trend for MIGA's role in extractive projects (MIGA 2006: 19).

The 2003 extractive review found that seventy-three per cent of extractive industry projects reviewed were consistent with MIGA safeguard policies at the time of Board approval and that almost all met MIGA's specific EA requirements. Yet eight of the twelve projects did not have adequate environmental and social compliance provisions included in the contract of guarantee. The report states that it is 'unclear why, in some of the projects reviewed safeguard policies were not triggered early enough – or at all – in the underwriting process' (Liebenthal *et al.* 2005: 182). Deficiencies were evident in applying the safeguards for indigenous peoples in all twelve projects; for involuntary resettlement and natural habitats in eight projects; and for dam safety in four projects. Finally, six of the projects had poor public consultation and information disclosure. The report argued that more needed to be done on due diligence, monitoring compliance, and reviewing social safeguard outcomes.

Reasons identified for these oversights included that MIGA became involved too late in the project; that it lacked sector expertise in identifying specific safeguards, and its underwriters lacked experience; that there were pressures to meet guarantee volumes; and that it did not re-evaluate the projects' scope and design after changes (Liebenthal *et al.* 2005: 181). Although MIGA formally included the right to terminate contracts for not being environmentally and socially compliant in 1999, there was no real monitoring within the Agency even for assessing the financial soundness for the projects they agreed to cover (MIGA 2004: 16, 23, 2003a: 8, 10). In July 2003 MIGA would formalise the requirement to monitor environmentally and socially 'sensitive' projects including all Category A and some B projects (MIGA 2003a: 16, n 26). Yet only five site visits were undertaken in 2003 and none in 2004. MIGA hired a social specialist in 2004 and in 2005 it increased its environmental and social monitoring of sensitive projects with twenty site visits to sensitive projects (MIGA 2005: 8).

In 2004 MIGA's environmental unit was brought into the new Economics and Policy Group as part of a wider organisational restructure to consolidate departments. The consolidation responded to a 'hardening' in the political risk market as a result of the terrorist attacks of 2001 and Argentina's financial crisis in 2002. The reorganisation was accompanied by MIGA's new strategic direction, which now emphasised the Agency's development mandate. Most policy changes within the organisation took place in 2004 and 2005. Under a newly created Chief Economist position, the Economics and Policy Group aimed to provide a 'one-stop shop for economic, environmental and social assessment of projects as well as country risk' (MIGA 2007f: 3, 7). The Economics and Policy Group currently houses three environmental and two social specialists (with one environmental specialist on secondment to the World Bank). MIGA also has an environmental consultant now working on its Environmental and Social Challenges Trust Fund; more are hired for MIGA's environmental review on a needs basis.[34] These specialists review all guarantees for their environmental and social impacts before they go to the Project Review Committee (PRC, formerly the Risk Management Committee or RMC). Thereafter all guarantee contracts are cleared by the EVP and then submitted to the Board for approval. The PRC now engages in advising underwriting teams much earlier than the RMC, which evaluated the contract guarantee 'at a very late stage in the project underwriting and Board approval process' (CAO 2005c: 11).

Although MIGA has scaled up its project compliance monitoring since 2005, ex-post evaluations still point to projects that have not been compliant with environment, social and health standards throughout their life (World Bank 2008a: 65–6). Indeed, recently matured projects evaluated in 2007 show that 'adequate monitoring arrangements ... were still not in place' (MIGA 2008c: 38). Although MIGA began discussing this in 2000, and approved a framework for one in 2005, the organisation has been slow in implementing it (MIGA 2007f: 7, 2003a: 11). The IEG recommends that MIGA do more to improve project performance through establishing 'environmental and social management systems and project management systems at a sufficiently early stage to effectively monitor impacts' and to '[c]onsistently incorporate provisions for regular reporting of safeguard performance during project implementation in MIGA's contract of guarantee' (World Bank 2008a: xlv; MIGA 2008c: 40).

The IEG recommends that MIGA pay more attention to baseline data with which to evaluate projects' environmental performance (World Bank 2008a: xxiii, 65). In 2006 MIGA created a self-assessment tool for *all* guarantees' quality-at-entry (MIGA 2007f: xi, 1–2, Annex I, 4). MIGA also now completes Closing Guarantee Notes for cancelled coverage but does not require them for expired insurance contracts, although these do not include development impact or project outcome information thus making further assessment of MIGA's impact difficult (MIGA 2007f: 7). The IEG-MIGA remains *the* source of monitoring and evaluation for MIGA.

In 2008 the IEG assessed MIGA's environmental and social project impact between 1990 and 2007 as part of the wider WBG sustainability review. Unlike the review of the World Bank and IFC, this period covers almost all of MIGA's lifespan incorporating 510 projects. Although, MIGA only began classifying projects for their environmental impact from 1999, it retroactively categorised pre-1999 projects (World Bank 2008a: 164). Notably, thirty-three per cent of MIGA's project portfolio throughout this period was in the finance sector, yet MIGA would not begin to track finance projects' environmental impact until 2007 under the new performance standards. Between 1990 and 2007 the second largest sector was infrastructure, constituting twenty-three per cent of projects, followed by manufacturing making up twenty per cent. Oil, gas and mining together constituted eight per cent of the projects MIGA covered (World Bank 2008a: 61).

The IEG discovered that the majority of projects during this period were classified as Category B, with less than fifteen per cent designated Category A. The review highlighted variation between Category A and B projects in that more Category B projects met their environmental action plans when evaluated at the time of approval (eighty-three per cent) compared to Category A projects (seventy-three per cent). However, this reversed when assessing their implementation with only sixty-three per cent Category B projects meeting their performance requirements compared to eighty per cent of Category A projects. Of course it was not until 2007 that MIGA required guarantee holders to provide information on the environmental impacts of Category B projects, meaning that in 'some cases MIGA was not even aware that projects failed to meet its guidelines' as they were not required to assess them (World Bank 2008a: 63, 64). Even now improvements are still needed for monitoring Category B projects to ensure their environmental and social compliance (World Bank 2008a: 64).

Overall, the IEG discovered that MIGA has used its contracts to identify environmental standards for remedial action by the guarantee holder but that MIGA's 'greatest weakness' has been in ensuring that its safeguards and required environmental management plans have been met (World Bank 2008a: 63). Problems include a lack of 'feasible project alternatives, inadequate attention to setting up of an EMS [environmental management system], and deficiencies in the way the issue-specific safeguards were applied' (World Bank 2008a: 62; MIGA 2006: 20). Recent improvements are evident in including environmental and social issues in MIGA's underwriting, in undertaking site visits for Category A projects during due diligence, making better use of the guarantee contract for identifying applicable safeguards, and outlining actions plans including resettlement and community plans prior to Board approval (World Bank 2008a: 66).

MIGA has changed over time from not reviewing and monitoring Category B and financial sector projects, to reviewing these while ensuring that environmental and social safeguards are included in all of its contract notes. The OEU/IEG-MIGA has extended its analysis of MIGA practices from reviewing projects after they were mature, to now tracking quality-at-entry for all new MIGA guarantees. Yet MIGA still does not have formal evaluations systems in place (MIGA 2006: 45). It routinely does not ensure compliance with safeguard measures, Category B projects often do not meet their safeguards during implementation, and worse, MIGA is often unaware of this (MIGA 2006: 19; World Bank 2008a: 63, 64). Although the IEG-MIGA points to improvements in the environmental management plans of guarantee holders over the life of projects, it states that this is because of the guarantee holder, not MIGA. In fact, the IEG-MIGA states that when there is not another MDB involved, MIGA scores low in what value it adds to the project (MIGA 2004: 21). It is therefore evident that MIGA 'lacks a more proactive approach for servicing clients on safeguards' while guarantee holders are often unclear of their environmental and social requirements and the specifics of the safeguards (MIGA 2006: 19, 46). This demonstrates that although MIGA has improved some oversight measures recently, it continues to lack environmental monitoring procedures to prevent further problem projects. The next section reveals how this affects MIGA's environmental accountability.

Environmental accountability

As a political risk insurer MIGA does not undertake environmentally and socially destructive development. The Agency operates in a competitive marketplace requiring 'timely and flexible responses from participants' while preserving business confidentiality.[35] According to TEANs, MIGA should still be held accountable for underwriting environmentally and socially destructive development via an accountability mechanism for people adversely or potentially affected by the projects it covers. Although removed from the development process and small in size, MIGA is part of the WBG and it does have a development mandate. TEANs therefore have argued that MIGA should not only have its own environmental and social safeguards, but that it should also be held accountable to peoples and ecosystems adversely affected by MIGA-insured projects.

While the Freeport campaign was not directly aimed at MIGA, this and other project campaigns in the 1990s cemented the need for an accountability mechanism covering MIGA as well as IFC. The World Bank's Inspection Panel rejected IFC's Pangue dam claim a few months after Freeport's social and environmental allegations emerged, and after TEANs engaged in the direct socialisation of MIGA. These events compounded the need for both WBG private sector organisations to be accountable. As discussed in the previous chapter, in the mid to late 1990s TEANs were heavily engaged in establishing the need for, and helped create, the Compliance Advisor/Ombudsman (CAO). TEANs offered drafts and suggestions on a proposed accountability mechanism to IFC and MIGA Boards. TEANs engaged in both direct and indirect socialisation. Indirect socialisation was based on the socialisation of the US-ED through the Tuesday Group to ensure that an accountability mechanism stayed at the top of the agenda for IFC and MIGA. Direct socialisation was furthered through the inclusion of CIEL on the selection committee for finding a candidate for the Office of the CAO. This is further demonstrated by the inclusion of a number of activists within the CAO's Reference Group who initially assisted in devising the operating procedures and guidelines for the CAO and who continue to provide advice during CAO operations. In addition, TEANs continue to monitor the CAO. This section examines how the CAO has contributed to shaping MIGA practices.

To date, four MIGA-backed projects have been brought to the CAO ombudsman: the Interagua Water Services project in Ecuador is currently in mediation (and is therefore not discussed here): the Orion pulp mill in Uruguay with a claim instigated in 2005; the Bulyanhulu mine in Tanzania in 2001; and the Antamina mine in Peru in 2000.[36] Of these four complaints, the Antamina mine claim would be reviewed by the compliance function of the CAO, while the Orion pulp mill would be subject to a full-scale compliance audit to assess whether MIGA met its environmental and social procedures.[37] One further MIGA-backed claim would be instigated by President Wolfowitz for a compliance audit: the Dikulushi mine in the Democratic Republic of the Congo in 2005. This section reviews the outcomes of the CAO ombudsman and compliance reports in relation to MIGA's environmental and social accountability.

The CAO's first MIGA-related claim in 2000 was the Antamina copper and zinc mine in Peru owned by Compania Minera Antamina (CMA) SA. The mine's impacts included the resettlement of local peoples with potential environmental damage. While the CAO found that the overall environmental performance of CMA was generally good and that its EIA was policy compliant, there were safeguard compliance gaps arising from miscommunications between CMA and its contractors. This is not an area required to be monitored, supervised, or assessed by MIGA's environmental team in its review, although the CAO highlighted that MIGA lacked a social specialist in its evaluation team. The CAO highlighted that MIGA's practice of only monitoring projects if 'events warrant it' meant that events may already have 'reached an explosive situation by the time such issues are brought to the attention of the company, lenders, politicians and NGOs' (CAO 2001b: 10). The report concluded with an acknowledgement by MIGA that it had 'identified tensions in being able to fully apply the Safeguard Policies, even as adapted by MIGA, in its role as an insurer', recommending that MIGA promptly resolve these tensions (CAO 2001b: 11). A second claim was made to the CAO in 2005 arguing that the mine's port facility was discharging metal concentrate into Huarmey Bay. Owing to the 'sour' relations between the mine and the community, the CAO independently investigated the allegations and the second mediation led to proposals for improving community access and understanding of the company's environmental monitoring.[38]

The second ombudsman claim for a MIGA-backed project was the Bulyanhulu gold mine in Tanzania. The CAO released an 'Assessment Report Summary' of the complaint in 2002, which assessed MIGA's due diligence of the mine in 1999 when the then mine owners, Barrick Gold, approached MIGA for political risk insurance. In 1996, prior to either Barrick Gold or MIGA's involvement in the mine, environmental and social allegations were made including the following: disputes over the mine's license; forced evictions; the failure to finance resettlement and compensate people for a loss of property; a lack of public consultation; land clearance; and the absence of proper EIAs with inaccurate and incomplete environmental and social plans. Similar allegations surfaced in 1998 as did claims that approximately fifty-two artisanal miners were murdered in July and August 1996.

The claim against MIGA was that it had failed to conduct

> a thorough and competent due diligence investigation regarding the facts surrounding the project sponsor's acquisition, possession and operation of Bulyanhulu to establish the veracity of information submitted and the soundness of conclusions drawn by project sponsors prior to making the decision to provide political risk insurance; and that MIGA failed to prepare and/or disclose to the complainants and other parties all material information pertaining to the facts and circumstances surrounding the project sponsor's acquisition, possession and operation of the project in spite of repeated requests to do so. (CAO 2002d: 3)

While a number of the allegations within the complaint could not be substantiated, and were not within the CAO's mandate to investigate, the CAO discovered that IFC had been involved briefly in Bulyanhulu in 1998 with the mine's previous owners.

IFC had 'noted in detail the remedies that would be required to bring the project into compliance with IFC policies'. IFC recognised the reputational risk for project sponsors and investors regarding the '1996 alleged incidents' (CAO 2002d: 8). MIGA informally discussed these issues with IFC in 1999 when approached by Barrick Gold and was aware of IFC's report. Yet there is no evidence to suggest that MIGA acted on the issues. The IFC report does not qualify as due diligence by MIGA because 'MIGA has asserted to the CAO that it based its work on IFC's and yet does not seem to have taken the issues the IFC note into account' (CAO 2002d: 9).

The findings of the CAO report suggest that 'the practice of IFC carrying out due diligence of IFC work product being used as a proxy for MIGA's due diligence be formalized and ... understood by all sides' (CAO 2002d: 9). The CAO was 'concerned at the informal arrangements that exist between IFC and MIGA regarding due diligence' and that 'when IFC performs the consultant's role in carrying out MIGA's due diligence, it should be covered by an agreement that waives it of responsibility if its recommendations are not acted upon'. Lastly, the report noted that 'MIGA did not carry out a more thorough review of the project following IFC's pre-appraisal visit' and that '[s]imply reviewing documents without a site visit, especially with changes in the project and a gap in time between IFC's and MIGA's reviews, is inadequate ... [and that] to date no environment or social specialist on contract to MIGA has visited Bulyanhulu' (CAO 2002d: 10). The case is reflective of MIGA's reliance on IFC for environmental and social assessments as well as its informal procedures in doing so and its lack of documentation in decision-making, something the IEG-MIGA repeatedly identifies as requiring improvement. The Bulyanhulu case demonstrated the need for MIGA to ensure that it had indeed verified the details of the situation at the mine site.

MIGA's third project assessed by the CAO ombudsman was the Orion pulp mill in Uruguay, which was also being considered for investment by IFC in conjunction with another pulp mill nearby. MIGA conducted an appraisal and stated that the Orion project met its environmental, social and information disclosure requirements even while a claim had been sent to the CAO on the project's likely environmental and social impacts and there was widespread public opposition to the project. Both MIGA and IFC conducted due diligence on the project, and EAs were released for both pulp mills. While MIGA determined that the Orion pulp mill met its environmental and social criteria, IFC asked for a further cumulative impact study of Orion and the other proposed pulp mill to determine both projects' impact. IFC's information disclosure practices during the appraisal process and the dissonance between IFC and MIGA actions triggered a compliance audit (CAO 2005b). In 2006 the CAO audit found that IFC was not in compliance with its information disclosure but that MIGA met its due diligence requirements and was compliant with its own policies and procedures. Again, the CAO stated that IFC and MIGA should improve and formalise their collaboration throughout the project appraisal process, while MIGA should ensure that the information it states is available to the public is accessible (CAO 2006d).

The final project assessed by the CAO, the Dikulushi mine in the Democratic Republic of Congo (DRC), was triggered in 2005 by the then President of the WBG, Paul Wolfowitz. This was the first time that a compliance audit was instigated by the President and it came as the result of social influence from NGOs led by Rights and Accountability in Development (RAID). They wanted to know whether MIGA had conducted due diligence before providing a contract of guarantee in September 2004 to the company controlling the mine, Anvil. This is because Anvil had provided logistical support to the DRC army in October 2004 as it retook the town of Kilwa from rebels, where the copper and silver from the mine is exported to Zambia. The Army was alleged to have engaged in human rights abuses including summary execution, the murder of civilians and illegal detention, as well as extortion and looting. The United Nations would go on to examine the Kilwa events (CAO 2005c: i, 4).

The CAO found that MIGA did meet its due diligence requirements and followed its environmental and social procedures although the CAO could not 'address whether the project may influence the dynamics of the conflict or whether security provision for a project such as Dikulushi could indirectly lead to adverse impacts on the local community' (CAO 2005c: i, 14). The CAO reported that MIGA was weak in its 'follow through on social aspects in some key areas' particularly that MIGA's environmental and social review process should have 'flagged the potential social impacts of the risk that the presence of the mine could exacerbate local tensions or attract rebel groups' (CAO 2005c: i–ii, 16). Although MIGA's assessment of the potential development impacts of the mine was sound, it was based on the assumption that the development impacts could actually be realised. The CAO questioned MIGA's reliance on Anvil in determining the method of consultation and how information was disclosed to the community, especially considering that open communication would have provided the company with information of the human rights abuse allegations (CAO 2005c: 16–18). Further, Anvil had signed the Voluntary Principles on Security and Human Rights, an international code of conduct established by states and the private sector. This should have broadened the company's security concerns to include the community although neither Anvil nor MIGA understood this, despite management response to the Extractive Industries Review committing MIGA to expect its new guarantors to follow these guidelines (CAO 2005c: ii, 9, 20).[39] These issues had previously been raised in the CAO's 2002 assessment of MIGA's environmental and social review procedures and remained unaddressed. Formal guidelines on how MIGA should address the concerns surrounding security forces and extractive industry projects were not available when MIGA was underwriting Dikulushi, nor when the CAO submitted its final report (CAO 2005c: 15).

The findings of the CAO's investigations into MIGA-insured projects detail that MIGA does meet its environmental requirements although the CAO points out the need to improve its social due diligence and to ensure the ability of companies to comply with their environmental and social requirements. Further, the CAO, as with the IEG-MIGA, has consistently called for MIGA to put in place more formal systems of collaboration between MIGA and IFC to ascertain where MIGA diverges from IFC environmental and social assessments. Most notable from the CAO reports is that many of the activities undertaken by project sponsors in relation to communities are beyond the remit of the CAO to investigate. The CAO can only assess whether the Agency met its own environmental and social procedures and standards and provide mediation to overcome conflict. Some of the claim concerns, including company capacity, security and human rights are addressed more fully in MIGA's 2007 performance standards. These may go some way towards providing MIGA with a means of positively and proactively addressing and monitoring the ongoing environmental and social impacts of the projects MIGA guarantees. The basis for MIGA is that this political risk insurer can add value to supporting projects that will facilitate development in developing countries. The next section examines whether MIGA can reconcile its insurer identity and sustainable development.

MIGA's identity shift?

Thus far MIGA's various components, its project operations, policies and institutions have been discussed in relation to TEAN efforts to directly and indirectly socialise this political risk insurer. In 1999 MIGA adopted formal environmental, social and disclosure policies and procedures and established institutions to further its environmental and social evaluation and accountability. It has therefore begun to institutionalise sustainable development but it is not yet clear whether this is leading MIGA to internalise sustainable development norms. This section brings together the analysis by assessing the effects of these changes including intersubjective and subjective understandings to argue that it has not internalised sustainable development norms.

TEANs first attempted to influence MIGA to halt problem projects as detailed in the Freeport McMoRan campaign. TEANs used persuasion through letters to MIGA and social influence through online campaigns to shape the organisation to stop its coverage of Freeport. Indirectly TEANs tried to influence the US OPIC to stop underwriting the mine. The campaign failed to halt the project or materially influence the project sponsor although it did contribute to OPIC's decision to cancel its coverage on environmental and social grounds, which was a landmark decision. This would lead MIGA to begin investigations into the project's impacts although Freeport then cancelled its MIGA coverage. TEANs therefore helped draw attention to the role that political risk insurers could play in preventing environmentally and socially damaging projects from continuing. It also highlighted the contingent nature of political risk coverage.

During this period both OPIC and MIGA would to draw up

their own environmental, social and information disclosure policies, which MIGA provisionally adopted in 1999 and permanently adopted in 2002. Its belated and reluctant stance demonstrated its unwillingness to engage with sustainable development norms. It initially rejected and then began to engage with TEANs, challenging their position in characterising MIGA practices as contributing to environmentally and socially damaging development. In 1997 MIGA established its own environment unit and undertook its first assessment of its environmental and development impacts in 1998. Yet TEANs argued that there was no consistent monitoring in place such that MIGA claims in 2002 to only cover good corporate citizens were challenged. Ongoing social influence through publications including the *Risky Business* report in 2001 and persuasion through letters to MIGA point to continued efforts by TEANs to question MIGA's understanding of development and to draw attention to its role in insuring companies that engage in environmental and social devastation. Direct and indirect socialisation, this time through the US Congress and Executive Director, focused on establishing environmental, social and disclosure policies for MIGA. TEANs also furthered the need for, and helped establish, the CAO to hold MIGA to account by peoples and ecosystems adversely affected by MIGA projects, again via processes of direct and indirect socialisation.

TEAN socialisation did have some effect. In 2004 the organisation outlined a new strategic direction that focused the Agency's attention on improving its development impact. Further, MIGA stated explicitly its aim to do so in an environmentally sustainable manner. While TEANs argued that these changes by MIGA did not really alter its behaviour, it did demonstrate a willingness to engage and respond to TEANs through annual meetings and more conciliatory letters. Yet the networks feel that these meetings have 'too much show and tell' leading some in the network to argue that TEANs should not engage with MIGA because it gives the Agency credibility while the organisation has done nothing.[40] MIGA also addressed criticisms from TEANs regarding its lack of proper evaluation and systematic monitoring. It released its 2001 Development Impact Review before establishing the OEU as an independent evaluation mechanism in 2003. It hired another environmental specialist and a social specialist in 2004. MIGA began to respond to TEAN criticisms over its perceived secrecy, aiming to make information about MIGA projects more publicly available, although no information was available for Category B, C or FI projects making it very difficult to determine exactly what MIGA was doing.

Most recently, in 2007 MIGA adopted its version of IFC's performance standards. These are seen as an 'important milestone' in outlining MIGA's 'vision in implementing sustainability' (World Bank 2008a: 64). The IEG notes that MIGA's ability to do good 'will no longer be the exception under the new policy framework' although it more likely represents the fact that MIGA along with thirty-five OECD export credit agencies has begun to follow IFC's market-based sustainable development (MIGA 2007f: 20). MIGA has begun some new initiatives including its first coverage of a carbon credit finance project in 2006 and a trust fund for environment-related technical assistance to African states established in 2007, a first for a political risk insurance agency (MIGA 2008c: 14; World Bank 2008a: xl).

While MIGA has undertaken all of these measures, it has not internalised sustainable development. It has recently improved but sustainable development is not a strategic aim of the Agency and there is no real discussion of how sustainability informs its mission 'to promote foreign direct investment into emerging economies to improve people's lives and reduce poverty' (MIGA 2006). A staff survey undertaken in 2003 noted that all staff interviewed thought that environmental and social safeguards were important and that they were adequately addressed even though 'twenty-seven per cent of EI [extractive industry] projects had substantial gaps and were not fully consistent with environmental and social safeguards' (Liebenthal *et al.* 2005: 193). The 'greatest weakness' of the organisation remains ensuring environmental and social compliance of the projects it covers. This has not improved although there has been an increase in monitoring and evaluation within MIGA and by the IEG-MIGA from 2003.

Equally importantly, the subjective and intersubjective elements of the IO's identity demonstrate that this organisation has not consumed norms of sustainable development. The TEAN attempting to socialise MIGA does not believe that MIGA's identity has changed as evidenced not only by the exchange between TEANs and MIGA in 2002 but as repeated in letters to MIGA in

2004 and reports in 2006. This contrasts with the recognition that various networks give to both the Bank and IFC regarding their respective identity changes. Perhaps most revealing however, is the view of the CAO. The CAO stated that there is a disconnect between MIGA's environmental and social review procedures and its core business practices and that its ability to encourage good practices is limited by the minimal 'do no harm' approach of the environmental and social review procedure (2002e: v–vi, 2003c: 1). Further, the CAO 2002 review noted that 'MIGA does not believe it has the leverage to require' measures that go beyond compliance to its clients (2002e: 7). Findings from recent compliance audits have led the CAO to argue that MIGA should 'systematically assess a client's capacity for managing social and environmental issues' and 'more systematically evaluate and report on social and environmental risks beyond those explicitly addressed in MIGA's policies' (CAO 2006c: 23). This reinforces the network's view that MIGA has outmoded views of development and is not interested in internalising sustainable development. The crux of the issue for TEANs was their attempts to socialise a political risk insurer to incorporate sustainable development. TEANs questioned whether this was even possible (Harmon *et al.* 2005). Indeed the challenges in doing so were begrudgingly recognised by the Agency (MIGA 2000). Some activists like Friends of the Earth remain convinced that MIGA should be shut down.[41]

Like IFC, MIGA may not have much leverage to shape investors in ensuring environment and social project impacts are addressed, although there is evidence that MIGA could improve a project's environmental performance even despite its minor role (MIGA 2007f: 19; World Bank 2008a: 66). Both the IEG and MIGA agree that the organisation can do more to provide environmental advice to project sponsors to bring them 'closer to industry best practices' (World Bank 2008a: xliii). The IEG states that MIGA's policy aims include that it help clients go beyond a strict interpretation of its safeguards and move towards best practice, and that it help other financial institutions 'do good', stating that MIGA has the opportunity to be a standard-setter in the investment insurance industry (World Bank 2008a: 64). The external advisory panel for the 2008 WBG sustainability review also states that MIGA 'needs to strengthen the implementation of its environmental safeguards as well as embrace a stronger commitment to proactively "do good"' (World Bank 2008a: xxvii).

The IEG recommends that MIGA 'move beyond safeguard performance to promote sustainability in its projects' while observing that MIGA 'does not have a strategy or business line to actively promote free-standing environmentally beneficial guarantee projects' (World Bank 2008a: 64, 66–7). Indeed, 'few MIGA operations specifically intended to avoid damage to the environment' (World Bank 2008a: xvii, 61). The CAO argues that compared to MIGA, IFC's 'business model and related environmental and social review procedures provides for a more in-depth and longer-term relationship between clients and environmental and social specialists' which it argues 'increases the prospects for constructive engagement and exerting a positive influence' (CAO 2003c: iv).

MIGA's role as an international political risk insurer is at odds with its development mandate as part of the WBG. TEANs aimed to internalise norms of sustainable development within MIGA as various networks had with regard to the World Bank and IFC. The effect has been the initial creation of the form of sustainable development within MIGA through policies and institution (which may flow through to future projects), but MIGA's inability to monitor the projects it covers while claiming that it does not encourage environmentally and socially damaging development means that MIGA has not internalised the norm of sustainable development. Whether MIGA's political risk identity can be reconciled with its development mandate merits continued scrutiny.

Conclusion

This chapter analysed how sustainable development norms have begun to be diffused within MIGA by assessing its projects, policies and institutions. MIGA initially responded negatively to the norm diffusion process. TEANs emerged to socialise this IO, and indirectly influenced states and their agencies in the process. Yet MIGA's political risk insurance identity remains at odds with norms of sustainable development. The chapter analysed the processes of direct and indirect socialisation by TEANs to diffuse norms of sustainable development within MIGA. While the first problem project campaign involving MIGA had no impact in diffusing norms of sustainable development, it was the first of a number of problem project campaigns against MIGA. The emergence of these campaigns was followed by attempted direct and indirect socialisation of MIGA to make safeguard and information disclosure policies part of what political risk insurers do. TEANs attempted direct socialisation to pressure MIGA to establish safeguard policies, and then to ensure that they would be monitored, while attempted indirect socialisation pressured for MIGA to have its own information disclosure policies distinct from IFC. While MIGA made significant changes to its policy framework, it has not internalised the norm of sustainable development.

The socialisation of MIGA has been furthered by the establishment of an accountability mechanism for MIGA-insured projects. The CAO has indicated areas where MIGA would benefit in internalising norms of sustainable development. What is notable about this chapter is not that TEANs used the same processes against MIGA as they had with both the Bank and IFC, but that MIGA is only beginning to fully institutionalise a market-based sustainable development. Processes of socialisation continue as the networks attempt try to diffuse norms of sustainable development within MIGA. TEANs established a pattern of socialising the World Bank Group; MIGA's political risk identity determines how the organisation understands norms of sustainable development. The identity of the organisation provides a compelling reason as to how and why this IO has begun to shift towards a market-based sustainable development that does not actively attempt to further norms of sustainable development. The next chapter questions how changed understandings of sustainable development fit within broader patterns of international development lending, investing and underwriting, and what role remains for TEANs.

Notes

1 Two types of international political risk insurance exist: investment insurance as undertaken by MIGA and export credit insurance, which is dominated by national export credit agencies (Stephens 1998: 150–1).

2 MIGA has limited technical assistance to further the implementation of environmental standards and this has not been the focus of TEAN socialisation (World Bank 2008a: 5).

3 Personal communication with Judith Pearce, Lead Operations Officer, External Outreach and Partners Group, MIGA, dated 31 October 2008.

4 MIGA underwrites investments for fifteen years, while the private sector initially maintained three-year guarantees (Shihata 1988: 148).

5 Confidential interview with BIC activist, 15 February 2006.

6 'West Papua' is used by the traditional owners of the western area of the island of New Guinea; Indonesia renamed it Irian Jaya.

7 This section is from Freeport's historical account (Freeport 2003).

8 Personal Communication with Denise Leith, 7 February 2003.

9 The next section, unless otherwise stated, is from Leith (2003).

10 Personal communication with Denise Leith, 7 February 2003.

11 The campaign highlights the human rights concerns of the traditional owners of West Papua. As their lives are entwined with the land, and as both human rights and environmental degradation were both explicitly the concerns of the campaign, this does not invalidate the use of this case in analysing sustainable development. The human rights aspects are detailed in Abrash and Kennedy 2001; Leith 2003; ProjectUndergound 1998.

12 Letter from Emmy Hafield of WALHI to Mr Wolfensohn as President of MIGA, dated 16 February 1996.

13 MIGA, 1995, 'Statement by the Vice President and General Council of the Multilateral Investment Guarantee Agency (MIGA)', 15 December 1995, to the MIGA Directors.

14 One network activist stated that there were heated debates as to how much to pressure MIGA while relying on the IO to diffuse norms of sustainable development and human rights to Freeport. Confidential interview, Australian activist on the Freeport Mine Campaign, dated 23 May 2003.

15 MIGA also adopted the *Pollution Prevention and Abatement Handbook* and sector specific environmental guidelines as well as the Policy on Harmful Child Labour (MIGA 1999).

16 Letter by MIGA to Friends of the Earth, dated 26 July 2001.

17 Letter by MIGA to Friends of the Earth, dated 28 September 2001.

18 Letter from Carol Welch from Friends of the Earth, Heffa Schuking from Urgewald and Antonio Tricarico from Reform the World Bank Campaign to Moina Vakrie, Chief of MIGA's Corporate Relations Group, dated 3 April 2002.

19 Letter from Moina Vakrie, Chief of MIGA's Corporate Relations Group to Carol Welch of Friends of the Earth, Heffa Schuking from

Urgewald and Antonio Tricarico from Reform the World Bank Campaign, dated 14 June 2002.

20 Friends of the Earth, 'Multilateral Investment Guarantee Agency Fact sheet', www.foe.org (accessed 2 December 2003).

21 For more on the TEAN campaign of export credit agencies through the OECD see www.eca-watch.org/ (accessed October 2008). That TEANs use indirect socialisation in relation to persuading and using social influence on member states to influence the OECD to in turn shape corporation practices, points to the broader applicability of this approach.

22 The lead author of this report, James Harmon, worked for the US Export-Import Bank while another contributor, Jon Sohn, formerly worked for OPIC (Harmon *et al.* 2005: 46).

23 MIGA, Response to NGO stakeholder comments, note 64, public discussion ending 5 February 1999, cited at www.miga.org (accessed 2 December 2003).

24 Letter from Carol Welch, dated 3 April 2002.

25 Letter from Carol Welch, dated 3 April 2002.

26 Letter from Moina Vakrie, dated 14 June 2002.

27 Letter from Moina Vakrie, dated 14 June 2002.

28 Letter from Moina Vakrie, dated 14 June 2002.

29 All annual reports are available at www.miga.org (accessed October 2008).

30 Interview with Environmental Defense activist, 14 February 2006.

31 Letter from Friends of the Earth, 'Letter to MIGA's Executive Vice President Yukiko Omura on Behalf of 90 NGOs', dated 24 September 2004.

32 Letter from MIGA EVP Yukiko Omura to Ms Colleen Freeman, Friends of the Earth, dated 17 October 2004.

33 Letter from Moina Vakrie, dated 14 June 2002.

34 Personal communication with Judith Pearce, Lead Operations Officer, External Outreach and Partners Group, MIGA, dated 31 October 2008.

35 IFC/MIGA 'Proposed Inspection Mechanism for Private Sector Projects: IFC and MIGA Inspection Panel', Report to the Committee on Development Effectiveness for the World Bank, IFC and MIGA, 27 June 1996.

36 As IFC took the lead on Orion it is only discussed here in relation to MIGA's actions.

37 See www.cao-ombudsman.org (accessed October 2008).

38 See www.cao-ombudsman.org (accessed October 2008).

39 For more see www.voluntaryprinciples.org/ (accessed November 2008).

40 Interview with BIC activist, 15 February 2006; interview with WRI activist, 9 September 2006.

41 Confidential interview with a staff member of BIC, dated 21 September 2001.

6

Conclusion: lending, investing and guaranteeing sustainable development

International organisations are important in international politics because they undertake tasks that states either do not or cannot undertake themselves. Thus far I have argued that IO actions and identities cannot be explained merely through unpacking the interests of their member states. As such, the central thrust of this book has been to posit that IOs can consume or internalise ideas, that is, they can take up different ways of thinking about and operationalising their state determined mandates. In some ways examining how IOs change is therefore unique. They are made up of member states, but they have their own management and staff, which often give them the autonomy to act on states' behalf. This autonomy gives IOs the ability to act independently of member states and yet they are beholden to them, even when member states have conflicting interests. This may give IOs room to shape international agendas and to construct different ways of understanding changing events. The ability to provide independent advice, often based on specialist expertise in a given area, provides IOs with authority. For rationalist scholars the focus has been on how this autonomy can lead to 'slippage' where IOs begin to do things not anticipated or desired by member states.

As documented throughout this book, I too examine why IOs behave the way they do. However, I go beyond the realm of analysing how member state interests determine IO actions. In doing so, I argue that IOs are not only shaped by materially powerful member states but also by non-materially powerful non-state actors. I pointed to the central role that non-state actors such as transnational environmental advocacy networks (TEANs) can play in influencing IOs by challenging their actions and providing alternative ways of understanding the world. This demonstrates that non-state actors can shape world politics through spreading norms that change how states view IO actions, and how IOs themselves understand how they should operationalise their mandates. To unpack these arguments the book examined the three organisations within the World Bank Group: the World Bank, constituted by the International Bank for Reconstruction and Development and the International Development Association (IBRD/IDA); the International Finance Corporation (IFC); and the Multilateral Investment Guarantee Agency (MIGA).

These three IOs were all given development mandates but they have separate identities. As discussed below, all initially resisted but then were influenced, to some degree, by norms of sustainable development. Recall that an IO's identity is constituted by the organisation's mandate and bureaucratic culture and is both subjective and intersubjective. The World Bank, IFC and MIGA all have a mandate and a bureaucratic culture based on their dominant profession which influences how they undertake their functions, but this is also informed by how they perceive themselves and are perceived by others. The World Bank is primarily an economists' bank with a multilateral development mandate to provide knowledge and leadership on how to lend official development assistance. IFC on the other hand is comprised of international financiers that aim to facilitate private sector investments and loans within developing countries. Lastly MIGA is made up of political risk analysts who underwrite direct foreign investment for projects in developing countries. Each perceives differently, and is perceived differently by, their member states, the private sector and TEANs because they have different ways of seeing the world based on their dominant collective professional view about how to undertake their operations.

An IO's identity is formed through social interaction during its creation, when states establish its mandate and constitution and hire its original staff. Identity is therefore formed by social processes, and 'once crystallized, it is maintained, modified or even reshaped by social relations' (Berger and Luckman 1987: 194). Identity is important because it determines actors' interests and preferences, thus shaping how they will behave in any given situation. Here we point to the mutual constitution of agents and structures, IOs and international norms. Through their interactions actors collectively create social structures such as international norms, rules, and institutions to regulate their behaviour and make ongoing and repeated interaction possible. Norms, rules and institutions are therefore social facts that define expectations for behaviour (Searle 1995: 24–7). As we know, norms are 'collective expectations about proper behaviour for a given identity' (Jepperson *et al.* 1996: 54; Finnemore and Sikkink 1998: 89). International norms therefore institutionalise knowledge about an actor's identity which in turn further stabilises interactions between actors because they behave as expected.

As a result, an IO's identity influences not only its actions but how it responds to new ideas. Much of the constructivist literature examines how actors, primarily states, are shaped by international norms. Often the mutual constitution of international norms and actors, where they influence and shape each other, is lost in documenting the structural power of ideas in changing states' behaviour. This book demonstrated how international norms of sustainable development emerged in the form of TEANs to counter the activities of the World Bank, IFC and MIGA in lending, investing and underwriting environmentally damaging development in developing countries. TEANs emerged to challenge the activities of these organisations on the basis of the World Bank, IFC and MIGA practices. They highlighted their destructive nature and used micro-processes of persuasion, social influence and coercion through member states to make these IOs aware of their behaviour and to change it.

In doing so, TEANs aimed to socialise IOs, shaping their identities to become sustainable development lenders, investors and underwriters. Recognisably then, IO identities are not static but fluid. They evolve over time and may change through interaction. Socialisation is a process whereby international norms influence IO behaviour by reconstituting their identities. IOs therefore begin to establish new roles to conform to new norms. The social structure therefore informs how agents behave but does not necessarily determine what they will do. Socialisation is a key concept for understanding how actors alter their behaviour and identity, and embrace new ideas in international politics.

The organisations' behaviour is not wholly based on the social structure within which they exist, nor do they exist entirely outside of social interaction. Rather, IO identities are informed by social interaction, and identity change results from socialisation, but how they change is distinct to each organisation. Again the mutual constitution of identities and norms comes to the fore. Actors do not just respond to new ideas, they internalise them and reconstitute them, making them part of their identities, thus changing them in the process. Engagements between TEANs and the World Bank led the organisation to establish a rules-based sustainable development. In ongoing interactions with TEANs the Bank created detailed environmental, social and information disclosure rules which it agreed to be bound by. It established elaborate environmental and social monitoring and evaluation functions to ensure that it met these agreed-upon rules and created an accountability mechanism to ensure that its practices did not adversely affect people at or near the development project site. Changes to those environmental rules and practices continue to evolve in relation to social interactions between the Bank, states and TEANs.

This process would be repeated in relation to IFC. By the early 2000s IFC had begun to internalise how it could be a leader in sustainable finance. It determined that the best means to do so was not through the rules-based sustainable development that it had emulated from the World Bank as a result of interactions with TEANs, but through reconstituting sustainable development for a private sector financier. This ultimately led to a market-based sustainable development for a private sector investor that clearly identifies the business case for sustainability and advocates international best practice. Each organisation's identity therefore determined how it would engage with norms of sustainable development and TEANs, reconstituting the norm in the process. MIGA's response was based on the assumption that sustainability had nothing to do with political risk insurance. Repeated engagements with TEANs had little traction until the organisation restructured in 2004, providing some space for new ideas. The changes undertaken by the organisation since then do accord with the market following of its political risk insurance identity, which follows shifts in investor identities. MIGA, along with thirty-five OECD export credit agencies, has begun to follow IFC in meeting minimum standards for underwriting political risk in developing countries.

Each of these cases demonstrates how TEANs engaged in ongoing processes of socialisation. The aim of the book was never to argue that ideas matter all the way down but to state that purely material explanations of IO change mischaracterise how the WBG organisations found different ways of doing development through interactions with TEANs and states. Indeed, the book demonstrates that international norms do shape how material factors are understood and used. I distinguished between direct and indirect socialisation where TEANs directly engage with the IO using persuasion including letters, emails and faxes to change the behaviour of these institutions, as well as social influence to shame and shun them through the use of protests, marches, and media stunts. Additionally, TEANs used indirect socialisation to persuade materially powerful member states such as the US, but also others, to shape their understanding of how IOs like the Bank, IFC and MIGA should act, and to use their material power to force them to change. Both direct and indirect socialisation are used simultaneously and arguing that one is more powerful than the other does not fully encapsulate how and why these IOs changed their understandings of what was appropriate behaviour for lenders, investors and underwriters of international development.

In documenting how these IOs engaged with TEANs and states, each of the cases details how the WBG organisations initially rejected TEAN characterisations of their actions. They ignored TEANs before rejecting their assertions that their activities contributed either overtly or indirectly to environmentally and socially destructive development. Concerted problem project campaigns demonstrated that this was not the case. As discussed in the theory chapter, the initial impetus for the shift from ignoring and rejecting TEAN claims, to then responding to them and engaging in dialogue, may have been for tactical reasons in alleviating the pressure from social influence and member state coercion. However, in the cases of the World Bank and IFC, the norm later became an entrenched aspect of their identities, changing their understanding of what is acceptable behaviour for multilateral development lenders and investors. It is too early to say with MIGA, although there is evidence to date to suggest a shift toward market-following behaviour.

This is not to state that these shifts in identity by the Bank and

IFC have been easy, complete or permanent. Most actors and activists when pressed would recognise that these institutions have changed markedly since the beginning of TEAN engagement. They have demonstrated changes in their policies, institutions and practices. Of course there remain difficulties in operationalising sustainable development. The Bank, IFC and MIGA all continue to engage in sectors of development known for their high environmental and social impact. The Bank has returned to sectors such as high dams and logging and continues to engage in oil, gas and mining. IFC has its high-risk, high-reward strategy whereby it knowingly engages in high-risk, potentially highly environmentally and socially damaging projects on the basis that it can contribute the most to development in doing so. Although the majority of MIGA's portfolio remains finance based, it too is heavily involved in infrastructure and manufacturing sectors not known for their positive environmental impact (although most claims against MIGA remain in mining).

In this sense then, although sustainable development means going beyond 'do no harm' towards 'doing good' and going 'beyond compliance' this is still predicated on large-scale development being fundamental to these institutions. Furthering sustainable development still means the Bank, IFC and MIGA engaging in development activities that either borrower states or project sponsors want funded. It means they attempt to mitigate the environmental and social ill effects of these projects and offset them with positive environmental and social components, but it does not mean that they will stop lending for, investing in or underwriting development projects. At the heart of this is the recognition that sustainable international development is determined by shared agreement over what is acceptable practice for multilateral development institutions – and most states, most IOs and even many NGOs in TEANs accept that this is still based on modernisation and industrialisation. In this respect, the very idea of sustainable development accords with what Steven Bernstein has called the 'compromise of liberal environmentalism' where environmental mitigation measures have been wedded to capitalist economic development (2001). Others rail against this form of 'green neoliberalism' (Goldman 2005) although this fails to adequately appreciate the extent to which the Bank, IFC and perhaps now even MIGA are changing to accord sustainability a role in their decision-making and operations.

Admitting that environmental ideas have been reconciled with economic concerns in this way does not mean that the Bank and IFC have completely solved how this works in practice. Indeed, their operations and activities continue to evolve but weaknesses remain. For some this constitutes IO 'hypocrisy' (Weaver 2008) where IOs attempt to reconcile the competing member states' demands but remain impeded by their own organisational culture. The World Bank, for example, often does not meet its own standards for sustainability as demonstrated in its QAG and IEG evaluations, while IFC posts consistently lower environmental, social, health and safety results. Although rejecting that this is merely a result of top-down change from member states, it is true that there is always more that each organisation can do, and both the Bank and IFC continue to devise new ways to track, monitor and evaluate their efforts. Critics continue to call for independent evaluators to ensure development organisations like the Bank remain accountable. Indeed, this would go some way to ensuring greater environmental and social transparency, effectiveness and accountability (Birdsall 2006; Woods 2006). Yet the Bank continues to experiment with alterative means of incorporating sustainability through sectoral and country environmental analyses that take a more holistic approach to sustainable development, while IFC has devised new means of tracking development impacts for projects in real time. MIGA has just announced that it will provide information for highly sensitive development projects. There is more that all of these organisations can do in furthering sustainable development and the process of internalising externally driven norms is not easy, fluid or continuous. Arguably however, until there are ecological economists, ecological financiers and ecological political risk analysts, sustainable development will remain somcthing that each organisation attempts to further through its own devising with TEAN and member state interactions (despite their differences). As a result, we can point to WBG practices, and interactions with TEANs and states, in reconstituting international norms of sustainable development.

While identity shifts have taken place in the World Bank and IFC, and there have been more recent changes in MIGA, the very basis for TEAN campaigns was to reshape international development to become sustainable through socialising the WBG. The Bank introduced a rules-based sustainable development for official development assistance. This would pale into insignificance compared to the very dramatic rise in FDI in the 1990s and again in the mid-2000s, leading to the expansion of IFC and MIGA. Both grew substantially in this period and now play important roles in furthering investment in developing countries in ways that contribute to development. IFC now has considerable normative sway in terms of international sustainable development through the Equator Principles and having its performance standards recognised in the OECD's common approaches for export credit agencies and MIGA. In some ways the rise in FDI and the role of private sector investors is even rebounding back on the World Bank, where the organisation has scaled up its private sector development (Miller-Adams 1999) and engaged in further collaboration with IFC and MIGA.[1] The Bank has begun to initiate the reconstitution of its rules-based sustainable development as it tries to compete with FDI to middle income countries, leading the organisation to begin to reinterpret sustainable development according to national equivalent standards through the use of a country systems approach.

As a result, while TEANs aimed to ensure that all investors and political risk insurers met the *World Bank*'s rules, all investors and political risk insurers are now following *IFC*'s market-based standards (Hunter 2008). While improvements in sustainable international development financing and even increasingly political risk insurance are demonstrable, these are not enough to prevent environmental degradation. Greening these IOs can alter practices in the industries in which they operate but they will never fundamentally shape the drivers of market competition, for one important structurally deficient reason: contract-based financiers and insurers of development, financial downturns or even individual project sponsor decisions to prepay loans or cancel their political risk coverage will not ultimately protect communities and ecosystems under threat from environmental degradation. Recognisably, these market events and subsequent behavioural responses limit the ability to ensure sustainability through international political economy instruments without fundamentally internalising environmental costs into the global political economy. While greening these IOs is a move in the right direction, much broader shifts within all market actors and industries needs to take place.

Yet attempting to transform the international political economy of development has been the focus of TEANs. The book traced how TEANs engaged with the WBG organisations to shape their identities to become sustainable. Identifiably, TEANs used a 'boomerang pattern' to combine forces between northern and southern NGOs, indigenous groups, activists and the media to influence powerful states to shape IOs to then stop or mitigate the environmental and social damage taking place in developing countries (Keck and Sikkink 1998). In cases like Narmada this worked spectacularly well in halting Bank lending and triggering organisational change. While TEANs would go on to socialise the Bank and IFC, the boomerang pattern did not always succeed in actually changing the situation on the ground as was the case in Polonoroeste/Rondonia (Rodrigues 2004) and Narmada for the Bank (Khagram 2004), Pangue for IFC (Alywin 2002), or Freeport for MIGA (Leith 2003).

From the evidence presented in this book, we now know that TEANs have been able to shape IOs but that this does not always prevent environmental and social destruction from taking place. Moreover, middle income countries are no longer dependent on the WBG, and multilateral, bilateral and private lenders are now proliferating in the international development market, many with lower or no environmental standards (OECD 2008; Woods 2008). The cases here show that TEANs may succeed in further spreading norms of sustainable development to these financiers although the examples of the World Bank, IFC and MIGA are historically and socially specific, and as such may not be replicable (although evidence suggests that the same processes of socialisation are being enacted in relation to the OECD and export credit agencies).

Does this mean that TEAN activism and the process of direct and indirect socialisation following the boomerang pattern is no longer a viable means of reshaping international development? Direct and indirect socialisation will remain an important means for non-state actors to shape world politics through reconstituting state and IO practices. As discussed throughout this volume, states are not always generators of ideas, nor are they sufficiently interested in changing their practices or those of their agents such as IOs without sufficient persuasion from non-state actors. Therefore, TEAN involvement in spreading international norms of sustainable development remains as important as ever. The boomerang pattern on the other hand may – owing to the changing fortunes of middle income countries like Brazil, Russia, India and China among others – no longer be a pathway to changing powerful actors' behaviour and identities in the twenty-first century. New paths to socialisation will need to be forged to radically reconstitute the broader international political economy towards ecologically driven development for all states, IOs and non-state actors alike. It remains to be seen whether crises, either ecological or financial, open these paths.

Note

1 IFC announced in 2008 a $500 million transfer of a total $1.75 billion commitment to IDA demonstrating that it is now beginning to influence other parts of the World Bank: see www.ifc.org (accessed November 2008).

Bibliography

Abbott, K. and Snidal, D., 1998, 'Why States Act through Formal International Organisations', *Journal of Conflict Resolution* 42 (1): 3–33.

Abrash, A. and Kennedy, D., 2001, 'Repressive Mining in West Papua', in G. Evans, J. Goodman and N. Landsbury (eds), *Moving Mountains: Communities Confront Mining and Globalisation*, The Protest and Globalisation Research Project, The Mineral Policy Institute and the University of Technology Sydney, Otford Press: 59–74.

Adler, E., 1998, 'Seeds of Peaceful Change: The OSCE's Community Building Model', in E. Adler and M. Barnett (eds), *Security Communities*, Cambridge, Cambridge University Press: 119–60.

—— 1997, 'Seizing the Middle Ground: Constructivism in World Politics', *European Journal of International Relations* 3 (3): 319–63.

Alderson, K., 2001, 'Making Sense of State Socialisation', *Review of International Studies* 27: 415–33.

Alter, K., 1998, 'Who are the "Masters of the Treaty"? European Governments and the European Court of Justice', *International Organisation* 59 (1): 121–47.

Alywin, J., 2002, 'The Ralco Dam and the Pehuenche People in Chile: Lessons from an Ethno-environmental Conflict', Paper presented to the Conference: Towards Adaptive Conflict Resolutions: Lessons from Canada and Chile, University of British Columbia, Canada, 25–27 September.

Ascher, W., 1983, 'New Development Approaches and the Adaptability of International Agencies: The Case of the World Bank', *International Organisation* 37 (3): 415–39.

Associated Press, 1996, 'OPIC, Louisiana Mine Company Settle Dispute', Washington, DC, 19 April.

Atkinson, C., 2006, 'Constructivist Implications of Material Power:

Military Engagement and the Socialisation of States, 1972–2000', *International Studies Quarterly* 50 (3): 509–38.

Auferheide, P. and Rich, B., 1988, 'Environmental Reform and the Multilateral Banks', *World Policy Journal* 5 (2): 301–21.

Australian Council for Overseas Aid, 1995, 'Trouble at Freeport: Eyewitness Accounts of West Papuan Resistance to the Freeport-McMoRan Mine in Irian Jaya, Indonesia, and Indonesian Military Repression, June 1994–February 1995', Canberra, ACFOA.

Ayers, R., 1983, *Banking on the Poor: The World Bank and World Poverty*, Cambridge, MA, MIT Press.

Baldwin, D.A. (ed.), 1993, *Neorealism and Neoliberalism: The Contemporary Debate*, New York, Columbia University Press.

Bank Information Center, 2003, 'Tuesday Group', cited at www.bicusa.org/usgovtoversight/tuesdaygroup.htm (accessed 7 November 2003; last updated: 2003).

—— 2001, 'The Ongoing Struggle for World Bank Transparency – The Outcome of the Information Disclosure Policy Review', *Bank Information Center Update*, 4 November, cited at www.bicusa .org/policy/InfoDisclosure/infodiscupdate.htm (accessed: 1 January 2002; last updated: 2002).

Barnett, M. and Coleman, L., 2005, 'Designing Police: Interpol and the Study of Change in International Organisations', *International Studies Quarterly* 49 (4): 593–620.

Barnett, M. and Finnemore, M., 2004, *Rules for the World: International Organisations in Global Politics*, Ithaca and London, Cornell University Press.

—— 1999, 'The Politics, Power and Pathologies of IOs', *International Organisation* 53 (4): 699–732.

Bearce, D. and Bondanella, S., 2007, 'Intergovernmental Organizations, Socialization and Member-State Interest Convergence', *International Organization* 61: 703–33.

Bebbington, A., Woolcock, M., Guggenheim, S. and Olson, E.O., 2006, *The Search for Empowerment: Social Capital as Idea and Practice at the World Bank*, Bloomfield, CT, Kumarian Press.

Berger, P. and Luckman, T., 1987, *The Social Construction of Reality: A Treatise in the Sociology of Knowledge*, England, Penguin Books.

Bernstein, S., 2001, *The Compromise of Liberal Environmentalism*, New York, Columbia University Press.

Best, J., 2005, *The Limits of Transparency: Ambiguity and the History of International Finance*, Ithaca and London, Cornell University Press.

Bhaskar, R., 1998, *The Possibility of Naturalism: A Philosophical Critique of the Contemporary Human Sciences*, 3rd Edition [1979],

London and New York, Routledge.

Birdsall, N. (ed.), 2006, *Rescuing the World Bank: A Centre for Global Development Working Report and Selected Essays*, Centre for Global Development, Washington, DC.

Bissell, R., 1997, 'Recent Practice of the Inspection Panel of the World Bank', *American Journal of International Law* 91 (4): 741–4.

Blanton, T., 2007, 'The Struggle for Openness in the International Financial Institutions', in A. Florini (ed.), *The Right to Know: Transparency in an Open World*, New York, Colombia University Press: 243–78.

Boli, J. and Thomas, G. (eds), 1999, *Constructing World Culture: International Nongovernmental Organisations Since 1875*, Stanford, Stanford University Press.

Bosshard, P., 2004, 'NGO Concerns on the Use of National Safeguard Systems in World Bank Projects', International Rivers Network, cited at www.irn.org/ (accessed November 2006).

—— 1996a, 'The Private Sector Lending of the World Bank Group: Issues and Challenges', January 1996, The Berne Declaration, Switzerland, cited at www.2.access.ch/evb/bd/privlend.htm (accessed 20 January 2003; last updated: 1999).

—— 1996b, 'A Case Study about MIGA's Lihir Island Goldmine Project in Papua New Guinea', February 1996, The Berne Declaration, Switzerland, cited at www.2.access.ch/evb/bd/privlend.htm (accessed 20 January 2003; last updated: 1999).

Bowles, I. and Kormos, C., 1999, 'The American Campaign for Environmental Reforms at the World Bank', *The Fletcher Forum of World Affairs* 23 (1): 211–25.

Bowles, I., Rosenfeld, A., Kormos, C., Reining, C.S., Nations J.D. and Ankersen, T., 1999, 'The Environmental Impact of International Finance Corporation Lending and Proposals for Reform: A Case Study of Conservation and Oil Development in the Guatemalan Peten', International Environmental Symposium, *Environmental Law* 29: 103–32.

Bradlow, D., 2005, 'Private Complainants and International Organisations: A Comparative Study of the Independent Inspection Mechanisms of International Financial Institutions', *Georgetown International Law Journal* 36: 403–94.

Bramble, B. and Porter, G., 1992, 'Non-Governmental Organisations and the Making of US International Environmental Policy', in A. Hurrell and B. Kingsbury (eds), *The International Politics of the Environment: Actors, Interests, and Institutions*, Oxford, Clarendon Press: 313–53.

Bratton, M., 1989, 'The Politics of Government – NGO Relations in

Africa', *World Development* 17 (4): 569–87.

Brenton, T., 1994, *The Greening of Machiavelli: The Evolution of International Environmental Politics*, London, Earthscan Publications.

Broad, R., 2006, 'Research, Knowledge and the Art of Paradigm Maintenance: The World Bank's Development Economics Vice Presidency (DEC)', *Review of International Political Economy* 13 (3): 387–419.

Bryce, R., 1995, 'US Cancel's Indonesia's Mine Insurance', *New York Times*, 2 November: 6.

Bunge, M., 1985, *Treatise on Basic Philosophy*, vol. 7, Boston, Dordrecht.

Caldwell, L., 1991, 'International Responses to Environmental Issues: Retrospect and Prospect', *International Studies Notes* 16 (1) Supplement: 3–7.

Campbell, J. and Pedersen, O., 2001, *The Rise of Neoliberalism and Institutional Analysis*, Princeton and Oxford, Princeton University Press.

Carson, R., 1962, *The Silent Spring*, London, Hamish Hamilton.

Catholic Church, Jayapura, 1995, 'Violations of Human Rights in the Timika Area of Irian Jaya, Indonesia, August 1995', Report, Jayapura Catholic Church, Indonesia.

Caufield, C., 1996, *Masters of Illusion: The World Bank and the Poverty of Nations*, UK, Macmillan.

Centre for International Environmental Law, 2004, *Matrix of World Bank Operational Principles – A Comparison of Annex A Objectives and Operational Principles for Country Systems Approach with Existing World Bank Operational Principles*, cited at www.ciel.org (accessed 3 September 2008; last updated: 2008).

—— 2000, 'Victory! World Bank Effort to Support China's Population Transfer into Tibet is Defeated!', Press Release, cited at www.ciel.org/ (accessed 13 September 2000; last updated: 2000).

—— 1997, 'World Bank Threatens Chilean Dam Builder with Default', Press Release 26 February, cited at www.irn.org (accessed 25 July 2001; last updated: 2001).

Chamberlain, C., 1998, 'Public Access to Information: The State of Disclosure at the Multilateral Development Banks', Bank Information Center, Washington, DC, cited: www.bicusa.org/ (accessed 29 January 2003; last updated: 2002).

—— 1997, 'Public Access to Information at the International Finance Corporation and the Multilateral Investment Guarantee Agency: A Bank Information Center Review', Bank Information Center, Washington, DC, cited at www.bicusa.org/ (accessed 28 February

2002; last updated: 2002).

Chatterjee, P., 1996, 'Company Cancels Insurance for Irian Jaya Gold Mine', *World Rivers Review* 8, September, cited at www.irn.org (accessed January 2003; last updated: 1999).

—— 1995a, 'World Bank Arm Insures Destructive Mining from Peru to Indonesia', *Inter Press Service*, 14 August, cited at www.mindsprings.com/~altafb/worldbn.txt (accessed 20 January 2003; last updated: 2002).

—— 1995b, 'World's Largest Gold Mine is Causing Unreasonable Environmental Hazard', *Inter Press Service*, 11 March, cited at www.forests.org/archive/indomalay/unrehaza.htm (accessed 17 January 2002; last updated: 2002).

—— and Finger, M., 1994, *The Earth Brokers: Power, Politics and World Development*, London and New York, Routledge.

Checkel, J., 2005, 'International Institutions and Socialisation in Europe', *International Organisation* 59 (4): 801–1079.

—— 2003, 'Going Native in Europe? Theorizing Social Interaction in European Institutions', *Comparative Political Studies* 36 (1/2): 209–31.

—— 2001, 'Why Comply? Social Learning and European Identity Change', *International Organisation* 55 (3): 553–88.

—— 1999a, 'Norms, Institutions, and National Identity in Contemporary Europe', *International Studies Quarterly* 43: 83–114.

—— 1999b, 'Social Construction and Integration', *Journal of European Public Policy*, 6 (4): 545–60.

—— 1998, 'The Constructivist Turn in International Relations', *World Politics* 50 (2): 324–48.

—— and Moravcsik, A., 2001, 'A Constructivist Research Program in EU Studies?' *European Union Politics* 2 (2): 219–49.

Chwieroth, J., 2008, 'Normative Change from Within: The International Monetary Fund's Approach to Capital Account Liberalisation', *International Studies Quarterly* 52: 129–58.

Civic, M., 1997–8, 'Prospects for the Respect and Promotion of Internationally Recognised Sustainable Development Practices: A Case Study of the World Bank Environmental Guidelines and Procedures', *Fordham Environmental Law Journal* 9: 231–60.

Clark, D., 2003, 'Understanding the World Bank Inspection Panel', in D. Clark, J. Fox and K. Treakle, *Demanding Accountability: Civil-Society Claims and the World Bank Inspection Panel*, Lanham, Rowman and Littlefield, 1–24.

Clausen, J., 1968, *Socialization and Society*, Boston, Little Brown.

Club of Rome, 1972, *Limits to Growth*, London, Earth Island.

Cockburn, A., 1997, 'Wolfensohn, Indian Killer', *The Nation*, 30 June.

Compliance Advisor/Ombudsman, 2007a, 'IFC's Policy and Performance Standards on Social and Environmental Sustainability and Information Disclosure Policy: Commentary on IFC's Progress Report on the First 18 Months of Application', Advisory Note December 17, cited at www.cao-ombudsman.org (accessed October 2008).

—— 2007b, *Annual Report 2006–2007*, Washington, DC, IFC.

—— 2006a, 'The Pangue Complaint Settlement Agreement between CAO and UNIMACH', 9 February 2006, cited at www.cao ombudsman.org (accessed November 2006).

—— 2006b, 'IFC's Review of Safeguard Policies and Policy on Disclosure of Information: CAO Comments on the January 25 2006 Drafts of IFC's Policy and Performance Standards on Social and Environmental Sustainability and Policy of Disclosure of Information', Washington, DC, IFC.

—— 2006c, *A Retrospective Analysis of CAO Interventions, Trends, Outcomes and Effectiveness*, Washington, DC, IFC.

—— 2006d, 'CAO Audit of IFC and MIGA's Due Diligence for Two Pulp Mills in Uruguay', *CAO Final Report*, IFC and MIGA, CAO, cited at www.cao-ombudsman.org (accessed October 2008).

—— 2005a, 'Safeguard Policy Review Revisited: Has IFC Addressed the Recommendations of the CAO Safeguard Policy Review?' CAO, cited at www.cao-ombudsman.org (accessed November 2006).

—— 2005b, 'Preliminary Assessment Report: Complaint Regarding IFC's Proposed Investment in Celulosas de M'Bopicua and Orion Projects Uruguay', Washington, DC, IFC and MIGA, CAO, cited at www.cao-ombudsman.org/env (accessed October 2008).

—— 2005c, 'CAO Audit of MIGA's Due Diligence of the Dikulushi Copper-Silver Mining Project in the Democratic Republic of the Congo', *CAO Final Report*, Washington, DC, IFC and MIGA, CAO, cited at www.cao-ombudsman.org/env (accessed October 2008).

—— 2003a, 'A Review of IFC's Safeguard Policies: Core Business, Achieving Consistent and Excellent Environmental and Social Outcomes', Washington, DC, IFC and MIGA, cited at www.cao -ombudsman.org/env (accessed October 2003; last updated: 2003).

—— 2003b, 'Assessment by the Office of the Compliance Advisor/Ombudsman in relation to a Complaint Filed against IFC's Investment in Endesa Pangue SA', *CAO Assessment Report*, Washington, DC, IFC and MIGA.

—— 2003c, *Extracting Sustainable Advantage? A Review of How Sustainability Issues have been Dealt with in Recent IFC and MIGA Extractive Industries Projects*, Washington, DC, IFC and MIGA, CAO.

—— 2002a, 'Review of IFC's Safeguard Policies: Draft for Comment', *CAO Report,* Washington, DC, IFC and MIGA, CAO, cited at www.cao-ombudsman.org/env (accessed September 2002; last updated: September 2002).
—— 2002b, 'Review of IFC's Safeguard Policies, IFC Staff Survey: Draft for Comment', *CAO Office Report*, Washington, DC, IFC and MIGA, CAO, cited at www.cao-ombudsman.org/env (accessed September 2002; last updated: September 2002).
—— 2002c, *Annual Report: 2001–2002*, Washington, DC, IFC and MIGA, CAO.
—— 2002d, 'Assessment Report Summary Complaint Regarding MIGA's Guarantee of the Bulyanhulu Mine, Tanzania', Washington, DC, IFC and MIGA, CAO.
—— 2002e, 'Insuring Responsible Investments? A Review of the Application of MIGA's Environmental and Social Review Procedures', *CAO Final Report*, Washington, DC, IFC and MIGA, CAO, cited at www.cao-ombudsman.org/env (accessed January 2003; last updated: January 2003).
—— 2001a, 'Review of IFC's Safeguard Policies: Final Approach Paper', CAO Office Report November 28, 2001, Washington, DC, IFC and MIGA, CAO, cited at www.cao-ombudsman.org/env (accessed September 2002; last updated: September 2002).
—— 2001b, 'Preliminary Audit Review of MIGA in Relation to Compania Minera Antamina SA, Public Report', *CAO Office Report*, Washington, DC, IFC and MIGA, cited at www.cao-ombudsman.org/env (accessed September 2002).
Cortell, A. and Davis Jr., J., 2001, 'Understanding the Domestic Impact of International Norms: A Research Agenda', *International Studies Review* 2 (1): 65–90.
Covey, J., 1998, 'Is Critical Cooperation Possible? Influencing the World Bank through Operational Collaboration and Policy dialogue', in J. Fox, and D. Brown (eds), *The Struggle for Accountability: The World Bank, NGOs and Grassroots Movements*, Cambridge, MA and London, MIT Press: 81–119.
Cowell, A., 1991, *The Decade of Destruction: The Crusade to Save the Amazon Rain Forest*, New York, Anchor Books.
Cox, R.W. and Jacobson, H.K., 1973, *The Anatomy of Influence: Decision Making in International Organisations*, New Haven, Yale University Press.
Crawford, L., 1997, 'Chile Dam Row Shows IFC Problem with Projects', *Financial Times*, 8 August.
Dames and Moore, 1996, 'PTFI Environment Audit Report', 25 March Dames and Moore.

Davis, G., 2004, 'A History of the Social Development Network in the World Bank, 1973–2002', *Social Development Chapters*, no. 56, Washington, DC, World Bank.

Dessler, D., 1989, 'What's at Stake in the Agent-Structure Debate?' *International Organisation* 43 (3): 441–73.

Donnan, S., 2003, 'Mine Admits $5.6m Payment to Indonesian Army', *Financial Times*, 14 March.

Down to Earth, 2001, 'The Multilateral Investment Guarantee Agency (MIGA): Whose Interests are Served and at What Cost?', *Down to Earth Fact Sheet Series* 16, cited at www.dte.gn.apc.org/ (accessed 21 January 2003; last updated: 2002).

Downing, T., 1998, 'A Call for an Independent Evaluation of the Use of Science by the World Bank Group', American Association for the Advancement of Science Committee on Freedom and Scientific Responsibility, Society for Applied Anthropology Newsletter, 9 September.

—— 1996, 'A Participatory Interim Evaluation of the Pehuen Foundation', International Finance Corporation 2067, AGRA Earth and Environment, Downing and Associates.

Durban, A., 1998, 'World Bank's Private Sector Agenda', *Foreign Policy In Focus* 3 (40), cited at www.fpif.org/briefs/vol3/v3n40bank.html (accessed October 2008).

Dysart, B., Murphy, T. and Chayes, A., 2003, 'Beyond Compliance? An External Review Team Report on the Compliance Advisor/Ombudsman Office of IFC/MIGA', prepared for Meg Taylor, IFC/MIGA Compliance Advisor Ombudsman, 24 July 2003, Washington, DC, The World Bank Group.

Einhorn, J., 2006, 'Reforming the World Bank', *Foreign Affairs* 85 (1): 17–22.

—— 2001, 'The World Bank's Mission Creep', *Foreign Affairs* 80 (5): 22–35.

Elliot, L., 1998, *The Global Politics of the Environment*, London, Macmillan.

Elster, J., 1989, *Nuts and Bolts for the Social Sciences*, Cambridge, Cambridge University Press.

Endesa, 1997, 'Pangue Prepays $150 million Loan to the IFC', Endesa Press Release, 11 March.

Environmental Defense, Friends of the Earth, and the International Rivers Fund, 2003, 'Gambling with People's Lives: What the World Bank's New "High Risk/High Reward Strategy" Means for the Poor and the Environment', cited at www.environmentaldefense.org (accessed 2 December 2003; last updated: September 2003).

Epstein, C., 2008, *The Power of Words in International Relations: The*

Birth of an Anti-Whaling Discourse, Cambridge, MA, MIT Press.

Erlich, P., 1968, *The Population Bomb*, New York, Buccaneer Books.

Evans, G., Goodman, J. and Lansbury, N., 2001, 'Politicising Finance', in G. Evans, J. Goodman and N. Lansbury (eds) *Moving Mountains: Communities Confront Mining and Globalisation*, The Protest and Globalisation Research Project, The Mineral Policy Institute and the University of Technology Sydney, Otford Press: 37–57.

Extractive Industries Review, 2003, 'Consultation on the Future Role of the World Bank Group in the Extractive Industries,' cited at www.eireview.org/ (accessed 28 January 2003; last updated: 2003).

Fearon, J., 1998, 'Bargaining, Enforcement, and International Cooperation', *International Organisation* 52 (2): 269–305.

Fidler, S., 2001, 'The Man Who Broke the Bank?' *Foreign Policy*, September/October: 40–50.

Financial Times, 1992, 'The World Bank Must Withdraw Immediately from Sardar Sarovar', 21 September: 6.

—— 1997, 'World Bank Arm Warns Endesa', 21 February: 3.

Finnemore., M., 1996a, *National Interests in International Society*, Ithaca and London, Cornell University Press.

—— 1996b, 'Constructing Norms of Humanitarian Intervention', in P. Katzenstein (ed.), *The Culture of National Security*, New York, Columbia University Press: 153–85.

—— 1996c, 'Norms, Culture and World Politics: Insights from Sociology's Institutionalism', *International Organisation* 50: 325–47.

—— and Sikkink, K., 2001, 'Taking Stock: The Constructivist Research Program in International Relations and Comparative Politics', *Annual Review of Political Science* 4: 391–416.

—— 1998, 'International Norm Dynamics and Political Change', *International Organisation* 52 (4): 887–917.

Fleetwood, S., 2002, 'Boylan and O'Gorman's Causal Holism: A Critical Realist Evaluation', *Cambridge Journal of Economics* 26: 27–45.

Flejzor, L., 2007, 'Explaining Change in the World Bank's Forest Strategy and Operational Policy', in Diane Stone and Chris Wright (eds), *World Bank and Governance: A Decade of Reform and Reaction* (London and New York, Routledge): 88–108.

Flockhart, T., 2006, 'Complex Socialisation: A Framework for the Study of State Socialisation', *European Journal of International Relations* 12 (1): 89–118.

Florini, A., 1996, 'The Evolution of International Norms', *International Studies Quarterly* 40: 363–89.

Fox, J., 2003, 'Introduction: Framing the Inspection Panel', in D. Clark, J. Fox and K. Treakle *Demanding Accountability: Civil-Society Claims and the World Bank Inspection Panel*, Lanham, Rowman and

Littlefield, ix–xi.
—— 2002, 'The World Bank Inspection Panel and the Limits of Accountability', in J.R. Pincus and J.A. Winters (eds), *Reinventing the World Bank*, Ithaca and London, Cornell University Press: 131–63.
—— 2000, 'The World Bank Inspection Panel: Lessons from the First Five Years', *Global Governance* 6 (3): 279–318.
—— and Brown, D.L. (eds), 1998, *The Struggle for Accountability: The World Bank, NGOs and Grassroots Movements*, Cambridge, MA, MIT Press.
Freeport McMoRan Copper and Gold, 2003, 'Historical Overview', cited at www.fcx.com/ (accessed: 10 January 2003; last updated: 2003).
Friends of the Earth, 2001, 'Not in the Public Interest: the World Bank's Environmental Record', cited at www.foe.org/ (accessed 29 January 2001; last updated: 2000).
—— 2000, 'Dubious Development: How the World Bank's Private Arm is Failing the Poor and the Environment', Washington, DC, Friends of the Earth.
—— Urgewald, and Campagna per la Riforma della Banca Mondialle, 2001, 'Risky Business: How the World Bank's Insurance Arm Fails the Poor and Harms the Environment', Washington, DC, Friends of the Earth.
Friends of the Earth International, Amigos de la Tierra Internacional and Grufides 2006, *The CAO in Peru: Lessons Learned from Dialogue as a Strategy to Reduce Conflict*, FOEI, Washington, DC.
Gallarotti, G., 1991, 'The Limits of International Organisation: Systemic Failure in the Management of International Relations', *International Organisation* 45 (2): 183–220.
Garrett, G., 1995, 'The Politics of Legal Integration in the European Union', *International Organisation* 49 (1): 17–182.
George, S. and Sabelli, F., 1994, *Faith and Credit: The World Bank's Secular Empire*, London, Penguin Books.
Giddens, A., 1979, *Central Problems in Social Theory: Action, Structure and Contradiction in Social Theory*, London, Macmillan.
Global Transparency Initiative, 2006, *Assessing World Bank Openness: A Transparency Scorecard*, cited at www.bicusa.org (accessed May 2007; last updated: 2007).
Goldman, M., 2005, *Imperial Nature: The World Bank and Struggles for Social Justice in the Age of Globalization*, Yale, Yale University Press.
Goldstein, J. and Keohane, R., 1993, *Ideas and Foreign Policy: Beliefs, Institutions, and Political Change*, Ithaca, Cornell University Press.
Gould, E., 2003, 'Money Talks: Supplementary Financiers and International Monetary Fund Conditionality', *International*

Organization 57: 551–86.

Gray, A., 1998, 'Development Policy – Development Protest: The World Bank, Indigenous Peoples and NGOs', in Jonathan Fox and David Brown (eds), *The Struggle for Accountability: The World Bank, NGOs and Grassroots Movements*, Cambridge, MA, MIT Press: 267–302.

Green K. and Raphael, A. 2002, *Third Environmental Assessment Review* (1996–2000), The Environment Department, Document 25577, the World Bank, cited at www.worldbank.org/ (accessed 2001; last updated: 2001).

Grigorescu, A., 2002, 'European Institutions and Unsuccessful Norm Transmission: The Case of Transparency', *International Politics* 39: 457–89.

Gruber, L., 2000, *Ruling the World: Power Politics and the Rise of Supranational Institutions,* Princeton, Princeton University Press.

Grupo de Action por el BioBio, 1995, 'The BioBio Dams in Chile: Violations of World Bank Policies and Lack of Accountability at the International Finance Corporation', Claim before the Inspection Panel and Petition before the IFC Board of Executive Directors, Chile, GABB.

Gutner, T., 2005a, 'Explaining the Gaps Between Mandate and Performance: Agency Theory and World Bank Environmental Reform', *Global Environmental Politics* 5 (2): 10–37.

—— 2005b, 'World Bank Environmental Reform: Revisiting Lessons from Agency Theory' *International Organisation* 59: 773–83.

—— 2002, *Banking on the Environment: Multilateral Development Banks and Their Environmental Performance in Central and Eastern Europe*, Cambridge, MA, MIT Press.

Guzzini, S., 2000, 'A Reconstruction of Constructivism in International Relations', *European Journal of International Relations* 6 (2): 147–82.

Gwin, C., 1994, 'US Relations with the World Bank 1945–92', *Brookings Occasional Papers*, Washington. DC, Brookings Institution.

Haas, E., 1990, *When Knowledge is Power: Three Models of Change in International Organisations*, Berkeley, California, University of California Press.

Haas, P., 1992, 'Introduction: Epistemic Communities and International Policy Coordination', *International Organisation* 46 (1): 1–35.

—— and Haas, E., 1995, 'Learning to Learn: Improving International Governance', *Global Governance* 1: 255–85.

—— Keohane, R. and Levy, M. (eds), 1993, *Institutions for the Earth: Sources for Effective International Environmental Protection*,

Cambridge, MA., MIT Press.
Hair, J., 1997, 'Pangue Hydroelectric Project (Chile): An Independent Review of the International Finance Corporation's Compliance with Applicable World Bank Group Environment and Social Requirements', IFC Internal Review, Washington, DC, IFC.
Halifax Initiative, 2006, *One Step Forward, One Step Back: An Analysis of the International Finance Corporation's Sustainability Policy, Performance Standards and Disclosure Policy*, Ottawa, Halifax Initiative.
Hall, A., 2007, 'Social Policies Inside the World Bank: Paradigms and Challenges', *Global Social Policy* 7 (2): 151–75.
Harmon, J., Maurer, C., Sohn, J. and Carbonell, T., 2005, *Diverging Paths: What Future for Export Credit Agencies in Development Finance?*, World Resources Institute, Washington, DC, cited at http://pdf.wri.org/iffe_eca.pdf (accessed October 2008).
Harre, R., 2002, 'Public Sources of the Personal Mind: Social Constructionism in Context', *Theory and Psychology* 12 (5): 611–23.
Hasenclever, A., Mayer, P. and Rittberger, V., 1997, *Theories of International Regimes*, Cambridge, Cambridge University Press.
Haurwitz, R., 1995, 'Freeport Threatens Action over Charges: Company Sends Letters to Those It Says Made "False and Damaging" Accusations against It', *Austin American Statesman*, 14 December: B1.
Hawkins, D., Lake, D., Nielson, D. and Tierney, M., 2006, *Delegation and Agency in International Organisations*, Cambridge, Cambridge University Press.
Herz, S., Genovese, K., Herbertson, K. and Perrault, A., 2008, 'The International Finance Corporations Performance Standards and the Equator Principles: Respecting Human Rights and Remedying Violations?' A submission to the UN Special Representative to the Secretary General on Human Rights and Transnational Corporations and Other Business Enterprises by CIEL, BIC, BankTrack, Oxfam Australia and the World Resources Institute, cited at www.ciel.org (accessed October 2008).
Higgott, R., Underhill, G. and Bieler, A., 2000, *Non-State Actors and Authority in the Global System*, London, Routledge.
Hobson, J.M., 2000, *The State and International Relations*, Cambridge, Cambridge University Press.
Holder, J., 2004, *Environmental Assessment: The Regulation of Decision Making*, Oxford, Oxford University Press.
Hollis, M. and Smith, S., 1991, 'Beware of Gurus: Structure and Action in International Relations', *Review of International Studies* 17: 393–410.

Hug, S., 2003, 'Endogenous Preference and Delegation in the European Union', *Comparative Politics Studies* 36 (1/2): 41–74.

Hunter, D., 2008, 'Civil Society Networks and the Development of Environmental Standards at International Financial Institutions', *Chicago Journal of International Law* 8 (2): 437–77.

—— 1994, 'The World Bank's New Inspection Panel', *Environment* 36 (9): 2–6.

Hurd, I., 1999, 'Legitimacy and Authority in International Politics', *International Organisation* 53 (2): 379–408.

Ikenberry, J. and Kupchan, C., 1990, 'Socialisation and Hegemonic Power', *International Organisation* 44 (3): 283–315.

International Finance Corporation, 2008, *IFC Annual Report 2008*, Washington, DC, IFC.

—— 2007a, *IFC Annual Report 2007*, Washington DC, IFC.

—— 2007b, 'IFC's Policy and Performance Standards on Social and Environmental Sustainability and Disclosure Policy: Progress Report on the First 18 Months of Application', December, IFC, cited at www.ifc.org (accessed October 2008).

—— 2006a, 'Strategic Directions Implementation Update and FY 07–09 Outlook', Report to the Board of Directors, IFC, 11 April, cited at www.ifc.org (accessed 1 November 2006).

—— 2006b, *Sustainability Report 2005*, Washington, DC, IFC.

—— 2006c, 'International Finance Corporation's Performance Standards on Environmental and Social Sustainability', IFC, 30 April, 2006 cited at www.ifc.org (accessed November 2006).

—— 2006d, 'International Finance Corporation's Policy on Disclosure of Information', IFC, 30 April, cited at www.ifc.org (accessed November 2006).

—— 2006e, *Lessons of Experience: External Monitoring of the Chad/Cameroon Pipeline Project*, No. 1, Environment and Social Development Department, Washington, DC, IFC.

—— 2006f, *Lessons of Experience: The Baku-Tbilisi-Ceyhan Pipeline Project*, No. 2, Environment and Social Development, Department. Washington, DC, IFC.

—— 2006g, 'Disclosure Policy of IEG-IFC's Products', 30 April, IFC, Independent Evaluation Group – IFC, cited at www.ifc.org (accessed November 2006).

—— 2005a, *IFC Annual Report 2005*, Washington, DC, IFC.

—— 2005b, *Lessons Learned: Pangue Hydroelectric Summary*, Environment and Social Development Department, Washington DC, IFC.

—— 2005c, *Sustainability Report 2004*, Washington, DC, IFC.

—— 2003, *IFC Annual Report 2003*, Washington, DC, IFC.

—— 2002a, *IFC Annual Report 2002*, Washington, DC, IFC.
—— 2002b, 'The Environmental and Social Challenges of Private Sector Projects: IFC's Experience', *Lessons of Experience Series* 8, Washington, DC, IFC.
—— 2002c, 'Annual Review of IFC's Evaluation Findings: FY 2001', *OEG Findings*, Washington, DC, IFC, Operations Evaluation Group.
—— 2001a, 'Building a Sustainable Development Roadmap: IFC's Strategy to Ensure Environmental and Social Responsibility', *Environment Matters*, IFC Annual Newsletter: 48–51.
—— 2001b, *IFC Annual Report 2001*, Washington, DC, IFC.
—— 2001c, IFC, *Strategic Directions Report*, Washington, DC, IFC.
—— 2000, 'Environment and Social Safeguard Policies', cited at www.ifc.org/about/ (accessed November 2000).
—— 1999, *IFC Annual Report 1999*, Washington, DC, IFC.
—— 1998a, *IFC Annual Report 1998*, Washington, DC, S&S Graphics, IFC.
—— 1998b, 'Policy on Disclosure of Information', IFC, cited at www.ifc.org (accessed September 1998; last updated: 1998).
—— 1997a, 'Pangue Prepays IFC', IFC Press Release No. 97/82.
—— 1997b, 'Agreement between IFC and Pangue SA', IFC Press Release No. 97/95.
—— 1997c, 'Statement of IFC about the report by Dr. Jay Hair on the Pangue Hydroelectric Project', Press Release dated 15 July, cited at www.ifc.org/press/1997/HAIR-E.HTM (accessed: 2 April 1999; last updated: 1999).
—— 1992, 'IFC Board Approves Pangue Dam', IFC Press Release No. 92/32.
International Financial Advisory Commission, 2000, 'Report of the International Financial Advisory Commission', United States Congress, cited: at www.house.gov/jec/imf/meltzer.pdf (accessed 15 January 2003).
International NGO Forum on Indonesian Development, 1996, 'INFID Statement on Freeport McMoRan Mining Operations on Irian Jaya', Tenth INFID Conference 26–28 April, Canberra, Australia.
International Organisation, Special Edition on the International Diffusion of Liberalism, 2006, 60 (4).
—— Special Edition on the Internationalization of Europe, 2005, 59 (4).
International Rivers Network, 2004, 'The World Bank Safeguard Policies Under Pressure', International Rivers Network, cited at www.irn.org (accessed October 2008).
—— 1998a, 'Anthropologists Slam World Bank for Indigenous Rights Abuses in Chile', International Rivers Network Press Release, Thursday, 2 April 1998, cited at www.irn.org (accessed September

1998; last updated: July 1998).

—— 1998b, 'Bio Bio Project Fact Sheet,' Cited at www.irn.org (accessed September 1998; last updated: September 1998).

—— 1997a, 'Chilean Dam Builders Slip Through the Noose: Endesa Pays Off World Bank to Avoid Loan Conditions', *World Rivers Review* 12 (2), April 1997, cited at www.irn.org (accessed September 1998; last updated: 2001).

—— 1997b, 'Independent Review Blasts World Bank over Chilean Dam Project', International Rivers Network Press Release, Wednesday, 30 July 1997, cited at www.irn.org (accessed September 1998; last updated: July 1998).

—— 1995, 'Insurance Cancelled for US Mining Operation: OPIC Cites Damage to Rivers as Prime Reason', *World Rivers Review* 10 (3), cited at www.irn.org (accessed September 1998; last updated: July 1998).

Jacobson, H.K., 1984, *Networks of Interdependence: International Organisations and the Global Political System*, 2nd Edition, New York, Alfred A. Knopf.

Jepperson, R.L., Wendt, A. and Katzenstein, P., 1996, 'Norms, Identity, and Culture in National Security', in P. Katzenstein (ed.), *The Culture of National Security: Norms and Identity in World Politics*, New York, Columbia University Press: 33–75.

Jervis, R., 1999, 'Realism, Neoliberalism, and Cooperation', *International Security* 24 (1): 42–63.

Johnston, A., 2001, 'Treating International Institutions as Social Environments', *International Studies Quarterly* 45: 487–515.

Johnston, B., and Turner, T., 1998, 'The Pehuenche, the World Bank Group and Endesa SA: Violations of Human Rights in the Pangue and Ralco Dam Projects on the Bio Bio River in Chile', Report of the Committee for Human Rights, American Anthropological Association.

Journal of Commerce, 1996, 'Freeport-McMoRan drops OPIC: Six Months after Winning the Coverage War, Company Declines Renewal of Risk Insurance', 18 December: 5A.

Kapur, D., 2002, 'The Changing Anatomy of Governance at the World Bank', in J.R. Pincus and J.A. Winters (eds), *Reinventing the World Bank*, Ithaca and London, Cornell University Press: 54–75.

Katzenstein, P., 1996, *Cultural Norms and National Security: Police and Military in Postwar Japan*, Ithaca, Cornell University Press.

—— Keohane, R. and Krasner, S., 1999, 'International Organisation and the Study of World Politics', in P. Katzenstein, R. Keohane and S. Krasner (eds), *Exploration and Contestation of World Politics*, Cambridge and London, MIT Press: 303–30.

Kay, D. and Jacobson, H., 1983, *Environmental Protection: the International Dimension*, Totowa, NJ, Allanheld, Osman and Co.

Keck, M., 1998, 'Planoflora in Rondonia: The Limits of Leverage', in J. Fox and D. Brown (eds), *The Struggle for Accountability: The World Bank, NGOs and Grassroots Movements*, Cambridge, MA,. MIT Press: 181–217.

—— and Sikkink, K., 1998, *Activists Beyond Borders: Advocacy Networks in International Politics*, Ithaca and London, Cornell University Press.

Kelley, J., 2004, 'International Actors on the Domestic Scene: Membership Conditionality and Socialisation by International Institutions', *International Organisation* 58: 425–57.

Kent, A., 2002, 'China's International Socialisation: The Role of International Organisations', *Global Governance* 8: 343–64.

Keohane, R., 1993, 'Institutional Theory and the Realist Challenge after the Cold War', in D.A. Baldwin (ed.), *Neorealism and Neoliberalism: The Contemporary Debate*, New York, Columbia University Press: 269–300.

—— 1984, *After Hegemony: Cooperation and Discord in the World Political Economy*, Princeton, NJ, Princeton University Press.

Khagram, S., 2004, *Dams and Development: Transnational Struggles for Water and Power*, Ithaca, Cornell University Press.

Kiewiet, D.R. and McCubbins, M., 1991, *The Logic of Delegation: Congressional Parties and the Appropriations Process*, Chicago and London, The University of Chicago Press.

Kingsbury, B., 1999, 'Operational Policies of International Institutions as Part of the Law-Making Process: The World Bank and Indigenous Peoples', in G. Goodwin-Gill and S. Talmon (eds), *The Reality of International Law: Essays in Honour of Ian Brownlie*, Oxford, Clarendon Press.

Klotz, A., 1995, *Norms in International Relations: Struggles Against Apartheid*, Ithaca, Cornell University Press.

Kohn, D., 2002, 'Setting a Standard: Environmental Impact Assessment Policies of Multilateral Development Banks and Export Credit Agencies', *Environmental Law* 9: 281–306.

Kolk, A., 1996, *Forests in International Environmental Politics: International Organizations, NGOs and the Brazilian Amazon*, The Netherlands, International Books.

Koremenos, B., Lipson, C. and Snidal, D., 2004, *The Rational Design of International Institutions*, Cambridge, Cambridge University Press.

Koslowski, R. and Kratochwil, F., 1994, 'Understanding Change in International Politics: The Soviet Empire's Demise and the International System', *International Organisation* 48 (2): 215–47.

Kraske, J., 1991, *Bankers with a Mission*, World Bank, Washington, DC, Oxford University Press.
Krasner, S. (ed.), 1983, *International Regimes*, Ithaca and London, Cornell University Press.
Kratochwil, F., 2000, 'Constructing a New Orthodoxy? Wendt's "Social Theory of International Politics" and the Constructivist Challenge', *Millennium* 29 (1): 73–101.
—— 1994, 'Preface', in F. Kratochwil and E. Mansfield (eds), *International Organisation: A Reader*, New York, Harper Collins College Publishers: ix–xiv.
—— 1989, *Rules, Norms and Decisions: On the Conditions of Practical and Legal Reasoning in International Relations and Domestic Affairs*, Cambridge, Cambridge University Press.
—— and Ruggie, J.G., 1986, 'International Organisations: A State of the Art on the Art of the State', *International Organisation* 40 (4): 753–76.
Lawrence, S., 2005a, 'Marching Backwards into the Future', *Environmental Finance*, 10 (November): 13.
—— 2005b, *Retreat from the Safeguard Policies: Recent Trends Undermining Social and Environmental Accountability at the World Bank*, Washington, DC, Environmental Defense.
—— 2005c, *Comparison Matrix of the Management Response to the Extractive Industries Review and the September 2005 Draft IFC Policy and Performance Standards,* Washington, DC, Environmental Defense.
Le Prestre, P., 1989, *The World Bank and the Environmental Challenge*, Selinsgrove, Susquehana University Press; London, Associated University Presses.
—— 1982, *The Ecology of the World Bank: Uncertainty Management and Environmental Policy*, PhD Dissertation, Indiana University, Microfilms.
Lee, C., 2001, 'International Finance Corporation: Financing Environmentally and Socially Sustainable Private Investment', in S. Schlemmer-Schulte and K.Y. Tung (eds), *Liber Amoricum Ibrahim F.I. Shihata: International Finance Development Law*, Kluwer Law International, The Hague and London: 469–81.
Legro, J., 1997, 'Which Norms Matter? Revisiting the "Failure" of Internationalism', *International Organisation* 51 (1): 31–63.
Leiteritz, R., 2005, 'Explaining Organisational Outcomes: The International Monetary Fund and Capital Account Liberalisation', *Journal of International Relations and Development* 8: 1–26.
Leith, D., 2003, *The Politics of Power: Freeport in Suharto's Indonesia*, Honolulu, University of Hawaii Press.

—— 2000, *The Politics of Power: Freeport in Suharto's Indonesia*, PhD Dissertation, University of Macquarie, Sydney.

Lerrick, A., 2006, 'Is the World Bank's Word Good Enough?' Statement presented to the Committee on Foreign Relations of the United States Senate, 28 March, cited at http://foreign.senate.gov/ (accessed September 2008).

Lewis, J., 2003, 'Institutional Environments and Everyday EU Decision Making: Rationalist or Constructivist?', *Comparative Political Studies* 36 (1/2): 97–124.

Leys, C., 1996, *The Rise and Fall of Development Theory*, London and Bloomington, Indiana, James Currey and Indiana University Press.

Liebenthal, A., 2002, *Promoting Environmental Sustainability in Development: An Evaluation of the World Bank's Performance*, Operations Evaluation Department, Washington, DC, World Bank.

—— Michelitsch, R. and Tarazona, E., 2005, *Extractive Industries and Sustainable Development: An Evaluation of World Bank Group Experience*, Operations Evaluation Department, Operations Evaluation Group and the Operations Evaluation Unit, Washington, DC, World Bank and IFC.

Linden, R. (ed.), 2002, *Norms and Nannies: The Impact of International Organisations on the Central and East European States*, Lanham, MD, Roman and Littlefield.

Lipshutz, R., 1996, *Global Civil Society and Global Environmental Governance: The Politics of Nature from Place to Planet*, Albany, State University of New York Press.

Lipson, C., 1993, 'International Cooperation in Economic and Security Affairs', in D.A. Baldwin (ed.), *Neorealism and Neoliberalism: The Contemporary Debate*, New York, Columbia University Press: 60–84.

Lupia, A. and McCubbins, M., 1994, 'Learning from Oversight: Fire Alarms and Police Patrols Reconstructed', *Journal of Law, Economics and Organisation* 10 (1): 96–125.

Maddux, J., 1981, *The Development Philosophy of Robert S. McNamara*, Washington, DC, World Bank.

Malik, M., 1995, 'Do We Need a New Theory of International Organisations?', in R.V. Bartlett, P.A. Kurian and M. Malik (eds), *International Organisations and Environmental Policy*, Westport, Connecticut, Greenwood Press: 223–39.

Mallaby, S., 2004, *The World's Banker: A Story of Failed States, Financial Crises and the Wealth and Poverty of Nations*, New York, Penguin.

Marcussen, H., 1996, 'NGOs, the State and Civil Society', *Review of African Political Economy* 69: 405–23.

Marschinski, R. and Behrle, S., 2007, 'The World Bank: Making the Business Case for Environment', Global Governance Working Paper No. 21, cited at www.glogov.org (accessed September 2008).

Marsh, D. and Sharman, J., 2007, 'Policy Diffusion and Policy Transfer', unpublished paper, on file with author.

Martin, L. and Simmons, B., 1999, 'Theories and Empirical Studies of International Institutions', in P. Katzenstein, R. Keohane and S. Krasner (eds), *Exploration and Contestation of World Politics*, Cambridge and London, MIT Press: 89–119.

Marwick, S., 1998, 'Trends in Political Risk for Corporate Investors', in T. Moran (ed.), *Managing International Political Risk*, Blackwell, MA: 44–56.

Mason, E.S. and Asher, R.E., 1973, *The World Bank Since Bretton Woods*, Washington, DC, The Brookings Institution.

Matecki, B.E., 1957, *Establishment of the International Finance Corporation and United States Policy: A Case Study of International Organisation*, London, Thames and Hudson.

Mattli, W. and Slaughter, A., 1998, 'Revisiting the European Court of Justice', *International Organisation* 52 (1): 177–203.

McCubbins, M., and T. Schwartz, 1984, 'Congressional Oversight Overlooked: Police Patrols Versus Fire Alarms', *American Journal of Political Science* 28: 165–79.

—— R. Noll and B. Weingast, 1989, 'Structure and Process, Politics and Policy: Administrative Arrangements and the Political Control of Agencies', *Virginia Law Review* 75 (2): 431–82.

—— —— —— 1987, 'Administrative Procedures as Instruments of Political Control', *Journal of Law, Economics and Organisation* 3: 243–77.

McCully, P., 2001, *Silenced Rivers: The Ecology and Politics of Large Dams*, 2nd Edition, London and New York, Zed Books.

Meadows, D. *et al.*, 1972, *The Limits to Growth*, Report for the Club of Rome, New York, Universe Books.

Mearsheimer, J., 1994/5, 'The False Promise of International Institutions', *International Security* 19 (3): 5–49.

Mercer, J., 1995, 'Anarchy and Identity', *International Organization* 49 (2): 229–52.

Meron, T., 1976, *Investment Insurance in International Law*, New York and Leiden, Oceana Publications and A.W Sijthoff.

Meyer, J., Boli, J., Thomas, G. and Ramirez, F., 1997, 'World Society and the Nation-State', *The American Journal of Sociology* 103 (1): 144–82.

Miller, G., 2005, 'The Political Evolution of Principal-Agent Models' *Annual Review of Political Science* 8: 203–25.

Miller-Adams, M., 1999, *The World Bank: New Agendas in a Changing World*, London, Routledge.

Mining Journal, 1995, 'Truth Travels Badly', 22–29 December: 483.

Mohammed, A., 2005, 'Who Pays for the World Bank?', in A. Buira, (ed.), *The IMF and the World Bank at Sixty*, London, Anthem Press: 181–98.

Momani, B., 2005, 'Limits on Streamlining Fund Conditionality: The International Monetary Fund's Organizational Culture', *Journal of International Relations and Development* 8: 142–63.

Moran, T., 1998, 'Political Risk Insurance as a Tool to Manage International Political Risk', in T. Moran (ed.), *Managing International Political Risk*, Blackwell, MA: 139–47.

Morgera, E., 2007, 'Significant Trends in Corporate Environmental Accountability: The New Performance Standards of the International Finance Corporation', *Colombia Journal of International Environmental Law and Policy* 18 (1): 151–88.

Morse, B. and Berger, S., 1992, *The Independent Review of the Sardar Sarovar Projects*, Ottawa, Resource Futures International.

Multilateral Investment Guarantee Agency, 2008a, *Annual Report 2008*, Washington, DC, MIGA, cited at www.miga.org/ (accessed October 2008).

—— 2008b, 'Izumi Koyabashi Appointed to Head MIGA', *MIGA Press Release* 2008/126, cited at www.miga.org/ (accessed October 2008).

—— 2008c, *IEG MIGA Annual Report 2008*, MIGA, Independent Evaluation Group, Washington, DC, cited at www.miga.org/ (accessed October 2008).

—— 2007a, *Annual Report 2007*, Washington, DC, MIGA, cited at www.miga.org/ (accessed October 2008).

—— 2007b, 'Policy of Social and Environmental Sustainability', cited at www.miga.org/ (accessed October 2008).

—— 2007c, 'Policy on Disclosure of Information', cited at www.miga.org/ (accessed October 2008).

—— 2007d, 'New Disclosure and Safeguard Policies to Take Effect October 1, 2007', *miganews* no. 10, July/August, cited at www .miga.org/documents/miganews/issue4_07.htm (accessed: October 2008).

—— 2007e, 'MIGA to Engage Stakeholders in Review of New Safeguard and Disclosure Policies', *miganews* no. 10, January/February, cited at www.miga.org/documents/miganews (accessed October 2008).

—— 2007f, *Independent Evaluation Group MIGA 2007 Annual Report*, MIGA, Independent Evaluation Group, cited at www.miga.org/ (accessed October 2008).

—— 2006, *Independent Evaluation Group (MIGA) Annual Report*

2006, MIGA, Independent Evaluation Group, cited at www.miga.org/ (accessed October 2008).

—— 2005, *Operations Evaluation Unit 2005 Annual Report*, Washington, DC, MIGA, Operations Evaluation Unit, cited at www.miga.org/ (accessed October 2008).

—— 2004, *2004 Review of Development Effectiveness in MIGA*, Washington, DC, MIGA, Operations Evaluation Unit, cited at www.miga.org/ (accessed October 2008).

—— 2003a, *2003 Report on Operations Evaluation in MIGA*, Washington, DC, MIGA, Operations Evaluation Unit, cited at www.miga.org/ (accessed October 2008).

—— 2003b, *Extractive industries and Sustainable Development – MIGA's Experience* MIGA, Operations Evaluation Unit, cited at www.miga.org/ (accessed December 2003).

—— 2002, *MIGA's Interim Issue-Specific Safeguard Policies*, cited at www.miga.org/ (accessed November 2002; last updated: 2002).

—— 2001a, 'MIGA: The First Ten Years', cited at www.miga.org/ (accessed June 2001; last updated: 2001).

—— 2001b, 'Commentary on the Convention Establishing the Multilateral Investment Guarantee Agency', cited at www.miga.org/ (accessed May 2001; last updated: 2001).

—— 2001c, 'MIGA to Follow Multi-Niche Path', *MIGA News and Events*, September 28 2000, Washington, DC, cited at www.miga.org/ (accessed May 2001; last updated: 2001).

—— 2000, 'MIGA 2000 Review, In Accordance with Article 67 of the MIGA Convention', Revised November 3 for Publication, MIGA, Washington, DC.

—— 1999, 'MIGA Environmental Assessment Policy, Disclosure Policy and Environmental and Social Review procedures', Approved by the Board of Directors May 1999 for Implementation 1 July 1999, MIGA, Washington, DC.

Naim, M., 2000, 'Washington Consensus or Washington Confusion?' *Foreign Policy* 118: 87–103.

Nash, N., 1992, 'On a Remote Chilean River, Fight Over Dam', *New York Times*, 10 February: 8.

Nelson, P., 2001, 'Transparency Mechanisms at the Multilateral Development Banks', *World Development* 29 (11): 1835–47.

—— 1997, 'Deliberation, Leverage or Coercion? The World Bank, NGOs and Global Environmental Politics', *Journal of Peace Research* 34 (4): 467–72.

—— 1996, 'Internationalizing Economic and Environmental Policy: Transnational NGO Networks and the World Bank's Expanding Influence', *Millennium* 25 (3): 605–33.

—— 1995, *The World Bank and Non-Governmental Organisations*, UK, Macmillan.

New York Times, 1992, 'Why Thousands of People will Drown Before Accepting the Sardar Sarovar Dam', 21 September: B10.

New Zealand Press Association, 2006, 'Rights Committee to Examine Papua Torture Allegations', 10 October.

Nielson, D. and Tierney, M., 2005, 'Theory, Data and Hypothesis Testing: World Bank Environmental Reform Redux', *International Organisation* 59: 785–800.

—— 2003, 'Delegation to International Organisations: Agency Theory and World Bank Environmental Reform', *International Organisation* 57 (2): 241–76.

—— —— and Weaver, C., 2006, 'Bridging the Rationalist-Constructivist Divide: Re-engineering the Culture at the World Bank', *Journal of International Relations and Development.*

Niskanen, W., 1971, *Bureaucracy and Representative Government*, Chicago and New York; Aldine, Atherton.

O'Brien, R., Goetz, A.M., Aart Scholte, J. and Williams, M., 2000, *Contesting Global Governance: Multilateral Institutions and Global Social Movements*, Cambridge, Cambridge University Press.

OECD, 2008, 'Financing Development 2008: Whose Ownership?', OECD Development Centre, cited at www.oecd.org/dev/publications /finance/2008 (accessed 30 October 2008).

—— 2007a, 'Total Net ODA Dataset', *OECD Statistics*, cited at http://stats.oecd.org/wbos/default.aspx?DatasetCode=REF_TOTALO DA (accessed 8 February 2007).

—— 2007b, 'Revised Council Recommendation on Common Approaches on the Environment and Officially Supported Export Credits', Working Party on Export Credits and Export Guarantees, OECD. Document TAD/ECG(2007)9, cited at www.olis.oecd .org/olis/2007doc.nsf/LinkTo/NT00002B8E/$FILE/JT03228987.PDF (accessed October 2008).

Overseas Private Investment Corporation, 'OPIC Environmental Handbook – February 2004', cited at www.opic.gov/ (accessed October 2004).

—— 1999, 'OPIC Environmental Handbook – April 1999' cited at www.opic.gov/ (accessed January 2003).

Paarlberg, R., 1993, 'Managing Pesticide Use in Developing Countries', in R. Keohane, P. Haas and M. Levy (eds), *Institutions for the Earth*, Cambridge, MA, MIT Press: 309–50.

Park, S., 2007a, 'World Bank Group: Championing Sustainable Development?', *Global Governance* 13 (4): 461–8.

______ 2007b, 'Becoming Green: Diffusing Sustainable Development

Norms throughout the World Bank Group', in D. Stone and C. Wright (eds), *The World Bank and Governance: A Decade of Reform and Reaction*, London, Routledge: 168–88.

—— 2006, 'Theorising Norm Diffusion within International Organisations', *International Politics* 43 (3): 342–61.

Paul, S. and Israel, A., 1991, *Nongovernmental Organisations and the World Bank: Cooperation for Development*, Washington, DC, The World Bank.

Payne, R., 1997, 'A Response to Nelson on "Deliberation, Leverage and Coercion"?', *Journal of Peace Research* 34 (4): 470–3.

—— 1996, 'Deliberating on Global Environmental Politics', *Journal of Peace Research* 33 (2): 129–36.

Perlez, J. and Bonner, R., 2005, 'Below a Mountain of Wealth, A River of Waste', *New York Times*, 27 December.

Piddington, K., 1992, 'The Role of the World Bank', in A. Hurrell, and B. Kingsbury (eds), *The International Politics of the Environment: Actors, Interests, and Institutions*, Oxford, Clarendon Press: 212–27.

Pincus, J.R. and Winters, J.A., 2002, 'Reinventing the World Bank', in J.R. Pincus and J.A. Winters (eds), *Reinventing the World Bank*, Ithaca and London, Cornell University Press: 1–25.

Pollack, M.A., 1997, 'Delegation, Agency and Agenda Setting in the European Community', *International Organisation* 51 (1): 99–134.

Porter, G. and Welsh Brown, J., 1996, *Global Environmental Politics*, 2nd Edition, Boulder, Westview Press.

Price, R., 1998, 'Reversing the Gun Cites: Transnational Civil Society Targets Land Mines', *International Organisation* 52 (3): 613–32.

—— 1997, *The Chemical Weapons Taboo*, Ithaca and London, Cornell University Press.

—— and Reus-Smit, C., 1998, 'Dangerous Liaisons? Critical International Theory and Constructivism', *European Journal of International Relations* 4 (3): 259–94.

Princen, T. and Finger, M., 1994, *Environmental NGOs in World Politics: Linking the Local and the Global*, London and New York, Routledge.

ProjectUnderground, 1998, 'Risky Business: The Grasberg Gold Mine', An Independent Annual Report on PT Freeport Indonesia, cited at www.moles.org/ProjectUnderground (accessed 11 January 2003; last updated: 1997).

—— 1996, 'Freeport Cancels World Bank Insurance: Lawyer and Activist Harassed as New Orleans Lawsuit Proceeds', *Drillbits and Tailings*, 9 September, cited at www.moles.org/ProjectUnderground /drillbits (accessed 14 January 2003; last updated: 1997).

Ratner, S.R., 2000, 'Does International Law Matter in Preventing Ethnic

Conflict?', *Journal of International Law and Politics* 32: 591–698.
Reed, D., 1997, 'The Environmental Legacy of Bretton Woods: The World Bank', in O. Young (ed.), *Global Governance: Drawing Insights from the Environmental Experience*, Massachusetts, MIT Press: 227–45.
Reinalda, B. and Verbeek, B. (eds.), 1998, *Autonomous Policy Making by International Organisations*, London and New York, Routledge.
Reus-Smit, C., 1996, 'The Constructivist Turn: Critical Theory After the Cold War', *Department of International Relations Working Paper 1996/4,* Canberra, The Australian National University.
Revkin, A., 1990, *The Burning Season: The Murder of Chico Mendes and the Fight for the Amazon Rain Forest*, Boston, Houghton Miffler.
Reynolds, A., 2000, 'Tibetan Takeover', *The Ecologist* 30 (6): 20–2.
Rich, B., 2002, 'The World Bank under James Wolfensohn', in J.R. Pinous and J.A. Winters (eds), *Reinventing the World Bank*, Ithaca, NY, Cornell University Press: 26–53.
—— 1995a, 'Statement of Bruce Rich on behalf of Environmental Defense Fund, National Wildlife Federation, Sierra Club, Greenpeace, before The United States Congress House Committee on Banking and Financial Services Subcommittee on Domestic and International Monetary Policy Concerning the World Bank', 27 March, Washington, DC, Environmental Defense Fund.
—— 1995b, 'The Emperor's New Clothes: The World Bank and Environmental Reform', in K. Conca, M. Alberty and G. Dabelko (eds), *Green Planet Blues*, University of Maryland, Westview Press: 188–98.
—— 1994, *Mortgaging the Earth: The World Bank, Environmental Impoverishment and the Crisis of Development*, Boston, Beacon Press.
—— 1989, 'The "Greening" of the Development Banks: Rhetoric and Reality', *The Ecologist* 19 (2): 1–9.
Riggirozzi, P., 2006, 'The World Bank as Conveyer and Broker of Knowledge and Funds in Argentina's Governance Reforms', in D. Stone and C. Wright (eds), *The World Bank and Governance: A Decade of Reform and Reaction,* New York, Routledge: 207–27.
Risse, T., 2000, '"Let's Argue!" Communicative Action in World Politics', *International Organisation* 54 (1): 1–39.
—— Ropp, S. and Sikkink, K. (eds), 1999, *The Power of Human Rights: International Norms and Domestic Change*, Cambridge, Cambridge University Press.
Robinson, S., 1998, 'Comment From Dr. Scott Robinson, IFC Consultant in the Planning Stage of the Pangue Project', American Anthropological Association, cited at http://ameranthassn.org /pehuenc2.htm (accessed September 1998; last updated: 1998).

Rodrigues, M.G., 2004, *Global Environmetalism and Local Politics: Transitional Advocacy Networks in Brazil, Ecuador and India*, New York, State University of New York Press.

—— 2000, 'Environmental Protection Issue Networks in Amazonia', *Latin American Research Review* 35 (3): 125–53.

Ruggie, J., 1998, 'What Makes the World Hang Together? Neo-utilitarianism and the Social Constructivist Challenge', *International Organisation* 52 (4): 855–85.

—— 1993, 'The Anatomy of an Institution', in H. Milner and J. Ruggie (eds), *Multilateralism Matters: The Theory and Praxis of an Institutional Form*, New York, Columbia University Press: 3–50.

—— 1986, 'Continuity and Transformation in the World Polity: Toward a Neorealist Synthesis', in R.O. Keohane (ed.), *Neorealism and Its Critics*, New York, Columbia University Press: 131–57.

Schein, E., 2004, *Organisational Culture and Leadership*, 3rd Edition, San Francisco, Jossey-Bass.

Schimmelfennig, F., 2005, 'Strategic Calculation and International Socialisation: Membership Incentives, Party Constellations, and Sustained Compliance in Central and Eastern Europe', *International Organisation* 59 (4): 827–60.

—— 2003, *Rules and Rhetoric: The EU, NATO and the Integration of Europe*, Cambridge, Cambridge University Press.

—— 2001, 'The Community Trap: Liberal Norms, Rhetorical Action, and the Eastern Enlargement of the European Union', *International Organisation* 55 (1): 47–80.

—— 2000, 'International Socialisation in the New Europe: Rational Action in an Institutional Environment', *European Journal of International Relations* 6 (1): 109–39.

Scholte, J.A. and Schnabel A., 2002, *Global Civil Society and Global Finance*, London, Routledge.

Schweller, R, and Priess, D., 1997, 'A Tale of Two Realisms: Expanding the Institutions Debate', *Mershon International Studies Review* 41: 1–32.

Searle, J., 1995, *The Construction of Social Reality*, New York, Free Press.

Seymour, F., 2006, 'Sustaining the Environment at the World Bank', World Resources Institute Policy Note, cited at www.wri.org (accessed 31 October 2006).

—— 2004, 'Mainstreaming and Infrastructure', *Environment Matters*, cited at www.worldbank.org/ (accessed 19 May 2006).

Shihata, I., 1995, *The World Bank in a Changing World: Selected Essays and Lectures*, Volume II, The Hague, London and Boston, Martinus Nijoff Publishers.

—— 1994, *The World Bank Inspection Panel*, Washington, DC, World Bank and Oxford University Press.

—— 1991, *The World Bank in a Changing World: Selected Essays*, Dordrecht, Boston and London, Martinus Nijhoff Publishers.

—— 1988, *MIGA and Foreign Investment: Origins, Operations, Policies and Basic Documents of the Multilateral Investment Guarantee Agency*, The Netherlands, Martinus Nijhoff Publishers.

Smith, S., 2000a, 'The Discipline of International Relations: Still an American Social Science', *British Journal of Politics and International Relations* 2 (3): 374–402.

—— 2000b, 'Wendt's World', *Review of International Studies* 26: 151–63.

Stein, R. and Johnson, B., 1979, *Banking on the Biosphere? Environmental Procedures and Practices of Nine Multilateral Development Agencies*, Massachusetts and Toronto, Lexington Books.

Stephens, M., 1998, 'A Perspective on Political Risk Insurance', in T. Moran (ed.) *Managing International Political Risk*, Blackwell, MA: 148–58.

Stevastopulo, D., 2003, 'Four Banks Adopt IFC Agreement', *Financial Times*, 7 April, cited at www.equatorprinciples.ifc.org (accessed 13 November 2003; last updated: 2003).

Stone, D., 2003, 'The "Knowledge Bank" and the Global Development Network', *Global Governance* 9: 43–61.

Streeck, W. and Thelen, K. (eds), 2005, *Beyond Continuity: Institutional Change in Advanced Political Economies*, Oxford, Oxford University Press.

Suganami, H., 2002, 'On Wendt's Philosophy: A Critique', *Review of International Studies* 28: 23–37.

Suzuki, E. and Nanwani, S., 2006, 'Responsibility of International Organisations: The Accountability Mechanisms of Multilateral Development Banks', *Michigan Journal of International Law* 27: 177–255.

Tallberg, J., 2000, 'The Anatomy of Autonomy: An Institutional Account of Variation in Supranational Influence', *Journal of Common Market Studies* 38 (5): 843–64.

Tarrow, S., 2001, 'Transnational Politics: Contention and Institutions in International Politics', *Annual Review of Political Science* 4: 1–20.

Thies, C., 2003, 'Sense and Sensibility in the Study of State Socialisation: A Reply to Kai Alderson', *Review of International Studies* 29: 543–50.

Thompson, A., 2006, 'Coercion through IOs: The Security Council and the Logic of Information Transmission', *International Organization* 60 (1): 1–34.

Toye, J. and Toye, R., 2005, 'The World Bank as a Knowledge Agency', Overarching Concerns Program Paper 11, UNRISD.

Treakle, K., Fox, J. and Clark, D., 2003, 'Lessons Learned', in D. Clark, J. Fox and K. Treakle (eds), *Demanding Accountability: Civil-Society Claims and the World Bank Inspection Panel*, Lanham, Rowman and Littlefield: 247–79.

True, J. and Mintrom, M., 2001, 'Transnational Networks and Policy Diffusion: The Case of Gender Mainstreaming', *International Studies Quarterly* 45: 27–57.

Udall, L., 1997, *The World Bank Inspection Panel: A Three Year Review*, Washington, DC, Bank Information Center.

—— 1995, 'Arun III Hydroelectric Project in Nepal: Another World Bank Debacle?', International Rivers Network, cited at www.hartford-hwp.com/archives/52/054.html (accessed 7 August 2001; last updated: 2001).

Umana, A., 1998, *The World Bank's Inspection Panel, 1994–1998*, Washington, DC, The World Bank.

UNCTAD, 2007, *World Investment Report 2007: Transnational Corporations, Extractive Industries and Development*, New York and Geneva, United Nations.

United Press International, 1995, 'OPIC Cancels Freeport Contract', 2 November, Washington DC, n.p.

United States Treasury, 2008, 'U.S. Position on Evaluation of the Initial Phase of the Pilot Program for Use of Country Systems for Environmental and Social Safeguards: Lessons Learned and Management Proposal for an Incremental Scale-Up of the Program, January 31', cited at www.treasury.gov/offices/international-affairs/multilateral_banks/operational_policies.shtml (accessed September 2008; last updated: March 2008).

—— 2006, 'The World Bank Group', US Treasury Office of Public Affairs, cited at www.treas.gov/offices/international-affairs/intl/fy2006/miga.pdf (accessed October 2008).

—— 2005, 'Report to Congress: Achievement of Certain Policy Goals with Respect to Transparency and Accountability in the Multilateral Development Institutions', 14 March, cited at www.treas.gov/offices/international-affairs/multilateral_banks/congress/sec581.pdf (accessed October 2008).

—— 2001, 'Annual Report to Congress on the Environment and the Multilateral Development Banks, FY 2001', US Treasury Press Release Report 3051, US Treasury Office of Public Affairs, cited at www.ustreas.gov/press/release/report3051.pdf (accessed 2 December 2002; last updated: 29 March 2002).

van de Laar, A., 1980, *The World Bank and the Poor*, Boston, The

Hague and London, Kluwer Nijhoff Publishing.
Van Veldhuizen, H., 2000, 'Multilateral Investment Guarantee Agency', *Environment Matters,* IFC Annual Newsletter, World Bank, Washington, DC.
Vaubel, R., Dreher, A. and Soylu, U., 2003, 'Staff Growth in International Organisations: A Principal-Agent Problem? An Empirical Analysis', *Public Economics*, EconWPA 0306006, IDEAS Research Papers in Economics: 1–27.
Verbeek, B., 1998, 'International Organisations: The Ugly Duckling of International Relations Theory?', in B. Reinalda and B. Verbeek (eds), *Autonomous Policy Making in International Organisations*, London, Routledge: 11–26.
Vetterlein, A., 2007, 'Change in International Organisations: Innovation or Adaptation? A Comparison of the World Bank and the International Monetary Fund', in D. Stone and C. Wright (eds), *The World Bank and Governance: A Decade of Reform and Reaction*, New York, Routledge: 144–63.
Volcker, Paul A. (Chair), Caviria, Gustavo, Githongo, John, Heineman, Ben W. Jr., Van Gerven, Walter and Vereker, Sir John, 2007, *Independent Panel Review of the World Bank Group Department of Institutional Integrity*, Washington, DC, 13 September, cited at www.independentpanelreview.com/release02.shtml (accessed October 2008).
Wade, R., 2009, 'Accountability Gone Wrong: The World Bank, NGOs and the US Government in a Fight Over China', *New Political Economy* 14 (1): 25–48.
—— 2003, 'Review: Promoting Environmental Sustainability in Development', *Environment and Planning* 35: 759–60.
—— 1997, 'Greening the Bank: The Struggle over the Environment 1970–1995', in D. Kapur, J. Lewis and R.C. Webb (eds), *The World Bank: Its First Half Century*, Washington, DC, Brookings Institute: 611–734.
Wall Street Journal, 1996, 'Freeport-McMoRan Copper and Gold Cancels Government Policy', 23 September: Section B, 10J.
Waltz, K., 1979, *Theory of International Politics*, Reading, MA, Addison-Wesley Publications.
Wang, Q., 2003, 'Hegemony and Socialisation of the Mass Public: The Case of Postwar Japan's Cooperation with the United States on China Policy', *Review of International Studies* 29: 99–119.
Wapenhans, W., 2000, 'Learning by Doing: Reflections on 35 Years with the World Bank', in J. Carlsson and L. Wolhgemuth (eds), *Learning in Development Cooperation*, Stockholm, Sweden, Expert Group on Development Issues (EGDI), Department for International

Development Cooperation, Ministry of Foreign Affairs.

—— *et al.*, 1992, *Effective Implementation: Key to Development Impact,* Portfolio Management Task Force, Washington, DC, World Bank.

Wapner, P., 1996, *Environmental Activism and World Civic Politics*, Albany, State University of New York Press.

Weaver, C., 2008, *The Hypocrisy Trap: The World Bank and the Poverty of Reform,* Princeton, Princeton University Press.

—— 2007, 'The Worlds Bank and the Bank's World', *Global Governance* 13 (4): 493–512.

—— and Leiteritz, R., 2005, 'Our Poverty is a World Full of Dreams: Reforming the World Bank', *Global Governance* 11: 369–88.

Wendt, A., 2000, 'On the Via Media: A Response to the Critics', *Review of International Studies* 26: 165–80.

—— 1999, *Social Theory· of International Politics*, Cambridge, Cambridge University Press.

—— 1992, 'Anarchy is What States Make of It: The Social Construction of Power Politics', *International Organisation* 46 (2): 391–425.

—— 1987, 'The Agent-Structure Debate in International Relations Theory', *International Organisation* 41 (3): 335–70.

West, G., 1999, 'Political Risk Investment Insurance: A Renaissance', *Journal of Project Finance* 5 (2): 27–36.

—— and Tarazona, E., 2001, *Investment Insurance and Developmental Impact: Evaluating MIGA's Experience*, Washington, DC, MIGA.

—— —— 1998, *MIGA and Direct Foreign Investment: Evaluating Developmental Impact*, Washington, DC, MIGA.

Williamson, J. 2003, 'From Reform Agenda to Damaged Brand Name: A Short History of the Washington Consensus and Suggestions for What to do Next', *Finance and Development* 40 (3): 10–13.

—— 1990, 'What Washington Means by Policy Reform', in J. Williamson (ed.), *Latin American Adjustment: How Much has Happened?,* Washington, DC, IIE.

Wirth, D., 1998, 'Partnership Advocacy in World Bank Environmental Reform', in J. Fox and D. Brown (eds), *The Struggle for Accountability: The World Bank, NGOs and Grassroots Movements*, Cambridge, MA and London, MIT Press: 51–79.

—— 1991, 'Legitimacy, Accountability, and Partnership: A Model for Advocacy on Third World Environmental Issues', *Yale Law Journal* 100 (8): 2645–66.

Woods, N., 2008, 'Whose Aid? Whose Influence? China, Emerging Donors and the Silent Revolution in Development Assistance', *International Affairs* 86 (4): 1205–21.

—— 2006, *The Globalizers: The IMF, the World Bank and their*

Borrowers, Ithaca, New York, Cornell University Press.

—— 2000, 'The Challenge of Good Governance for the IMF and the World Bank Themselves', *World Development* 28 (5): 823–41.

World Bank, 2008a, *Environmental Sustainability: An Evaluation of World Bank Group Support*, Washington DC, Independent Evaluation Group, World Bank.

—— 2008b, 'Sustainable Infrastructure Action Plan: FY2009–2011', July, Washington, DC, World Bank.

—— 2008c, *Evaluation of the Initial Phase of the Pilot Program for Use of Country Systems for Environmental and Social Safeguards: Lessons Learned and Management Proposal for an Incremental Scale Up of the Program*, Report 42105, Washington, DC, World Bank, cited at www.worldbank.org/ (accessed August 2008).

—— 2008d, *Annual Report*, Washington, DC, World Bank, cited at www.worldbank.org/ (accessed October 2008).

—— 2007a, *Annual Report of Portfolio Performance FY2006*, Washington, DC, Quality Assurance Group, World Bank, cited at www.worldbank.org/ (accessed October 2008).

—— 2007b, *Quality of Supervision in FY05–06 (QSA7): A QAG Assessment*, Washington, DC, Quality Assurance Group, World Bank, cited at www.worldbank.org/ (accessed October, 2008).

—— 2007c, *The Inspection Panel Annual Report 2006–2007*, Washington, DC, Inspection Panel, World Bank, cited at www.worldbank.org/ (accessed October 2008).

—— 2006a, *Annual Report*, Washington, DC, World Bank.

—— 2006b, *Quality at Entry in FY04–05: A QAG Assessment*, Washington, DC, Quality Assurance Group, World Bank, cited at www.worldbank.org/ (accessed October 2008).

—— 2005a, *Environment Matters 2005*, Washington, DC, World Bank, cited at www.worldbank.org/ (accessed November 2006).

—— 2005b, 'Enhancing World Bank Support to Middle Income Countries: Management Actions Plan Progress Memorandum', 1 February, Washington, DC, World Bank.

—— 2005c, *Annual Report on Operations Evaluation 2004*, Washington, DC, World Bank.

—— 2005d, 'IBRD Financial Instruments: Frequently Asked Questions', October 2002, updated 5 September 2005, cited at www.worldbank.org/ (accessed August 2008).

—— 2005e, *Focus on Sustainability 2004*, Washington, DC, World Bank.

—— 2004, 'OP8.60 Development Policy Lending', Operational Policies, World Bank Operational Manual, cited at http://wbln0018.worldbank.org/Institutional/Manuals/opmanual.nsf (accessed September 2008; last updated, December 2005).
—— 2003a *Putting our Commitments to Work: An Environment Strategy Implementation Progress Report*, Washington, DC, World Bank.
—— 2003b, *Accountability at the World Bank: The Inspection Panel 10 Years On*, cited at www.worldbank.org/ (accessed October 2008).
—— 2002, 'Mainstreaming Environment in Poverty Reduction Strategy Papers', *Environment Strategy Notes* No. 4, cited at www.worldbank.org/ (accessed November 2007).
—— 2001a, *Making Sustainable Commitments: An Environment Strategy for the World Bank*, Washington, DC, World Bank.
—— 2001b, *The Cost of Doing Business: Fiduciary and Safeguard Policies and Compliance*, Internal Draft Report, World Bank. On file with author.
—— 2001c, 'OED's Review of the Bank's Performance on the Environment', cited at www.worldbank.org/evaluation/sector (accessed July 2001; last updated: 2001).
—— 2001d, 'MIGA Corporate Overview', *World Bank Development News: Issue Briefs*, cited at www.worldbank.org/html/extdr/pb/miga.htm (accessed 5 June 2001; last updated: 2001).
—— 2000, *Entering the 21st Century: World Development Report 1999/2000*, New York, Oxford University Press.
—— 1997, *The Impact of Environmental Assessment: The World Bank's Experience, Second Environmental Impact Assessment Review*, Washington, DC, Environment Department, World Bank, cited at www.worldbank.org/ (accessed September 2008; last updated: 2008).
World Commission on Dams, 2001, 'Dams and Development: A New Framework for Decision Making', cited: at www.dams.org/ (accessed 11 April 2002; last updated: 2001).
World Commission on Environment and Development, 1987, *Our Common Future*, Oxford, Oxford University Press.
Wright, C., 2006a, 'From "Safeguards" to "Sustainability": The Evolution of Environmental Discourse within the International Finance Corporation', in D. Stone and C. Wright (eds), *World Bank and Governance: A Decade of Reform and Reaction*, London and New York, Routledge: 67–87.
—— 2006b, 'Public Rules for Private Consumption: The International Finance Corporation and the Equator Principles', draft article, on file with author.
—— and Rwabizambuga, A., 2006, 'Institutional Pressures, Corporate

Reputation, and Voluntary Codes of Conduct: an Examination of the Equator Principles', *Business and Society Review* 111 (1): 89–117.

Yerton, S., 1996, 'Digging Deeper: Newly Released Documents Show Federal Insurer Questioned Environmental Impact of Freeport Mine', *Times Picayune*, 28 July 28: F1.

Zehfuss, M., 2001, 'Constructivism and Identity: A Dangerous Liaison', *European Journal of International Relations* 7 (3): 315–48.

Index

EU authorised representative for GPSR:
Easy Access System Europe, Mustamäe tee 50,
10621 Tallinn, Estonia
gpsr.requests@easproject.com

www.ingramcontent.com/pod-product-compliance
Ingram Content Group UK Ltd.
Pitfield, Milton Keynes, MK11 3LW, UK
UKHW021823100926
8556IPUK00003B/130

* 9 7 8 0 7 1 9 0 7 9 4 7 4 *